HARD BALL

HARD BALL

THE ABUSE OF POWER
IN PRO TEAM SPORTS

JAMES QUIRK
and
RODNEY FORT

PRINCETON UNIVERSITY PRESS
PRINCETON • NEW JERSEY

Library of Congress Cataloging-in-Publication Data

Quirk, James P.
Hard ball : the abuse of power in pro team sports /
James Quirk and Rodney Fort.
p.   cm.
Includes index.
ISBN: 978-0-691-14657-7
1. Professional sports—Economic aspects—United States.
2. Professional sports—Moral and ethical aspects—United States.
I. Fort, Rodney D.   II. Title.
GV716.Q566   1999
796.04′4′0973—dc21   98-38409

This book has been composed in Adobe Trump Mediaeval
and Gill Sans

The paper used in this publication meets the minimum requirements of
ANSI/NISO Z39.48-1992 (R1997) (*Permanence of Paper*)

http://pup.princeton.edu

Printed in the United States of America

1 3 5 7 9 10 8 6 4 2

To
Shirley
and the kids: Gayle, Jim, Janice,
Jill, Colleen, and Tom
and to
Carl W. Schmidt,
for getting Rod started

CONTENTS

PREFACE

This is our second jointly authored book on the sports business and our second with Princeton University Press. Our first book, *Pay Dirt,* appeared in 1992 and was intended as a more-or-less encyclopedic treatment of certain topics in the economics of sports, from the point of view of two fundamentally mainstream economists.

The present book is quite different. This is a book about what has gone wrong in the pro team sports business and how to fix it, written for the general public and for policymakers. The argument of the book, that the underlying cause of the problems of pro team sports is the monopoly power of sports leagues and how leagues exercise that power, is documented by numerous examples and anecdotes and by data from the recent history of the pro sports business.

The most visible sign of the abuse of power by sports leagues is the widespread use of threats and coercion by teams to blackmail cities into providing elaborate, new, publicly financed stadiums and arenas, along with lease agreements that saddle state or local taxpayers with the costs of the facilities. When owners threaten cities that they will move their teams if new stadiums are not forthcoming, these are not idle threats, as the recent history of franchise moves documents. It is the monopoly power of leagues that puts teeth in the threats of team owners. There is an extensive treatment of the stadium issue in the book: Chapters 6 and 7 are concerned primarily with these matters.

However, owners and leagues are not the only actors with clout in the pro sports business. Television networks, unions, and players, among others, all possess market power. The earlier chapters of the book document the central role of television income in the pro sports business of the 1990s, the confrontational nature of labor relations in sports, the success of unions and players in capturing an increasing share of that income, and the consequences of this for the bottom line of teams, especially small-market teams. It is in this context that events such as the baseball strike of 1994–95, the selling off of the Florida Marlins after the 1997 World Series, and the downsizing of the Montreal Expos or the Orlando Magic can best be understood. The inability of leagues to solve their competitive balance problems has exacerbated these and related problems of pro team sports.

Finally, in the last chapter of the book, there is a detailed discussion of the pros and cons of our proposed solution to the problems of pro team sports.

Sources used in writing this book include the *New York Times, Sporting News, Sports Illustrated,* and a number of local newspapers. *Broadcasting and Cable* magazine was a prime source of information on the radio and television aspects of the sports business. Much of the data appearing in the tables is taken from the annual surveys of the sports business published by *Financial World* magazine since 1990. The story in Chapter 1 about the German shepherd and Chihuahua dogs comes from the "Bulletin Board" feature of the *St. Paul Pioneer Press.* Historical information, anecdotes, and other data appearing in the book come from a variety of sources, including our earlier joint book, papers the two of us have written on the economics of sports for academic journals, and consulting we have done in legal cases involving sports teams and leagues.

We thank Bruce Hamilton and Bruce Johnson for their very helpful reviews of an earlier version of the manuscript, as well as a third, anonymous reviewer whose comments also were helpful. Special thanks go to Dick Ruppert, Quentin Quirk, Roger Noll, and Tom Pahl. We also express our appreciation to Peter Strupp and the staff of Princeton Editorial Associates and to Ellen Foos and Janet Stern of Princeton University Press for their careful attention to the production of the volume. Finally, the original idea for this book came from our editor and friend Jack Repcheck, who has once again provided the support, suggestions, and oversight to help make this a much more readable book.

HARD BALL

THE SCENE OF
THE CRIME

Players say the owners are stupid, owners say the players are greedy, and they're both right. They make one pine for the simpler days when owners were greedy and players were stupid.

—Richard Corliss, *Time*, August 8, 1994, p. 65

In a familiar passage, often quoted by those who make a living from the sport, Jacques Barzun said, "Whoever wants to know the heart and mind of America had better learn baseball, the rules and realities of the game." If Barzun was right, this might help to explain why so many Americans are absolutely bewildered by what is going on in their own country. It's not that most of us don't understand the game of baseball—sure, the infield fly rule doesn't come immediately to mind, and just what constitutes a balk leads one inexorably into and through the bowels of existentialism, with even a nod to Hegel and Kant. But what happens on the playing field is not the problem. The problem is figuring out how to make sense of what goes on off the field in baseball (and in other pro team sports as well), why it happens, and what to do about it.

3

Bill Veeck, the greatest owner-promoter of pro team sports, once told one of the coauthors of this book that what he and the other owners were selling was not winning on the field nor superlative athletic performances nor even dramatic down-to-the-wire games. Instead, Veeck believed pro team sports was marketing "dreams," that intangible aura of sports that leads to the fans' identification with "their" teams and their favorite players, coaches, and managers. Veeck also thought that going to a game should be fun—more fun if your team won, of course, but still fun even if they lost. So if you went to a White Sox game at Comiskey Park in the late 1950s or early 1960s when Veeck owned the team, you saw the exploding scoreboard when Sherm Lollar or Ted Kluszewski hit a home run, you oohed and aahed at the infield magic of Nellie Fox and Louie Aparicio, you cheered the go-go Sox for every one of their infrequent runs, you especially cheered if the Sox were whipping the hated Yankees, you stayed after the game for the fireworks display, and, believe us, you had a ball. If you were a kid who made it to the game early enough, you could even fill a scorecard with the autographs of players—rookies through stars—who seemed to be having as much fun at the park as you were.

Bill Veeck, bless his soul, is gone now, which is a crying shame because major league baseball (MLB), the National Football League (NFL), the National Basketball Association (NBA), and the National Hockey League (NHL) all could use a large dose of his wisdom and sense of fun today. (But there is a possible light at the end of the tunnel—Bill's son, Mike, is making a name for himself as a minor league owner–general manager, following in his father's footsteps. At St. Paul, running the Saints in the independent Northern League, he sold out Midway Stadium year after year with a three-ring circus approach to baseball featuring a pig as ball boy [or girl?]; inserting races, raffles, sumo wrestling, and what have you between innings; keeping the stands in an uproar looking for what was coming next—and then ending every game with one of his dad's fireworks displays. While the Twins were losing money at the Metrodome [capacity 60,000], Mike was making money at Midway [capacity 5,000]. When the city of St. Paul offered to build a larger stadium for the Saints, their fans voted it down, and Mike Veeck went along with the fans. Is anyone in major league baseball even remotely aware of how baseball can be promoted, Mike Veeck– and St. Paul Saints–style?)

The "field of dreams" that Bill Veeck talked about is long since a thing of the past, and a lot of the fun has gone out of baseball and other pro team sports. Pro team sports has become big business, in which Vince Lombardi's rule that "winning is everything" holds and civility, tradition, and any sense of civic involvement and commitment be damned. Somehow the owners, the players, the leagues, the media, the lawyers, the agents, the unions, the politicians, and the fans, too, have each played a part in transforming sports into a Rube Goldberg monster machine that seems to have next to no redeeming social value, just the ability to generate big payoffs for the insiders. And, increasingly, the money that the insiders are raking in is coming not from the tickets bought by lower- and middle-income fans taking their families to the game, but from television, from big-bucks business executives with their corporate boxes and preferred seat licenses, and from taxpayers, most of whom can think of any number of better things to spend their taxes on than new gold-plated stadiums or arenas for rich owners, rich players, and that select group of fans rich enough to afford the luxury boxes.

The Bible tells us that the love of money is the root of all evil, and sports today is absolutely awash in cash. With billionaire owners, and players and coaches drawing multi-million-dollar salaries, they live in a different world from the rest of us. But money per se is not the root of the current problems of pro team sports. Instead, the market power that insiders in the industry possess, and the arrogant use of that power, is the real culprit. The most attractive feature of pro team sports is the fact that championships are determined by

5

open competition on the playing field; the only thing that counts is how well you play the game, not who you are or whom you know. The least attractive feature is the way that teams and leagues use their monopoly power to exploit fans and the general tax-paying public, and then squander their ill-gotten gains in outrageous salaries paid to mostly ungrateful players.

Without any apologies (and also without any retribution) teams use blackmail tactics, including threats to leave town often based on fictitious profit and loss claims, to extort public money from cities and states for new stadiums or arenas along with sweetheart rental agreements. Sports leagues routinely approve almost any franchise move desired by owners, with or without any determination of financial problems for the team at the old location. The long-term commitments of teams and owners to cities—if such ever did exist—are today a thing of the past; all that matters now is how much other cities are offering in the way of subsidies compared with what the team's current "home" city has on the table.

Players with multimillion-dollar contracts routinely use the same kind of blackmail tactics against owners, staging sit-outs and demanding renegotiation midway through a contract, whenever any other player signs for a better figure anywhere in the league. Too many star players ignore team and league rules with impunity, abuse officials, and treat fans like dirt. And it's not just fans, officials, and coaches who are trashed by these players. The Florida Marlins were invited to the White House to be congratulated by the president for winning the 1997 World Series. Half the team failed to show up for the ceremony.

Owners and unions engage in public relations battles in the press during labor contract negotiations and the inevitable strike or lockout that follows. And then, if a star player or the team performs badly on the field, owners and players can at least agree about one thing—it's the fans' fault for not supporting them.

In one of George Will's columns, there is a story relating to one of Will's abiding loves, baseball. The story goes something like this. Two old timers were reminiscing about the depression years. One mentioned Lou Gehrig, saying to the other, "You remember Lou Gehrig, right?" The other replied, "Of course, Lou Gehrig was the first baseman on those great Yankee teams of the 1920s and 1930s. What ever happened to him?" "Well, he died years ago, of Lou Gehrig's disease." The second friend whistled in astonishment: "Wow, what are the odds? Here's a guy named Lou Gehrig and he dies of Lou Gehrig's disease!"

Just to mention Lou Gehrig brings to mind an image of class both on and off the field, something that seems to be a rarity among players today. As time goes on, it is harder and harder to find players in the Gehrig mold with whom to identify—players like Kirby Puckett, Cal Ripkin, Tony Gwynn, or Roberto Clemente. Too often they are being replaced by in-your-face egoists who make it as clear as day that you as a fan should consider it a privilege to be allowed to witness them in action.

Having said all this, it also is true that pro team sports has been on a financial roll for the past twenty years, racking up record gate receipts, TV income, player salaries, and franchise prices each and every year. Pro team sports is front-page news now in most of the country, from the World Series and the Super Bowl to the latest list of drug arrests, drunk driving incidents, and wife beatings by star players and financial shenanigans by owners. It makes one wonder whether we fans, with our apparently insatiable appetite for sports, simply happen to be cursed as well with the least appealing group of players and owners in sports history or whether something else accounts for the problems pervasive in pro team sports.

Actually, anyone who knows anything about sports history is aware that even the worst of the current group of players look like models of deportment compared with that mean-spirited bigot of the early days of baseball, Ty Cobb, who is generally regarded as the greatest baseball player of all time. And the transgressions of the current crop of owners pale in comparison with those of the Robison brothers of the 1890s, who managed to acquire control of both the St. Louis and Cleveland franchises of the National League in 1899. St. Louis was drawing better than Cleveland, so the Robisons simply transferred all of the good players on the Cleveland lineup to St. Louis. Cleveland ended up with the worst won-lost record in National League history—20 wins, 134 losses! (even the 1961 Mets looked good next to this team)—and played 53 of its last 77 home games on the road. Cleveland was dropped by the league the next year.

This suggests that it is not the individuals who currently people sports, flawed as they might be, who are the villains of the piece. There is something more fundamental going on, something to do with the way in which the sports business is organized and operated. But can we identify the critical feature of the pro team sports business that is the ultimate source of its problems?

Is it the media for supplying the bucks? Or the unions for resisting the owners' demands for reasonable restrictions on free agency? Or the players for shaking down the owners and the fans for unbelievable salaries? Or the owners for bidding up player salaries to ridiculous levels and for exploiting the cities in which they have franchises? Could it be the leagues for allowing teams to move when and where they wish, regardless of the consequences for fans and localities? Or the politicians who pay the bribes to owners to keep teams in town? Or the fans who continue to support teams and players who provide absolutely no loyalty to them in return? And how do we clean up this mess?

We will argue in this book that essentially all of the many problems of the pro team sports business arise from one simple fact, namely the monopoly power of pro team sports leagues. Each of the major pro team sports is controlled by a monopoly league—MLB in baseball, the NFL in football, the NBA in basketball, and the NHL in hockey. Eliminate that monopoly power and you eliminate almost every one of the problems of the sports business. Allow that monopoly power to persist and any attempted partial solutions to the problems of sports are cures that will leave the disease still flourishing.

The monopoly power exercised by leagues is not the only market power being exercised in pro team sports. The media, unions, and players, among others, all have a modicum of market power as well. But what we will document here is that the market power of leagues enables them to capture the great bulk of the monopoly profits ("rents") that sports generates, from gate receipts, media income, sweetheart stadium deals and rental arrangements, and other sources. These monopoly profits in turn become the prize package over which owners and players, who are backed up by their player unions, fight.

Eliminate the monopoly power of leagues and you eliminate the blackmailing of cities to subsidize teams. Eliminate the monopoly power of leagues and you eliminate the sources of revenue that provide the wherewithal for high player salaries. Eliminate the monopoly power of leagues and you eliminate the problem of lack of competitive balance in a league due to the disparity in drawing potential among league teams. Eliminate the monopoly power of leagues and you transfer power from the insiders, owners and players alike, to the outsiders, fans and taxpayers. In this book, we present the arguments and documentation to back up each of these points and then propose our solution—what we argue is the only feasible solution—for achieving the elimination of league monopoly power. That's the modest program for this book.

But before doing this, it makes sense to take a look back in time to see where and when the seeds for the current crop of problems were sown. Sports fans, including the two of us, are mostly nostalgia nuts so some might think that what sports needs is a return to the "good old days" (fill in your favorite time period from the past). But even in the good old days pro sports had its share of problems involving money and market power, and the solutions that emerged for solving those earlier problems have led in turn to the problems we face today. So, before looking in detail at what is causing problems today, we should first look back to those great days of sports as they used to be during, say, the early 1950s.

The early 1950s was a golden age of sorts for New York City baseball fans. The Yankees continued their World Series–winning ways from the prewar and immediate postwar years, the Dodgers were the dominant team in the National League, and the Giants showed signs of recovery from the dismal days of the war and early postwar years. There was pennant fever for New York fans of either the American League (AL) or the National League (NL) year after year. At the glamour position, center field, Duke Snider had already arrived in Brooklyn by 1947, and Willie Mays was on the scene with the Giants and Mickey Mantle with the Yankees in 1951. Was there ever any better time for New York City baseball fans?

On the other hand, there were baseball fans in other parts of the country, especially those in the booming West and Southwest, who complained about being left out of the baseball action, with good reason. Baseball has always been the most traditional and conservative of sports. Nothing illustrates this better than the franchise picture of the early 1950s. In 1951, the same sixteen major league baseball teams resided in the same familiar locations where they had been since the end of the American League–National League war in 1903: New York (Yankees, Giants); Brooklyn (Dodgers); Boston (Red Sox, Braves); Philadelphia (Athletics, Phillies); St. Louis (Cardinals, Browns); Chicago (White Sox, Cubs); Pittsburgh (Pirates); Washington (Senators); Cleveland (Indians); Cincinnati (Reds); and Detroit (Tigers). The war and postwar shifts of population and industry to the West and Southwest, and the development of safe, reliable, low-cost air travel, had had no impact on the distribution of major league baseball franchises in the country.

Over in Brooklyn, one individual who had more than a passing interest in what was going on (not just with New York

City baseball but with baseball in general) was the long-time Democratic congressman from the borough, Emmanuel Celler. Celler was the powerful chairman of the House Judiciary Committee, the committee that deals with monopoly and antitrust issues. Celler had been receiving complaints from congressmen from all over the West and Southwest about the restrictive business practices of baseball and their effects on congressional districts and regions. In 1951, in response to these and other complaints, Celler initiated a series of hearings into the business of organized baseball, the first congressional investigation of the sport.

The resulting report, published as volume 6 of the committee's *Studies in Monopoly Power*, was the first, the best-researched, and the most penetrating of the many congressional investigations into various aspects of the economics of sports. Still, given that we now look back to the 1950s with some nostalgia as a time when everything seemed to be coming up roses in baseball and in the other pro team sports, it is natural to ask what in the world was so wrong with baseball in the 1950s to warrant a full-scale congressional investigation.

Well, things were not quite as rosy as you might think. In fact, there were a number of problems with baseball in those days, some relating to the vaunted traditionalism and conservatism of the sport and some relating to the monopoly power that the major leagues wielded. In 1951, it had been only four years since Branch Rickey managed to breach a seventy-year-old unwritten baseball rule by integrating the major leagues, bringing in Jackie Robinson to play second base for the Dodgers. But only the first steps had been taken to eliminate racism in the sport; there were teams such as the Boston Red Sox that would have to be dragged, kicking and screaming, into integrating their lineups. It would be years before black players began to move closer to "equal pay for equal work" status in baseball.

Those were also the days of the old "reserve clause" in pro team sports. Anyone wanting to play in the major leagues had to sign a standard contract that, in effect, gave the team owner exclusive rights to the services of the player for his entire playing lifetime. On the other hand, the owner committed himself to giving only a few weeks' notice to the player before dropping him from the team. The standard contract thus gave the owner an enormous advantage in bargaining with the player, and there were no player unions in existence to provide the clout to fight owners over the issue. Every other major pro sports league—the NFL, the NBA, and the NHL—used a similar player contract. So players had obvious grievances with the way that baseball and the other pro team sports operated in the 1950s.

Competitive balance was an ongoing problem within baseball, as it had been for more than fifty years. At the one extreme were small-city teams such as the Cincinnati Reds and the St. Louis Browns; at the other, blockbusters like the New York teams. The differences in revenue potential among league teams were enormous. Big-city teams drew, on average, larger crowds and charged higher ticket prices. This provided the wherewithal for big-city teams to spend more for talent, and it showed in the number of pennants won by teams such as the Yankees relative to those won by the small-city teams.

There was revenue sharing in baseball, but it didn't come near to closing the gap between big-city and small-city teams. In the very earliest days of baseball, back in the 1880s and 1890s, gate receipts were split roughly 50–50 between the home and visiting teams. Over time, though, the visitor's share kept decreasing until, by the 1950s, the split was about 80–20 in favor of the home team in the AL and 95–5 in favor of the home team in the NL.

In the early 1950s, the problem of competitive balance in baseball was getting worse, not better. TV was just coming on the scene, and baseball owners made the decision to treat TV revenues from local telecasts in the same way they treated radio revenues, that is, all TV revenues were assigned to the home team. Bill Veeck owned the St. Louis Browns at the time, and he was one of the few owners to fight this decision. For his efforts, he was punished by the New York Yankees who scheduled all home games with the Browns as afternoon rather than night games, reducing the gate and Veeck's visiting-team share on the Browns' trips to New York. TV revenues have continued to soar, constituting an ever larger fraction of total baseball revenues, but the 100–0 split rule on the sharing of local TV revenues has continued up to the present day, as has baseball's competitive balance problem.

What baseball owners had going for them was a long tradition as the national sport of the country, monopoly control of the baseball market, and an almost unfettered right to use that monopoly power as they wished. Back in 1922, Justice Oliver Wendell Holmes handed down a unanimous Supreme Court decision that held that baseball was exempt from the federal antitrust laws, because baseball was not "commerce" in the sense of the interstate commerce clause of the Constitution and hence not subject to the federal government's power of regulation. Later, Judge Henry Friendly would refer to this as "not one of Justice Holmes' happiest days," since later Supreme Court decisions held that boxing, pro football, pro basketball, pro hockey—all pro sports other than baseball, and college athletics as well—are subject to federal antitrust laws.

By 1951, the Supreme Court was willing to admit that it had made a mistake in 1922 in exempting baseball from the federal antitrust laws. However, the Court refused to overturn the earlier decision, arguing that baseball team owners had invested substantial sums of money in the sport relying on the earlier decision and that it would be unfair to reverse course and subject owners at this late date to antitrust prosecution. But, just to show that consistency is not necessarily a hallmark of judicial decisions, the Court noted that Congress had the right to overturn the earlier decision simply by passing a law making baseball subject to antitrust laws. Just why it was unfair for the Court to reverse the earlier decision but not unfair for Congress to accomplish the same thing was left hanging in the breeze.

In any case, in 1951, baseball was still exempt from antitrust. One of the issues that faced the Celler Committee was whether to recommend passage of a law that would eliminate the antitrust exemption for organized baseball. This would also be a central topic in at least five later congressional hearings into professional sports—it certainly has had an abiding and ongoing attraction for congressional investigators. Every time the issue came up, comments by congressmen got a lot of play in the press, too. Needless to say, this latter fact did not go unnoticed by those same congressmen, recalling Adlai Stevenson's famous line, "A politician is a statesman who approaches every question with an open mouth."

Turning to more immediate matters, the Celler Committee heard testimony that in the 1950 baseball season, every team in the AAA Pacific Coast League (PCL), a minor baseball league, had outdrawn the major league St. Louis Browns. At the time, the Pacific Coast League consisted of Seattle, Portland, Sacramento, San Francisco, Oakland, Los Angeles, Hollywood, and San Diego. The PCL was making noises about establishing itself as a third major league, with or without the approval of the existing two major leagues. The Celler Committee was clearly sympathetic to the complaints of the PCL teams. The commissioner of baseball, Happy Chandler, president Will Harridge of the AL, and president Ford Frick of the NL all were subjected to probing questions by members of the committee, and none of the three did a good job of defending his position.

In the end, despite the evidence unearthed by the Celler Committee concerning the market power that baseball exercised with respect to players and franchise locations, baseball retained its antitrust exemption. But, slowly and reluctantly, baseball did respond to the pressures, both external and internal, to adjust its lineup of franchises to bring it more into line with the changing U.S. economy. Along the way, the good old "law of unintended consequences" came into operation; forces unleashed by the process of changing the baseball lineup gave rise to even more egregious problems involving the national sport, as well as the other pro team sports—the problems we are trying to cope with today.

In 1953, the NL agreed to the first franchise move in the majors since the 1902 AL move of the Yankees from Baltimore to New York, when the league sanctioned a move of the Boston Braves to County Stadium in Milwaukee. County Stadium was a publicly owned facility built in 1950 to host games played in Milwaukee by the NFL Green Bay Packers on a split-season basis. The move itself was certainly significant, but it was also significant that the city and county had greased the skids for the move by providing a low-cost rental agreement to the Braves in a publicly owned stadium. At the time, every other baseball team played in a privately owned stadium (one owned either by the team itself or by some other major league team), with the sole exception of the Cleveland Indians, who set a major league attendance record in 1948 while playing in the publicly owned Municipal Stadium (which also housed the NFL Cleveland Browns).

The move of the Braves started the ball rolling. In 1954, the St. Louis Browns left for Baltimore to play in the publicly owned Memorial Stadium, built in 1950 for the NFL Baltimore Colts. And in 1955, it was the Philadelphia Athletics who left town for Kansas City, once again to move into a publicly owned facility, Municipal Stadium. The details of this move were a little more complicated. The stadium had been built in 1923 by the Kansas City Blues, a team that later became a Yankee farm club in the AAA American Association. The Athletics agreed to move to Kansas City only after the city committed to buy the stadium from the Yankees and to refurbish and enlarge it to meet major league standards. But once again, public money was involved in the franchise move.

The Braves, Browns, and Athletics all were perennial second-division teams in two-team cities, and there was little weeping and gnashing of teeth by supporters when they left for greener pastures—supporters of these teams at their old locations were few and far between.

Then, in 1958, came a bombshell, something that Emmanuel Celler in his wildest dreams could never have contemplated. It was a classic instance of the old adage that "No good turn goes unpunished." Having helped to pave the way for the moves of the weakest sisters of baseball, Celler now found that the next team to move was one of the strongest teams in the sport, financially and otherwise: none other than his own beloved hometown Brooklyn Dodgers.

The Dodgers had been on the ropes in the 1930s, racked by internal fights between the heirs of the Ebbets family and those of the Mckeever family, each owning exactly 50 percent of the team, with disputes every bit as vicious and damaging to the team as the battles between Tim and Wellington Mara over control of the NFL New York Giants fifty years later. In 1938, Larry McPhail came in to take charge of the front office and the team improved almost overnight. Branch Rickey took over from McPhail in 1943. In the 1940s and 1950s, the Dodgers were so successful that the team accounted for almost half of total NL profits for that period.

By 1950, the team's lawyer, Walter O'Malley, had acquired control of the team. In 1958, O'Malley broke the hearts of a generation of Dodger fans when he moved the team to Los Angeles, carting along with him Horace Stoneham and the NL New York Giants, bound for San Francisco. The Dodgers didn't get a publicly financed stadium, but Walter O'Malley's team received title to a big chunk of prime real estate near the downtown confluence of four major LA freeways—the Pasadena, the Harbor, the Golden State, and the Santa Ana—and a stone's throw away from the Hollywood Freeway, the San Bernardino Freeway, and the Santa Monica Freeway. As Roger Noll has noted, O'Malley had acquired something akin to the right to print money. The Giants did get a new publicly financed stadium, Candlestick Park, which unfortunately also came with a wind off the bay that has caused problems for the team and its fans for most of the past forty years.

In a final touch of irony, O'Malley justified his move of the Dodgers on the grounds that he had to find a location where the revenue potential could match that of the relocated and rejuventated Braves who were selling out County Stadium with those great teams of the 1950s. How else could the Dodgers hope to compete with the Braves? By 1966, the bloom was off the rose in Milwaukee and the Braves were gone, moved to Atlanta by the "carpetbaggers" who had bought the team in 1962.

The moves of the Dodgers and the Giants in 1958 provided the indirect trigger for the next break in baseball's traditions when, again for the first time since the AL–NL war, league expansion occurred. This took place in 1961, with teams in the Twin Cities, Houston, New York (Mets), and Los Angeles (Angels) added to the major leagues. It was the threat of a potential rival league, the Continental League, that led to expansion of the majors. The Continental League was organized by Branch Rickey and William Shea in 1958 with the main goal of filling the gap in New York City baseball caused by the departure of the Dodgers and Giants. An agreement was reached with the majors to admit the Mets and expansion teams in the other cities, and the Continental League disbanded without playing a game. As an indication of the future of baseball, all the 1961 expansion teams played in publicly owned stadiums, although it took the Angels five years to disentangle themselves from a prior commitment to O'Malley's Dodger Stadium before heading down the Santa Ana Freeway to the publicly owned Anaheim Stadium.

Finally, the modest beginnings of a baseball players' union developed in the late 1950s as well, in the form of an owner-financed organization to oversee the players' pension plan. This was a "company union" in all but name; it would take almost another decade for a legitimate players' union to be established in baseball.

Things weren't all that different in the other pro team sports leagues in the 1950s, all of which operated under much the same business rules as baseball and experienced many of the same problems. Way back in the 1920s, there had been prominent black players in the NFL, stars such as Duke Slater, Paul Robeson, and Bobby Marshall. But by the 1930s, the NFL had joined organized baseball as a strictly segregated league, reportedly in part because of the influence of George Marshall, owner of the Washington Redskins. It was the competitive pressure imposed by an integrated rival league, the All American Football Conference (AAFC, 1946–49), that caused the NFL to reintegrate. This was solidified by the incorporation of four integrated AAFC teams—the Browns, the 49ers, the Yankees, and the Colts—into the NFL when the AAFC–NFL war ended in a 1950 agreement.

That agreement re-established the NFL as the sole major pro football league in the country with the monopoly power over franchise locations and player markets that this implies. The NFL's standard contract was every bit as restrictive as that of baseball, despite some misleadingly softer language. The 1950s was not a good time for players in the NFL.

Following the AAFC–NFL war, the NFL decided to stick with its franchise list, rejecting petitions for expansion franchises from a number of cities in the Midwest, Southwest, and West, despite impressive increases in league attendance and TV income. The main opponents of expansion were George Marshall and Viola Wolfner, owner of the Chicago Cardinals. The Cardinals wanted to keep their options open for a franchise move (they ultimately went to St. Louis in 1961), while the Redskins were going through bad times on the field and at the gate following the admission of the Baltimore Colts into what had been the Redskins' territory. And, of course, George Marshall was beginning to show his age as well.

The NFL put off expansion for so long that the league found itself facing competition again in 1960 from a new rival league, the American Football League (AFL), organized by a wealthy Texas oil man, Lamar Hunt. That war wasn't settled until 1966 when, under a special congressional antitrust exemption, the AFL and NFL merged into a reconstituted NFL, with all the teams of the AFL joining the new NFL.

Television was both a promise and a problem for the NFL in the 1950s. Early experiments in the late 1940s with televising home games had been disastrous for the Los Angeles Rams and the Philadelphia Eagles, and the NFL reaction was to impose strict rules banning the televising of NFL games in any city on a Sunday when an NFL team in the city was playing a home game. This rule was struck down by a federal court in 1951. The court imposed an injunction forbidding the NFL from signing a league-wide season-long television contract with any network. In 1958, the national audience viewing the televised NFL championship game between the Giants and the Colts ("The Game" that the Colts won in a barn-burning finish) gave the first really clear indication of the enormous revenue potential from TV for the NFL. But it wasn't until 1962, when Congress exempted league-wide television contracts from antitrust prosecution for all sports, that the NFL signed its first league-wide contract (with CBS). Then, at the urging of long-time NFL owner George Halas of the Chicago Bears, the NFL adopted the rule of equal sharing of all national TV revenues among league teams, which became the pattern for the other leagues as well. Pro football turned out to be the absolutely ideal sport for television viewers, which led to ever-rising network TV revenues in contracts negotiated by league commissioner Pete Rozelle.

During the 1950s, the popularity of pro football continued to grow, but the NFL was still overshadowed in its own sport by college football and by major league baseball among pro team sports. Most NFL teams played in stadiums owned by major league baseball teams—for example, the Chicago Bears played in the Cubs' Wrigley Field and the Chicago Cardinals played in the White Sox's Comiskey Park. The rising popularity of pro football, however, combined with the move toward publicly owned stadiums, led to a wave of construction of multiple-use stadiums, facilities that could be used for either baseball or football. A prime example was Candlestick Park, which opened in 1960 and housed the NL San Francisco Giants and the 49ers of the NFL. The tap of public money had opened for both baseball and football teams; it would play a major role in the financial futures of both sports.

NBA basketball was still very much a minor sport in the 1950s. The NBA came into existence in 1949 as an outgrowth of the Basketball Association of America (BAA), founded in 1946, which added teams in 1948 and 1949 from the recently defunct National Basketball League. The BAA was organized by the owners of arenas with NHL teams as a sidelight to their main hockey operations, following the publicity and success of college basketball doubleheaders played at Madison Square Garden in New York City. The idea was to host pro basketball games on the nights that their NHL teams were on the road. Of the original members of the BAA, only two teams survived into the 1950s—the Boston Celtics and the New York Knicks. All the others dropped out because pro basketball didn't draw well enough to pay.

The dominant team of the early years of the NBA was the Minneapolis Lakers, featuring big George Mikan at center. After Mikan's retirement, the Celtics took over the league, with Red Auerbach's teams winning eight straight NBA titles (1957–65). This problem of competitive balance was reflected in the continuing upheaval and turnover among NBA franchises.

There were a few centers of basketball interest where the NBA flourished in the 1950s—Boston, of course, and New York—but the financial picture was dim for the rest of the league. At the time, college basketball completely dominated the sport, and NHL hockey provided in-season competition for the NBA at the pro team sports level. A major innovation introduced during the 1950s was the "24-second clock," which both eliminated the existing game's emphasis on ball control and distinguished the pro game from its college counterpart. Over time, the popularity of superstar players such as Wilt Chamberlain, Bill Russell, Bob Cousy, Elgin Baylor, and others, plus the development of an intense rivalry between the Celtics and the Los Angeles (née Minneapolis) Lakers, fed a growing interest in the pro game.

By the end of the 1950s, the surviving teams in the NBA had begun to break even, which was incentive enough for a rival league, the American Basketball League (ABL), to enter the field, bankrolled by Abe Saperstein, owner of the Harlem Globetrotters. But even with the money and clout of George Steinbrenner available (he was the owner of the ABL's Cleveland team), there weren't enough fans to support two leagues, and the ABL went under midway through its second season.

By 1950, the NHL had been around for almost thirty-five years and had a small but dedicated group of fans, especially in its Canadian member cities. (When Jack Kent Cooke, a Canadian himself, was awarded an NHL expansion franchise for Los Angeles in the mid-1960s, he was told that he had a gold mine, because of the number of Canadians who had emigrated to the LA basin. After a few years of low attendance, Cooke commented that he had discovered the reason the local Canadians had left Canada for LA—they hated hockey.) The NHL had undergone expansion in the 1920s and then been caught by the depression, with the list of franchises whittled down to a mere six by the end of World War II: the New York Rangers, Detroit Red Wings, Chicago Blackhawks, Boston Bruins, Toronto Maple Leafs, and Montreal Canadiens. The NHL membership remained at six until league expansion took place in 1966.

There were also competitive balance problems in the NHL —the Canadiens were every bit as dominant a team in the NHL as the Yankees were in the AL. But there were even more fundamental problems in hockey than in the other sports. For a period of almost ten years, the NHL was in the peculiar position of having three of its six teams owned or controlled by the same individual, James Norris. Norris was a major figure in the arena business from the 1930s until his death in 1966, and he also played a comparable role in the booking and management of the attractions that appeared at the arenas, including boxing and NHL hockey. Norris owned the Chicago Blackhawks outright and also controlled the Madison Square Garden corporation, which in turn owned the New York Rangers. Norris' daughter, Marguerite Riker, and his son, Bruce Norris, held controlling interest in the Detroit Red Wings. For obvious reasons, this was strictly against league rules, but the situation was allowed to continue for years. Officers of the league argued that these teams were losing money and that no one other than the Norris family was willing to take on the burden of keeping the teams afloat.

The NHL had an unchallenged monopoly in major league pro hockey and used the same devices that had been adopted in baseball, the NFL, and the NBA to restrict the bargaining rights of players in contract negotiations. As the national sport in Canada, hockey generated substantial radio and TV income for the two Canadian NHL teams under a national contract. These revenues were not shared with the American NHL teams, though, which served to increase the disparity in revenue among teams in the league.

The tradition in the NHL was for teams to be owned by the owners of the arenas in which the teams played. All during the 1950s, the six NHL teams played in team-owned arenas so that there was no direct infusion of public money into the sport in the form of arena subsidies. That changed with expansion in 1966; the new NHL teams coming into the league played in publicly owned arenas, and over time, as the original arenas got older, in the main the original NHL teams demanded and received publicly financed replacement facilities.

This is just a capsule summary, of course, of some of the circumstances that existed in the pro team sports business in the 1950s; we will return to examine the current counterparts of these and related issues in more detail in the chapters that follow. Here we simply note that by the 1950s TV was already emerging as an important source of income for pro team sports, so that the question of how that income would be shared among league teams was also an important matter. Competitive balance was an ongoing problem in the 1950s in all leagues. The approach that was supposed to correct competitive balance problems, namely the reserve clause, clearly was not working in that direction. However, the reserve clause did hold down player salaries, and this result provided incentives in spades for players to organize unions to combat the power that owners exercised in the player labor market. The experience gained by teams and leagues in the 1950s with respect to franchise moves showed that cities lacking sports franchises were willing to ante up sizable amounts of money to entice teams. And what worked for franchise moves also worked for league expansion, which was to become an important source of income for league teams from 1960 on. Pro sports also discovered that racial barriers were not impenetrable, that fans could identify with Willie Mays, Roy Campanella, and Joe Black, just as they did with Duke Snider, Mickey Mantle, and Whitey Ford. Notably, this occurred a decade or more before the big civil rights breakthroughs of the late 1950s and 1960s. It is of interest that market competition, from the All American Football Conference, played an important role in eliminating the implicit racial exclusion rules of the NFL.

The issues dealt with in this book concern money and economic power in pro team sports. By their very nature, they are contentious and controversial—they are bread and butter (or, better, baguette and caviar) issues for players, owners, the media, and other interested parties. Our conclusions will certainly be judged "radical" by some, maybe all, of the insider groups. The arguments we make to arrive at those conclusions are economic arguments, the stock in trade of your garden-variety economist. We plead guilty right off the bat to being card-carrying members of that reviled profession, the one that George Bernard Shaw described as being so convoluted that "If all economists were laid end to end, they still wouldn't reach a conclusion." Another sage has argued the other way: "Put four economists in a room to solve a problem, and they'll come up with five different answers." Yet another critic lamented the lack of one-armed members of the profession, economists who might at least feel awkward about offering the standard economist's bromide, "On the one hand . . . , and then, on the other hand. . . ." Well, at least we aren't lawyers.

Having said all that, there isn't anything at all complicated or technical about the arguments we make because they are based on two very simple ideas that underlie essentially all of economics.

First, we assume that everyone—owners, players, fans, the media, public officials, agents, the whole caboodle—acts "rationally" in the sense that, given a choice between two options, each person will pick the option that the person believes leaves him or her better off. This is the assumption that people act to further their own self-interest. For example, we assume that owners generally act so as to make as much profit as possible, and that players tend to sign with the teams that offer the highest salaries.

Second, we assume that "markets work": that supply and demand clear markets, where supply and demand reflect the self-interest-motivated decisions being made by the individuals who are participating in the market. That means, for example, that we view the average level of player salaries as reflecting what team owners think players are worth to them, that is, what the players can be expected to generate in revenue for a team. Franchise prices likewise reflect the profit potential of teams as viewed by current and prospective franchise owners.

That's it—this is the full extent of economic theorizing that we are working with in this book. You might agree or disagree with either of the above ideas, but the fact of the matter is that they really do a pretty good job of explaining and predicting quite a lot of what goes on in our world. But in any case, we hope you will withhold your judgments until after you've seen where these ideas are going to lead in the course of the book. Who knows, you might find that you end up changing your mind about one or two things along the way.

In applying economic reasoning, it is important to let yourself be carried wherever the reasoning will take you, not allowing any preconceptions to get in your way. There's nothing at all wrong with finding that you are going to arrive at some surprising conclusions—after all, that's what learning is all about. In fact, that's what much of humor is about, too—following the logic of a story to its sometimes surprising and funny conclusion, as, for example, in this story:

> There were two guys walking their dogs, one with a German shepherd, the other with a Chihuahua. After a half-hour or so, the two decided to stop in at a tavern. They sat down at the bar and the man with the German shepherd ordered a beer. The bartender said, "I'm sorry, sir, but I can't serve you. We don't allow pets in this place."
>
> Thinking quickly, the man replied, "Oh, that's not my pet, that's my seeing-eye dog." The bartender apologized and turned to the other individual: "I'm sorry, sir, but we don't allow pets in here." Taking a cue from his friend, the man said, "That's not a pet, that's my seeing-eye dog."
>
> The bartender looked at the dog and said, "You're telling me that you have a Chihuahua for a seeing-eye dog?"
>
> Without blinking an eye, the man replied, "You mean to say they gave me a Chihuahua?"

In this book, we are simply going to follow economic logic as it applies to the sports industry, wherever it may lead. We think you'll find it's an enlightening and interesting way to look at pro team sports. Our arguments are laced with examples and tables of data about teams and players as well, but to keep the body of the book as readable as possible we've consigned all the tables to the back of the book.

That's it. As Deep Throat said to Woodward and Bernstein in the Watergate investigation, "Follow the money!" And we will begin with what has become the most important source of money for pro team sports—the media.

2

THE MEDIA

Why is television like a steak? Because it is a medium where it's rare to find anything well done.

—Radio comic Fred Allen in the late 1940s

Fred Allen made his comment about television back in the days when TV was first coming onto the scene, before the coaxial cable and national TV networks. However, in our modern, technologically advanced, communications-centered society, things haven't changed all that much. With sixty or more channels to surf, who over the age of twelve can find a program worth watching—other than sports of course? On the other hand, TV (or, more generically, the media) today is routinely blamed for just about all of our current ills—crime on the streets, teenage obesity, the decline in school test scores, the deterioration of family values, racial strife, the drug culture, the war of the sexes, political campaign corruption. You name it, the media are implicated as the root of the problem. With such perceived power for good or evil in our society, and with the prominence of TV in the sports business, is there any doubt that the market power exercised by the media in the sports industry should be examined first in this book?

Those who criticize the media's power and the way it is exercised are of course following a long-hallowed American tradition of "blaming the messenger" for the disagreeable message. Needless to say, most of us, including the most vocal critics of the media, would be much happier with a society that was less confrontational and more public-spirited, one where individuals took personal responsibility for their actions. But our present-day society (like all societies from the past) doesn't quite live up to our ideals. When the media reflect the facts of the society we actually live in, often we blame the media rather than society itself.

There is another, more fundamental, apparent misunderstanding of the media. It might simply be semantics. When a term like "the media" is used, it gives the impression that there is some single entity out there making purposeful decisions, including the decisions to air programs or views with which we heartily disagree. Nothing could be further from the truth. In our present-day world there is an absolutely mindboggling array of information sources and entertainment available to us, ranging from local libraries through newspapers and magazines, movies, radio, television, and cable, to the Internet and beyond.

With a few notable exceptions, each of the purveyors of information and entertainment is in the business to make money, and the way you make money is by selling something that the audience wants to buy, at a price they are willing to pay. There are strong competitive pressures working on every media outlet, including the most prominent, such as network television.

Because of the enormous audiences that network television reaches, the implication is that network television has a corresponding degree of power to influence the views and behavior of those audiences. But this ignores the fact that a network retains its audience only if it presents programs that the audience wants to watch (and wants to watch more than the programs being presented on other stations). There are few industries in which competition is more intense than the media industry and the television industry in particular.

The competitive media market is the dominant factor that determines what kinds of shows a network will run, including its news shows, certainly in the long run and usually in the short run as well. Let's face it, we are getting on TV the kinds of shows we, the viewing audience, want to watch, as measured by viewer ratings, and not necessarily the kinds of shows that network executives, network anchors, or network owners would choose to watch themselves.

The competitive nature of the media market implies that the "power" possessed by a network or a station is in fact only the power to give the public what it wants—and woe betide any network or station that strays far from that path. As Pogo said, "We have met the enemy, and they are us."

So what has been the role of the media in the creation of the current raft of problems in pro team sports? It's a no-brainer: the networks, the superstations, the cable sports stations, and local TV stations have inundated pro team sports with a veritable monsoon of dollars, which has affected everything and everyone involved in pro team sports. Over the past twenty years, from 1980 on, the most important single factor responsible for the wild explosion in franchise prices and in player and coaching salaries is the huge increase in pro sports' television income. Like Topsy, TV income has grown and grown and grown. In case there are any doubts, some numbers might be in order.

Back in 1980, major league baseball earned a grand total of $80 million from local and network TV and radio. In 1990, major league baseball earned a whopping $612 million from TV and radio. Even after the fiasco of the cancelled 1994 World Series, *Financial World* magazine reported MLB TV and radio income of $706 million in 1996, which translates into an average of about $28 million per team per year, not too far from the average team payroll in baseball that year.

The NFL's story is even more dramatic. In 1960, NFL media income was $3 million, and the AFL was earning $1.6 million. By 1980, a decade after the AFL and NFL merged, media income for the combined league was up to $167 million. In 1990, the figure was $948 million. *Financial World* estimated that total TV income for the NFL in 1996 was $1.29 billion dollars, an average of $43 million per team for the year. And this was before the blockbuster eight-year $17.6 billion national TV contracts that the NFL signed in early 1998, providing for an average payment of around $73 million per year per team through 2005.

It took a while for the NBA to get on the bandwagon, but when it did things really took off. Back in 1964, ABC's network contract with the NBA paid $1.5 million to the league. In 1980, the NBA network contract was worth $18.5 million. In the 1980s, the NBA became a popular TV favorite. By 1990, total NBA TV income (NBC, TNT, and local telecasts) added up to $323 million. The estimated TV income for the NBA in 1996 was $615 million or an average of around $21 million per team. In late 1997, the NBA signed a four-year national TV contract with NBC and TNT that alone will pay the league $660 million per year ($23 million per team) through the 2001–2 season, without taking into account local TV revenues.

The one laggard so far is the NHL. Estimated 1996 media income for the NHL was $164 million, a far cry from that being earned in the other team sports. This amounts to only a little over $6 million per team per year. However, in August 1998, it was announced that a new national TV contract had been signed between the NHL and ESPN for $120 million per year, an increase of almost $100 million per year over the previous contract.

Of course, TV income is not the only source of revenue for sports teams and leagues—there are ticket sales, luxury box rentals, personal seat license fees, stadium income (from parking and concessions), and memorabilia sales. But according to *Financial World* estimates, media income in the 1996 season (almost exclusively from TV) accounted for 38 percent of MLB revenue, 55 percent of NFL revenue, 37 percent of NBA revenue, and 15 percent of NHL revenue. TV has become a major player in pro team sports.

Beyond the impact of TV money, the media have had other related effects. Back in 1964, a public outcry leading to a congressional investigation occurred when CBS became the first media company to enter the pro team sports business by buying the New York Yankees for $14 million. Owners feared overexposure of the sport through CBS telecasts of Yankee games, CBS money being used to buy pennants for the team, and conflicts of interest with CBS sitting in as an owner as well as a potential bidder in negotiations for the national TV contract.

As things turned out, CBS proved utterly incompetent in operating the Yankees, turning a traditional pennant winner and highly profitable team into a loser on the field and at the gate. CBS also didn't appear to get any other advantages from its ownership position. After a dismal 10-year period, CBS sold the team for $10 million—a $4 million loss, a rare event for a sports franchise—to a syndicate headed by an obscure shipping magnate from Cleveland named George Steinbrenner. The rest, of course, is history.

That was then and this is now, and my how things have changed. The growing influence of TV on pro team sports is indicated by the number of powerful owners of pro sports teams who have deep links to the TV industry. Thirty years ago, Jack Kent Cooke was one of the earliest of the cable TV magnates to get into the business of owning sports teams— Cooke bought the Los Angeles Lakers in 1965 and the Los Angeles Kings in 1966, built and operated the LA Forum where they played, and used televised Lakers' and Kings' games to promote his cable systems. After selling his LA properties in 1979, Cooke took over as the principal owner of the NFL Washington Redskins, which is still owned by his heirs. In effect, Jack Kent Cooke showed the way for a following wave of team owners with ties to TV.

The most notable of these is Ted Turner, who owns the Atlanta Hawks of the NBA and the Atlanta Braves of the NL. Turner's contributions to cable TV are legendary, including establishment of all those cable channels with "Turner" in their names—TNN, TNT, TCM, and the superstation WTBS—and CNN to boot. From the 1970s through the 1990s, Braves' and Hawks' telecasts became the vehicles for promoting WTBS and cable TV in general. In 1996, Turner sold the Turner Broadcasting operations to Time Warner, where he is now vice president. Time Warner remains a major player in cable TV, but Turner retains ownership of the Hawks and the Braves.

A second giant in the media industry with strong links to pro team sports is the Tribune Company of Chicago, which publishes the *Chicago Tribune* and owns the Chicago Cubs, along with another of the leading superstations, WGN, and a string of local television stations. At one time in the early 1990s, the Tribune Company did the local telecasts of the Cubs and the White Sox on WGN, the Angels and Dodgers on KTLA, the Yankees on WPIX, the Phillies on WPHL, and the Colorado Rockies on KWGN, all stations owned by the Tribune Company.

Yet another major player in the media and sports industries is the Disney Company, which owns ABC and ESPN along with its own cable channel and various local TV interests. Beginning in the early 1990s, Disney began to move into the pro sports business, acquiring an NHL expansion franchise, the Anaheim Ducks, and purchasing control of the AL Anaheim Angels. There have been reports in the press that Disney is one of the possible bidders for an NFL expansion franchise for the Los Angeles–Orange county territory when that becomes available.

The most recent addition to the list of team owners with ties to the media is the new owner of the LA Dodgers, Rupert Murdoch. Murdoch is president of the News Corporation, which owns the Fox network and its related cable offspring. Among other things, Fox has moved into local telecasting of major league baseball in a big way. *Sports Illustrated* (May 25, 1998, p. 46) reported that the Florida Marlins were "one of only six major league teams for which Fox hasn't yet gobbled up local broadcasting rights."

Other current or recent past team owners with interests in TV include Red McCombs, owner of Clear Channel Communications, the new owner of the NFL Minnesota Vikings; and Charles F. Dolan, a leading figure in the MSG (Madison Square Garden) cable network and at one time a part owner of the NHL New York Rangers and NBA New York Knicks. There is Wayne Huizenga, a past owner of Blockbuster Video, who also owns the NFL Miami Dolphins and the NHL Florida Panthers, and who owned the NL Florida Marlins until that team was put on the market in 1998. Huizenga also owns the Miami TV station that airs the local telecasts of those teams. In the 1980s, the Boston Celtics bought a Boston TV station and used the station as the outlet for their televised games, but the station has since been sold.

Links between the media and sports are not without their potential problems. When there is joint ownership of a team and a superstation, the revenue potential of a nationally televised team increases the incentive to the owner to field a championship team, which promotes forays by the team into the free-agent market, which in turn puts upward pressure on player salaries. The success story of the Atlanta Braves during the 1990s is a case in point, and some have expressed worries about the beefing up of the Dodgers' lineup since Murdoch acquired the team. On the other hand, the Braves were a dismal failure for years under Turner's ownership and nothing—including all that Tribune Company money—seemed to work for the hapless Cubs until their surprising success in the 1998 season.

TV and sports can lead to some interesting confrontations. In 1996, the Fox network decided to introduce a cable news channel, Fox News, as a direct competitor to Time Warner's established CNN cable news channel. Time Warner operates the largest New York city cable system and refused to include the new Fox News channel as part of its basic cable offering. As it turned out, the Fox network had contracts expiring at the end of 1996 with other Time Warner cable systems, including ones in Green Bay, Wisconsin, and Austin, Texas, neither of which had a local Fox station. Fox also had the rights to televise the Super Bowl in January 1997. After being rebuffed in its attempts to get Fox News on Time Warner's New York City cable system, the Fox network began running ads in December 1996 advising cable users in Green Bay and Austin (fans of two Super Bowl possibilities, the Packers and the Cowboys) that they might need to upgrade their old-fashioned TV antennas to pick up the Super Bowl over the air from some distant TV station, because Fox would not be renewing its contracts with their local cable systems, hence the Super Bowl would not be available on their cable systems. The threats paid off; Fox News was added to the New York City Time Warner system in time to save Super Bowl Sunday for those deliriously happy Green Bay fans, and for those pleased if somewhat less than deliriously happy Cowboys fans.

Bottom-line considerations also resulted in some notable battles in pro team sports involving the role of superstations in telecasting league games across the country. In the early 1990s, the Tribune's superstation WGN signed a contract with the Chicago Bulls under which WGN put twenty-five to thirty Bulls games per season on WGN—games that were then carried across the country on various cable systems. The WGN games competed with local telecasts by league teams and with national telecasts under the NBA's network contract. The NBA's first reaction was to pass a rule limiting the number of Bulls games that could be shown on WGN to twenty per year. Both the Bulls and WGN sued the NBA. The resulting case went to the U.S. Supreme Court, which ruled in favor of WGN. The NBA then adopted a different approach. The league signed a contract with NBC under which title to all nationally televised games was given to NBC, which then demanded payment from

WGN for any Bulls game aired on the superstation. This also resulted in a court case, with the decision going in favor of the NBA. In the current situation the leading superstations (WGN and WTBS) now have contracted with NBC and the NBA for the privilege of showing league games, with WTBS dropping its former policy of showing only Atlanta Hawks games and WGN reducing its scheduled number of Bulls games to around the level originally demanded by the NBA.

All of this leads us in a somewhat roundabout way to the media's role in the problem of competitive balance in pro sports leagues. Competitive balance has been a problem plaguing pro team sports from its earliest days—this is not something peculiar to the era of free agency and television. After all, it was back in the pre–free agency and pre-television days that the Yankees simply owned the American League, George Halas' Bears dominated the NFL, and the Montreal Canadiens had a lock on the Stanley Cup.

At the root of this problem is the lack of balance in drawing potential among franchises: Kansas City, Cincinnati, Pittsburgh, and similar small-market teams are trying to compete against teams located in New York, Chicago, and Los Angeles, but without the revenue potential of the big-city teams.

While the lack of balance in drawing potential is a fact of life in sports, the introduction of local television into the picture has exacerbated the problem. This is especially true for the two sports that are in the most trouble so far as the bottom line is concerned, namely major league baseball and the NHL. These also happen to be the two sports where local TV plays a more important role in league finances than national TV.

All leagues share national TV income equally among league members (except for temporary arrangements discriminating against new expansion teams), so that national TV revenues act to promote the survival of small-market teams. On the other hand, local TV revenue goes exclusively to the home team in all leagues, which can create additional problems for small-market teams beyond those caused by a difference in gate revenue potential among franchises.

Tables 2-1 through 2-4 in the back of the book present the *Financial World* estimates of media income by teams in all major sports leagues, 1990 through 1997. The one league in which TV's impact on competitive balance is not an issue is the NFL, where local TV income is generated only during the preseason and is miniscule compared with national TV income. For 1996, excluding the expansion teams from Jacksonville and Carolina, which were short-changed on national TV revenue sharing, the narrow range of NFL team media income was from a low of $42.8 million (Indianapolis) to a high of only $48.0 million (Chicago).

By contrast, the 1996 statistics for MLB show that average media income per team was $25.2 million, but the range was from a low of $15.1 million (Milwaukee) to a high of $69.8 million (New York Yankees). Predictably, the low media income teams were mainly those from the smaller cities—Kansas City, Milwaukee, Pittsburgh, San Diego, and Minnesota— while the Yankees' TV income towers far above that of all other teams.

In the NBA, the average media income in 1996 was $21.2 million per team. The Lakers led all teams with $36.5 million in media income, while the expansion Vancouver Raptors, with $14.5 million, had the lowest media income figure. The highest media income teams were mainly from large cities— the Los Angeles Lakers, Chicago Bulls, and New York Knicks —while the lowest media income again went mainly to small-market teams such as Indiana, Milwaukee, Sacramento, and Utah.

Finally, the estimated NHL average media income in 1996 was $6.3 million per team. The top team was the Boston Bruins with $11.8 million; at the bottom, Colorado had $3.0 million in media income. Among the other top teams were the New York Islanders, the New York Rangers, and the Detroit

Red Wings. The other bottom teams included Hartford, Dallas, and San Jose.

Generally speaking, the more important local TV (as compared with national TV) is in media income, the wider is the gap in media income between the have-teams, the big-market teams, and the have-nots, the small-market teams.

A simple way to eliminate most of the bad effects of local TV on the imbalance of revenue potential in a league, of course, would be to institute something approaching equal sharing of local TV income between the home and visiting teams. But this requires cooperation from the big-market teams, who have no interest at all in moving in that direction. In any case, as of 1998, none of the major sports leagues has adopted local TV revenue sharing between home and visiting teams.

Before leaving this issue, we should note that the estimates of media income provided by *Financial World* are estimates of what the team is receiving in media income. When a team owner also has TV interests, as in the case of WGN or WTBS, there can be important "spill-over" income benefits to the owner that do not appear as income for the team itself. We will return to this topic in Chapter 5.

Thus far, we've been looking at the income that teams and leagues derive from television, but there is another side to the television revenue picture as well—that of the networks and cable stations that air the games. How are they faring in the booming sports television market of the late 1990s?

We've already emphasized that TV is a highly competitive industry, peopled by firms that are very much motivated by profits—they'd better be or they're out of business. And the offerings on TV are absolutely driven by demographics, the number of viewers in various age and income groups, because the firms that advertise on TV channel their advertising money to reach specific demographic groups. The 1970s and 1980s were decades in which the baby-boomer generation, the first to be raised on TV and the first couch-potato generation, became a targeted audience for TV programming. Pro football and pro basketball, the two sports that are most TV-friendly, were prime beneficiaries of the evolving demographics. Baseball benefited as well, with big increases in viewership of pro team sports programming.

So the underlying reason for the huge increases in TV income in sports over the past twenty years is the emergence of a large group of individuals who are avid TV watchers, who have money to spend, and who find pro team sports, especially pro football and pro basketball, a desirable TV offering. That audience in turn attracts big bucks in the form of advertising dollars for networks televising pro team sports. Given this situation, it stands to reason that a sizable share of the money that flows through the TV spigot must end up with the networks or the cable giants, right? Well, no—that's not quite what the record tells us.

In 1990, CBS signed a four-year contract with MLB in part to provide some in-season coverage of the sport, but primarily to acquire rights to the premiere events on the baseball schedule —the All Star game, the playoffs and LCS (League Championship Series), and the World Series. CBS paid $1.06 billion for the national TV rights for four baseball seasons (1990–93). CBS reportedly ended up losing roughly $500 million on its baseball contract and announced that it had no interest in getting involved in the sport ever again.

Also in 1990, the NFL signed its own four-year TV contracts (with CBS, NBC, ABC, ESPN, and TNT) for around $1 billion per year. In 1993, when testifying in the *WGN v. NBA* superstation trial, Dick Ebersol, president of NBC Sports, said that NBC was considering dropping the NFL when contract negotiations came up in 1994. He estimated that NBC would lose $88 million on its NFL contract in 1993 alone. Total losses under NBC's 1990 four-year NFL contract were estimated to run something on the order of $200 million. It also was reported that CBS was losing roughly twice as much as NBC on its NFL contract, with ABC losing approximately the same amount as

NBC. In 1991, CBS wrote off sports losses of $322 million on its various TV contracts, most of which represented losses on its baseball contract.

By 1994, when it came time to negotiate the new NFL TV contract, NBC had changed its mind and entered a (successful) bid of $868 million for four more years of televising the AFC games of the NFL package. ABC anted up $920 million for its Monday Night Football program plus a Super Bowl, and ESPN and TNT remained players for secondary games on Sunday and Thursday nights, for $524 million and $496 million, respectively. Left out of the NFL picture was CBS, which was outbid to the tune of over half a billion dollars by Fox. Fox put up a cool $1.58 billion for four years of telecasting NFC football games. Within a year, Fox wrote off $350 million in losses under its new NFL contract, while CBS announced that it was going to make every effort to return to NFL telecasting the next time contract negotiations came around.

In 1998, the NFL TV contracts came to an end, and the bidding war began on new eight-year contracts, covering the 1998 through 2005 seasons. The final scorecard looked something like this:

1. ABC retained its Monday Night Football show, along with three Super Bowl telecasts, for $4.4 billion ($550 million per year).
2. ESPN outbid TNT to obtain sole possession of Sunday and Thursday night football, paying $4.8 billion ($600 million per year).
3. Fox kept its NFC contract and will telecast three Super Bowls, paying $4.4 billion ($550 million per year).
4. CBS outbid NBC for the AFC contract, including two Super Bowl games, spending $4 billion ($500 million per year).

In summary, the 1998 NFL national TV contracts added up to a grand total of $17.6 billion for the eight-year period, or $2.2 billion per year.

When the results were announced, Dick Ebersol of NBC Sports stated that the contracts would result in "catastrophic losses" for the networks involved, up to between $150 million and $200 million per year. On the other side, Sean McManus, president of CBS Sports, was quoted as saying, "We are not going to lose money on this deal. . . . [because of] the value it brings to our stations, the savings in promotional time, the extra value to our affiliates."

Given the past results under the baseball and football contracts, are the winning bids the actions of rational, profit-oriented businessmen, or do we have here a gang of TV executives who can't shoot straight or add up the numbers on an income statement? What in the world is going on if network pro sports, one of the most popular attractions on television, can't earn any money for the networks showing the games?

One explanation is that at least some of the losses reported aren't really losses. What has been reported are the losses chalked up by the sports divisions of the networks, that is, the difference between ad revenue generated by the games and the cost of the games to the network (the rights fee plus salaries of play-by-play announcers, commentators, and off-camera personnel, and other costs of production). That does not mean that the network necessarily lost money on its sports contract, because, as CBS Sports president McManus had noted, there are indirect payoffs to the network from any such contract. An important payoff is the network's ability to use game telecasts to promote other network programs, through its own ads during the game, to a particularly desirable audience, namely eighteen- to thirty-four-year-old middle- to upper-income individuals, primarily males, who are big spenders on items such as cars, computers, and beer.

A second side benefit of sports programming is its attractiveness to network affiliates. The Fox case showed this most dramatically. When Fox acquired its NFC contract, it also acquired a number of new VHF affiliates (in the valuable two to thirteen channel range), affiliates that switched from independent status or CBS to Fox, increasing the viewership for nonsports programming on Fox. The NFC contract also served to increase the market value of existing Fox stations.

Sports programming was Fox's marketing strategy for expanding the Big Three (ABC, NBC, and CBS) into the Big Four, and it was a highly successful move. Although Fox wrote off $350 million in losses in 1994 on its NFL contract, the network as a whole showed an increase in profits (after the $350 million writeoff) from $511 million for the last six months of 1993 to $610 million for the last six months of 1994.

So there are indirect as well as direct revenues to be gained by a network from sports contracts. Network executives aren't necessarily weak in the head when they pay more for TV rights to sports than they can recover in advertising revenues for the games they televise.

Having said this, though, there also can be pressures on the networks to go overboard and simply bid too much in the competitive environment that surrounds TV rights auctions. In a sealed bid auction such as that conducted for TV rights, the winning bid can be subject to what is known as "the winner's curse": if you are the lucky winner in such an auction, you will have agreed to pay more for the item (TV rights in this case) than any of the other interested bidders thought the property was worth. This suggests that you have simply bid too much for the property—if it's as valuable as you think, how come nobody else thought it was worth enough to match or beat your bid?

The notion of a winner's curse shouldn't be pushed too far. There are legitimate reasons why an item might be worth more to one bidder than to others. This was certainly true of Fox's bid for the NFC contract in 1994, and there was some verification of this in the increase in profits for Fox following the acquisition of the NFC rights.

In fact, the logic underlying the winner's curse has a kissing-cousin relationship to a story told about two economists walking down the street. One spies something that looks like a $20 bill. As he bends down to pick it up, the other says, "Don't bother—if it really were a $20 bill, somebody would have already picked it up."

While the Fox bid in 1994 was not an instance of the winner's curse, there still must have been some heads rolling at Fox after the auction results were announced. Once Fox had committed itself to entering the NFL TV market, the main problem Fox faced was coming in with a winning bid as close as possible to the next highest bid, to minimize the amount of money "left on the table" in the parlance of the bidding game. And it appears that Fox did miss the boat on that part of its 1994 deal, bidding almost $600 million more than CBS, and hence leaving the $600 million "on the table" to be scooped up by the NFL. Despite this, Fox ended up better off following its 1994 NFL bid.

On the other hand, sometimes genuine winner's-curse mistakes have been made in bidding for sports TV rights. One apparent instance of this involved the then semipermanent acting commissioner of baseball, Bud Selig, and his band of merry men, the owners of major league baseball teams. When CBS threw in the towel after the 1993 baseball season, after losing $500 million on its $1.06 billion four-year baseball deal, Selig came up with the bright idea of having the baseball owners bypass the middle men and get directly into the business of running the TV side of baseball. MLB joined with NBC and ABC to form TBN, an acronym for The Baseball Network. Under the TBN joint agreement, the three partners would share production costs and ad revenues from "Game of the Week" telecasts during the regular season and from the All Star, playoff, LCS, and World Series games.

Given the less than sparkling record of baseball owners in making money running their own teams, this was the height of chutzpah to think that they could make more money in the TV end of the business than the networks could. Nonetheless, TBN came into operation for the 1994 baseball season with its novel idea of regionalizing national baseball telecasts so that, for example, West Coast fans only got to see West Coast teams playing in the Game of the Week. Also, by simultaneous scheduling of playoff games, TBN insured that fans were not permitted to see all playoff games on TV, only those involving regional teams, a sort of "let them eat cake" approach to the baseball TV audience.

When the owners announced TBN, Bud Selig was quoted as saying, "This is the wave of the future." With MLB under TBN sharing the considerable financial risks associated with running a television operation, the owners proceeded to shoot themselves in the foot by turning the 1994 labor negotiations with the players' union into the strike that wiped out the 1994 World Series. The year 1995 wasn't much better, even after they settled the labor dispute, because baseball fans had been turned off by the events of the year before. In August 1995, NBC and ABC announced that they were pulling the plug on TBN, which met its richly deserved death after the 1995 season. NBC Sports then made a public announcement that because of the poor ratings performance of TBN and because MLB had reneged on various commitments it had made when the original agreement was signed, NBC wanted nothing more to do with baseball for the foreseeable future.

Three months later, in November 1995, the new baseball national television package was announced, to cover the 1996 through 2000 seasons. The whole TBN approach was abandoned, as baseball returned to the old practice of letting TV executives rather than baseball owners run the TV business. The total five-year package came in at $1.68 billion, with Fox anteing up $575 million for the Game of the Week, three World Series, and several playoff and LCS games; Fox-Liberty paying $172 million for two regular-season night games per week; ESPN paying $465 million for Sunday and Wednesday night regular-season games and several playoff games; and, lo and behold, NBC paying $475 million for two World Series, and All Star, playoff, and LCS games.

The first NBC World Series under the new contract, in 1997, featured two small-market teams, Cleveland and Florida.

The TV ratings were miserable, much worse in fact than NBC was getting with its regular programming. One NBC executive even stated publicly that he hoped the Series would go only four games to get it over with, so that NBC could go back to its regular programming. Don Ohlmeyer, president of NBC West Coast operations, was particularly down on baseball and the NBC contract, stating, "This is a sport where you get 10 days for spitting on a ball, and five days for spitting on an umpire," not really the way to promote a product appearing on your own network. It took only two years for NBC to recognize that it has now committed the same mistake twice in a row, and that simply throwing money at sports programming, especially MLB sports programming, doesn't necessarily pay off.

Okay, so there have been some mistakes made by people in the TV business who have at times apparently paid more for television rights to sports games than those games turned out to be worth. This would help to account in part for the low levels of profits earned by the networks and sports cable channels in their TV deals with the leagues. But there is another more basic factor at work, namely the monopoly power of the leagues.

Back in 1962, when Congress was considering a bill (which it later passed) exempting league-wide television contracts from antitrust prosecution, Pete Rozelle, commissioner of the NFL, testified before a congressional committee. At the time, the NFL was operating under a court injunction forbidding it from signing a league-wide national TV contract. Thus, individual teams had signed their own contracts with local stations or networks, and the big-market teams such as the New York Giants were earning substantially more TV income than small-market teams. Rozelle argued that only a league-wide contract would allow the NFL to share television revenues equally among teams, permitting small-market teams such as the Green Bay Packers to survive.

Rozelle must have been persuasive because the antitrust exemption for national television contracts became law that year. However, what Rozelle did not mention was the advantage to the NFL of replacing all those individual team-specific TV contracts with one league-wide contract. In effect, this converted what was essentially a competitive television rights market into a monopolized one. Whereas before the exemption was passed fourteen NFL teams competed with one another to obtain television contracts, after the exemption there was one rights contract to market, controlled by the NFL.

In 1961 under the old regime, total TV income for NFL teams was $3.5 million. In 1964 under the new regime, the national TV contract brought in $16.2 million, with fewer games being telecast. Competition among teams under the old regime reduced the value of TV rights for each team, since there were more games on the air involving other NFL teams to compete with any given NFL game, and because teams were competing with one another to obtain television contracts.

A characteristic of monopolistic markets is that output of the product (TV games in this case) is set at the point where the profits (revenue minus cost) of the monopolist are as large as possible. As compared to competition, output is reduced and the income of the supplier goes up. The NFL case is just one example. The same principle was involved (in reverse) back in 1984 when the National Collegiate Athletic Association (NCAA) was sued by the University of Georgia and the University of Oklahoma. At the time, the NCAA had the authority to control television appearances by college football teams and to act as a monopolist in negotiating television contracts with networks. The NCAA was sued under the antitrust laws and lost the case, with the Supreme Court ruling seven to two that the NCAA actions were violations of the Sherman Antitrust Act.

The court decision abrogated the contracts the NCAA had signed, contracts that were to pay $65 million per year to the college members of the group. Conferences and teams were set free to negotiate their own television contracts. There was an explosion in TV rights signings and in the number of college games on television. After the smoke had cleared and the numbers added up, it turned out that the total value of the contracts negotiated by the various teams and conferences added up to only half of the $65 million that the NCAA had been able to obtain as a monopoly supplier. The gains from monopoly power are not simply a theoretical concept—they are very real.

In brief, under present conditions, the NFL is the monopoly supplier of major league pro football national television rights in the U.S. market, with the same sort of monopoly power exercised in the other pro team sports. When NFL TV rights are auctioned, networks and cable systems bid against one another to obtain these rights. The number of games offered under the rights contract and the terms of the rights, for example the blackout rules, are chosen so as to maximize the potential income for NFL teams. Competitive bidding has the effect of transferring to the monopoly rights holder—the league— the great bulk of the income that can be earned from sale of the rights, over and above a market rate of return on investment by a bidder in the rights. The monopoly power of the league more or less ensures that it is the league and its member owners, rather than the TV networks, who capture the profits from TV contracts. The contracts themselves are framed to make those profits as large as possible. As important as TV money is in the operation of pro team sports, TV networks in effect simply collect the money from advertisers and pass it on to the team owners, after covering their own costs.

The intrusion of TV onto the playing field has changed the way that sports are played. Would there be those celebrations and dances after every tackle and catch, however insignificant, if it weren't for TV? It has also certainly changed the way that sports are marketed. TV should bear its full share of the blame for lionizing those players and owners who people the sports talk shows and beer commercials, but there is much more blame to assign to the fans who provide the audience that keeps the shows and commercials on the tube. Despite all the rhetoric about the power of the media in modern life, TV's main role in pro team sports is to act as a conduit channeling advertising revenues from telecasts to the leagues. The media turn out to be just a highly visible bit player so far as the problems of pro team sports are concerned.

3

UNIONS

Either Miller or baseball has to go. We need to make it the way it
was when Judge Landis was commissioner.

—A comment by Paul Richards in 1969
(Richards had been a major league catcher but was
best known as the manager of the White Sox
[1951–54] and of the Orioles [1955–61])

Back in 1970, a conference
was held in Washington, D.C., at the Brookings Institution.
Brookings's conferences are typically concerned with basic
issues of national and international military, economic, and
political matters, including national security and the government's role in the domestic and world economy. The conference we are concerned with, however, did not deal with
politics or national security matters. Instead, this was the first
conference ever held to deal with the economics of pro team
sports. The conference proceedings appeared several years later
in a book, one of Brookings's all-time bestsellers: *Government
and the Sports Business*, edited by Roger Noll.

Following Brookings's usual practice, the conference list featured academics who presented papers on various aspects of the sports industry. But Brookings also invited members of the industry itself, including owners and heads of the player unions. No active owners from any of the major sports leagues showed up at the conference. Phil Wrigley, then owner of the Chicago Cubs, supposedly wanted to come but was dissuaded by his fellow owners. There were reports that they had argued, with some justification, that joining in the conference would just add a touch of prestige to a gathering of fuzzy-minded economists who inevitably were going to come up with some disagreeable conclusions concerning the anticompetitive practices of pro team sports. So no current owners came, but (also inevitably!) all of the leagues sent their lawyers to observe what was going on and report back.

On the other hand, the leaders of all of the player unions made it to the conference. At the time, this meant Marvin Miller of the Major League Players Association (MLPA), Ed Garvey of the NFL Players Association (NFLPA), Larry Fleischer of the NBA Players Association (NBAPA), and Alan Eagleson of the NHL Players Association (NHLPA). And there was one ex-owner at the conference, too: the legendary Bill Veeck, who was out of baseball at the time but who came in from his Maryland farm to sit in on every one of the conference sessions, chain smoking and putting out his cigarettes in an ash tray he had built into his wooden leg.

There were lots of prominent academics at the conference, but the two individuals who stood head and shoulders above the rest in the room were Veeck, with his wit and his iconoclastic insight into the inner workings of sports leagues, and Marvin Miller, the most intense person in the room and unquestionably the brightest, too.

On the other side from Miller was the lawyer representing major league baseball, a former U.S. senator from California, one of a long-since vanished breed—a moderate Rockefeller Republican—named Tom Kuchel. Watching Miller manhandle

Kuchel in arguments about disputed items, one conference participant whispered to another, "This is murderous. The [baseball] owners have major, major problems in their future. Their best strategy might be simply to let Miller run baseball, and hope for the best." As things turned out, this might not have been a bad idea.

The player unions were still in their infancy in 1970; it was a time when the owners had the undisputed upper hand in all of the major sports leagues. Players were generally very naive about their collective bargaining rights, and the leagues had long-established practices of treating labor laws as something that applied to the rest of the business world, not to sports leagues.

For example, up until mid-1966 when Miller was hired as the executive director of the MLPA, the baseball players' union operated in effect as a "company union," with the owners paying the expenses of the union as well as the salary of Judge Robert Cannon, the director who preceded Miller. Both actions were clear-cut violations of the Taft-Harley Act. Under Judge Cannon, the MLPA did not engage in collective bargaining with owners; instead its main concern centered on preserving the players' pension plan, which was administered by the owners. Owners set the rules without consulation with the players, and those rules were subject to change without notice. Players weren't even provided with copies of the rules ("the laws of baseball") that applied to them. Instead, they were expected to rely on the good faith of the owners and of the commissioner, who was hired by the owners.

At the time, the very idea of a player union was something with which most players felt uncomfortable; after all, they weren't blue-collar workers punching a time clock—they were skilled professionals spending their working hours playing a game, doing something that most men in the country would kill to be able to do. And many of the players believed that the owners were genuinely looking out for the players' interests.

One problem for the players was that Judge Cannon, who supposedly represented their interests, instead came across in his public statements and actions like a cheerleader for the owners. For example, at a 1964 hearing before a congressional committee, Cannon was asked what plans the MLPA had. He replied, "If I might, Senator, preface my remarks by repeating the words of Gene Woodling . . . 'we have it so good we don't know what to ask for next.' I think this sums up the thinking of the average major league ballplayer today." With a friend like this, the players didn't need enemies. Judge Cannon was voted out of office by the players two years later.

On the owners' side, railroad baron George Baer best expressed their position much earlier in time when he made the following classic remark during a coal strike in 1902: "The rights and interests of the laboring men will be protected and cared for, not by the labor agitators, but by the Christian men to whom God in his infinite wisdom has given control of the property interests of the country."

Actually, even as late as 1970, you might have found a sizable number of players who agreed with old George Baer and the owners, which gives some idea of just how far we have come from those not-so-distant days.

It was during the 1970s that player unions came to the fore as principal actors in the pro team sports drama. Since that time there is absolutely no doubt that the unions have played a critical role in setting the stage for the continuing explosive escalation of player salaries in all sports leagues. Along the way, the labor disputes associated with the emergence of unions in sports have led to a deterioration of relations between players and owners, with predictable spin-off effects on fans. Moreover, the rise in union power has led as well to an erosion in the power of coaches, owners, and league commissioners to discipline players, with arbitrators chosen jointly by owners and unions mainly taking over this function. All of these trends within sports, aided and abetted by unions, suggest that the market power possessed by player unions is certainly worth examining. The question then is, to what extent can we pin the blame for the current problems of pro team sports on Marvin Miller and his fellow labor agitators?

Traditionally, outside the sports industry, labor unions have been organized to insulate member workers from competition from outsiders, to make it possible to negotiate pay and benefit packages for members in excess of what they could earn on their own doing their own bargaining. The standard justification offered for unions relates to the presence of market power on the hiring side, possessed by one or perhaps a few large firms, with the union providing a means for exerting "countervailing power" against that possessed by the hiring firms. But as firms and workers have become more mobile, both geographically and technically, competition has tended to eliminate or markedly reduce the market power of firms and of unions as well. Likewise, competition has reduced the perceived benefits of unions to workers. In today's global marketplace, the competitive labor market determines the pay-benefit packages of the vast majority of workers, rather than union-negotiated contracts.

During the very time that traditional unions have been losing members and market power, player unions in pro team sports have flourished. The explanation lies in several facts. First, the large infusion of television income into sports, documented in the previous chapter, provided the strongest incentive for players to act jointly to get as large a share of those revenues as possible. Second, player unions wield more bargaining power in negotiations than do more conventional unions because of the unique skills possessed by their members. And third, player unions have quite different bargaining objectives and often different bargaining tactics than those of conventional unions. These all complement the fact that global competition has not yet eroded the monopoly power of leagues, so that there remains a perceived need for unions on the part of players, as a counter to the market power of the owners.

In contrast to conventional unions, player unions do not negotiate salary contracts for their members—each player negotiates his own contract. Player unions do negotiate league-wide minimum salaries for their members and standard benefit packages (e.g., pension, health insurance, dental insurance, accident insurance) as well as working conditions. But a striking difference between player unions and other unions is that player unions have as a primary objective creating something approaching a competitive labor market for their members. So, while the United Auto Workers or the Teamsters work to shield their members from competition, the player unions have tried to make the player labor market more rather than less competitive. In a switch from the usual situation, it is the owners who have been fighting against the creation of competitive labor markets for players, in opposition to the player unions.

In making a freely competitive labor market for players a prime goal, the player unions that came on the scene in the late 1960s were working to dismantle a set of owner-created rules from the far distant past—in the case of baseball, dating all the way back to the 1870s. The centerpiece of those rules was the so-called "reserve clause" (or "option clause" in sports other than baseball). This was a clause in the standard player's contract in all the sports leagues that stated that, so long as the team submitted a new contract to the player by some specified date prior to the next season, the current contract was extended for one more playing season. If the contract was extended for one more season, the owners interpreted this to mean that the reserve clause of the contract was extended as well, even if the player had not signed the new contract. The upshot was that under the owners' interpretation of the reserve clause, once a player signed his first contract with a team, that team (or any team to which the contract was sold or traded) owned his services for the remainder of his playing career. On the other hand, the player could be dismissed by the team with minimal (two weeks or one month) notice.

The owners' interpretation of the standard player contract was so blatantly one-sided and unfair that the contract was unenforceable in the courts. However, it was very effectively enforced within sports leagues by the member teams. When a sport is controlled by a monopoly league, the typical situation in the history of pro team sports in the United States, a player taking his team to court discovered that even if he won in the court and was released from his contract, no other team in the league would offer him a contract—he was blacklisted in the sport. Thus, right up to the 1970s, as a practical matter the only times players brought court cases against owners concerning the legitimacy of player contracts was when rival leagues were in operation (e.g., during the American League–National League war of 1901–3 or the Federal League war of 1914–15).

The original reserve clause was invented in 1879 by Arthur Soden, one of the owners of the NL Boston Braves. It was adopted within the NL as a device to control player salaries by restricting competitive bidding for players by league teams. It did a pretty fair job of this. However, as the reserve clause came under court challenge during later baseball wars and interleague wars in other sports, owners and their lawyers invented two other justifications for the reserve clause: First, the reserve clause was needed to preserve the public's faith in the "integrity of the sport." Second, the reserve clause was needed to preserve "competitive balance" within a league.

The reasoning underlying the "integrity of the sport" argument has always been a little murky, but apparently the idea was that if players were free to move from team to team, they might throw games in order to curry favor with a prospective employer. In a less extreme scenario, they might not give their all for their current team if they were planning to move, or at least raise doubts in the minds of fans that they might do this. Just why any owner would trust a player who threw games or didn't play all out for his current team, even if it benefited that owner, is hard to figure out. But, in fact, the only well-documented instance of throwing games in major league baseball (following its very early years) occurred in the 1919 World Series, when members of the Chicago White Sox (the infamous "Black Sox") were bribed by gamblers to throw the series.

After buying the White Sox in the late 1950s, Bill Veeck came across the books of the team for 1919 and discovered that the Sox owner, "Old Roman" Charles Comiskey (whom Veeck described as "the cheapest skate in town"), had been paying penurious salaries to his superstar players, who might well have thrown the series as much to get back at Comiskey as for the money they hoped to make for themselves. And it was the reserve clause and other restrictions on player mobility, of course, that made it possible for Comiskey to pay his players so much less than what they were worth and what they would have been paid playing for other teams in the league. During the same period, persistent rumors had it that Ty Cobb and Tris Speaker, two hallowed Hall-of-Famers, were routinely bribing players on other teams to play so as to help Cobb's or Speaker's teams win pennants. These assaults on "the integrity of the game" came during the height of the reserve clause era; the evidence suggests that the reserve clause actually acted to promote cheating and thrown games by players, rather than to discourage it. In particular, in today's free agency player markets, players with large salaries really have a lot to lose if they are caught throwing games, so that free agency acts as a disincentive to cheat. So much for the "integrity of game" argument.

The competitive balance issue is another kettle of fish entirely. The idea is that with a freely competitive market for players, the big-market teams (such as the Yankees or the Dodgers) would acquire a disproportionate share of the playing talent in a league, because star players are worth more to big-market teams (they can generate more money for the big-market team owner) than they are to small-market teams. The resulting lack of "competitive balance" would lead to a fall in gate receipts at small-market teams as their won-lost records declined, and might even lead to bankruptcy and exit from the league for some small-market teams. In fact, if a league becomes too imbalanced, the gate receipts of even strong big-market teams drop, due to the lack of exciting competition from other league teams.

All of this makes a lot of sense. However, it is not at all clear that imposing restrictions on player mobility is the answer to the competitive balance problem. Restrictions on player mobility simply don't work to create competitive balance, as is amply demonstrated by the past history involving its use.

Why? The imbalance of drawing potential among the teams in a league creates incentives for the big-market teams to acquire a disproportionate share of the playing talent of the league, whether there is a reserve clause in place or not. Under a reserve clause setup, the big-market team could not make a higher salary bid for a player signed by a small-market team because the player wasn't free to move. But the big-market team could negotiate with the small-market team to buy the player's contract. Because the player is worth more to the big-market team than to the small-market team, in principle it should be possible to negotiate a price for the contract such that both teams are better off, in bottom-line terms, with a sale of the player from the small- to the big-market team. This is the condition that leads to the movement of players from small- to big-market teams, even under a reserve clause.

Did this actually happen in the history of sports? It certainly did. Branch Rickey sold players by the carload to big-market teams when he was operating the small-market St. Louis Cardinals in the 1920s and 1930s. Boston Red Sox fans still talk about the curse on their team dating back to the disastrous sale of one Babe Ruth to the Yankees after the 1919 season. Connie Mack unloaded two outstanding pennant-winning teams, the Philadelphia Athletics of 1910–11–13–14 and 1929–30–31, to the highest bidders. Clark Griffith sold the best players from his 1933 AL champion Washington Senators, including his own son-in-law, Joe Cronin, to teams with more cash. Later on in the reserve clause era, sales of players by the small-market Kansas City Athletics to the Yankees were so controversial that a congressional committee held a meeting to look into the matter.

The latest instance of star players moving from a small-market to a big-market team through sales or trades—even in the free-agency era—was the "trade of the century" in May 1998 when the Dodgers traded Mike Piazza ($8 million salary) to the Florida Marlins for Gary Sheffield ($10 million salary), Charles Johnson ($3 million salary), Bobby Bonilla ($5.9 million), and Jim Eisenreich ($1.4 million). This is a classic example of what Roger Noll describes as an "unbalanced trade" —the Marlins gave away a lot more in game-winning potential than they received, as indicated by the disparity in salary numbers. The whole point of the trade was to reduce the Marlins' payroll to a level commensurate with its small-market status, as owner Wayne Huizenga was downsizing the team in preparation for selling it. Piazza's career with the Marlins lasted just one week before he also was traded, for two rookies, to yet another big-market team, the Mets. Piazza is a sure-fire Hall-of-Famer, leading Tom Fitzgerald of the *San Francisco Chronicle* (May 27, 1998) to raise the tongue-in-cheek question, "Do you think the Marlins will retire Mike Piazza's number?"

Despite the history of leagues being dominated by their big-market teams under a reserve clause setup, owners continued to convince sportswriters, judges and juries, fans, and even the players themselves that any attempt to junk the reserve clause in favor of free agency, with open competitive markets for players' services, would be disastrous for small-market teams. Economists examining the issue disagreed; in fact, they predicted that free agency would have no effect at all on competitive balance. Why? Because sales and trades of players among teams under a reserve clause system would effectively undo any positive effects of the reserve clause on competitive balance. Switching to free agency wouldn't have any effect on competitive balance, which was already skewed in favor of big-market teams under the reserve clause. It would simply mean that money that previously went to the owners (from the sale of players' contracts) now would go to the players themselves, in the form of higher salaries.

Once player unions became the recognized bargaining agents for players, which happened in all four major sports leagues by the early 1970s, the unions centered in on the reserve clause–free agency issue, with Marvin Miller and the MLPA in the forefront of this battle.

The first collective bargaining agreement in baseball was arrived at in 1968. Miller and the MLPA put aside a direct attack on the reserve clause, but in 1970 they did manage to get an agreement from the owners for arbitration to settle contractual disputes between players and owners, to apply to players with two or more years of service since their last arbitration hearing. In particular, arbitration was available to such players when there was a dispute between the player and the owner over the player's salary for the next season. If the two couldn't reach an agreement through head-to-head negotiations between the player's agent and the team's general manager, the case could go before an arbitration board. In the case of salary disputes, the arbitration process, still in place in major league baseball, is one in which the player and the owner each submit a proposed salary to an arbitration board, which consists of a representative from the union, one from management, and an independent member chosen by the two sides. The arbitration board then has to choose one of the two proposed salaries with arbitration binding on both parties.

The rules of the arbitration process move both sides toward advancing "reasonable" proposals, since an "unreasonable" proposal is almost guaranteed to be rejected by the arbitration board. And this procedure also promotes negotiated settlements. Table 3-1 in the back of the book gives the arbitration results for 1996. There were 76 players who asked for arbitration that year, but in 66 cases (87 percent), the dispute was settled before arbitration. In the ten cases in which arbitration actually occurred, players won seven and teams won three.

Over time, salary arbitration wins have been pretty evenly divided between players and owners. There is next to no evidence that the independent member, the deciding vote in just about every dispute, has been biased in favor of one side or the other. There's a simple explanation for this—either side can fire the independent member without having to specify cause; so, to keep his or her job, the arbitrator had better be unbiased.

Salary arbitration performs one of the important tasks of a competitive market for player services in that it tends to bring the salaries of players with similar playing records into rough equality with one another. ("Old Roman" Comiskey couldn't have gotten by with those minimal salaries if there had been arbitration in 1919.) The documentation used by players and owners in justifying their arbitration claims is playing records (e.g., earned run average [ERA], batting average, runs batted in [RBIs]) and information as to the salaries of players with comparable playing records. The best evidence that an owner's (or player's) proposal is unreasonable is that it does not match up with salaries paid by other owners to players with similar records. Because of the critical importance of salary information to the arbitration process, one of the first steps taken by the MLPA, over the objections of the owners, was to convince its members to make all playing salaries public information for use by all players in arbitration hearings. Thus, each year, the *New York Times* publishes a list of the players for all major league teams and their salaries for the previous season, as supplied by the MLPA.

The point made by Marvin Miller in instituting this policy was that the owners shared salary information among themselves. If players did not share salary information, they would be at an important informational disadvantage in negotiating with any owner. Interestingly, the MLPA is the only union that follows this approach; in the NFLPA, for example, it is a breach of union rules for any player to disclose salary information about other players to outsiders, including the press.

Once salary arbitration was in place, average baseball salaries were bumped up somewhat, as players on the poorer-paying teams were able to force owners to pay salaries comparable to those of the better-paying teams. But of course even the better-paying teams were still availing themselves of the bargaining power advantage the reserve clause provided. The real breakthrough for players' salaries came almost five years later, in an arbitration case involving Andy Messersmith of the Dodgers and Dave McNally of the Montreal Expos. Both had refused to sign contracts for the 1975 season, so their clubs had simply used the terms of their 1974 contracts to pay them for the 1975 season. Messersmith and McNally decided to make a test case of the reserve clause in their contracts, arguing that since the clause only covered the next year after a contract had been signed, the two of them were now free agents—they had played out their "option" year. Miller and the MLPA came out in full support of the two.

The arbitrator in the case, Peter Seitz, ruled in favor of the players, holding that the proper interpretation of the reserve clause in the player contract was that it gave the club the right to the services of the player for the current year and one succeeding year, and then was null and void. The owners appealed the arbitration award to the courts, but Seitz's decision was upheld in the courts, and Seitz was promptly fired by the owners. Three hundred players announced that they were planning to play out their options the next season.

There was some fast footwork by both sides following the Seitz decision. Owners thought they were going to be bankrupted paying competitive market salaries to players, and Miller and the MLPA were concerned that if too many free agents hit the market at the same time, competition among the players would erode the potential gains from free agency. A compromise was reached under which players could exercise free agency only once each six years, with expanded arbitration rights during the intermediate periods. Despite some major confrontations since 1976, this basic compromise (with some minor modifications) continues to be the free agency rule in major league baseball.

Arbitration accomplished what one hundred years of baseball history had been unable to do, namely eliminating the reserve clause. The role of the MLPA was crucial. The MLPA had won arbitration rights in its labor negotiations with management, and once free agency was declared, the MLPA had the clout in the form of strike threats to counter any attempt by the owners to return to the old reserve clause days.

With free agency, even if restricted, in place in major league baseball, player salaries were free to respond to market forces, to the competitive bids of teams for players. This led to an initial spurt in salaries, unrelated to anything that was going on at the box office or in TV contracts but simply a reflection of the move to a more competitive market. Since the introduction of free agency into baseball in 1976, there has been a spectacular rise in player salaries, as discussed and documented in the next chapter. Contrary to popular belief, however, this continuing rise in salaries is not due to escalating demands by unions. Instead, with something approaching a competitive player market in place, the rise in salaries reflects primarily the increases in gate and TV revenue that have taken place over time, and only secondarily the transfer of some monopoly profits ("rents") from owners to players. In brief, what is going on in the market for players is the same thing that goes on in any competitive market for any scarce resource—as the resource (major-league-caliber players) becomes more valuable, it earns more.

The introduction of free agency in baseball also provided a laboratory experiment of sorts concerning the claim of owners that free agency would destroy competitive balance in baseball. Did it? In a comparison of the ten-year (1966–75) period preceding free agency to the ten-year (1976–85) period following free agency, the list of pennant-winning teams in the AL and NL, together with the number of pennants won, is as follows:

I. Pre–Free Agency (1966–75)				II. Post–Free Agency (1976–85)			
NL		**AL**		**NL**		**AL**	
Cincinnati	3	Baltimore	4	LA	3	New York	4
LA	2	Oakland	3	St. Louis	2	Baltimore	2
St. Louis	2	Boston	2	Philadelphia	2	KC	2
New York	2	Detroit	1	Cincinnati	1	Milwaukee	1
Pittsburgh	1			Pittsburgh	1	Detroit	1
				San Diego	1		

Note: Between 1986 and 1997 (excluding 1994 when the seasons were not completed), the breakdown of pennant winners was as follows: NL: Atlanta 4, Philadelphia 1, Florida 1, New York 1, St. Louis 1, LA 1, San Francisco 1, Cincinnati 1; AL: Oakland 3, Minnesota 2, Cleveland 2, Toronto 2, Boston 1, New York 1.

If the owners were right, period II, the post–free agency period, would show a drastic rise in the concentration of league championships. In fact, the two appear almost identical, except that the post–free agency period actually shows a little more competitive balance than the pre–free agency period. The note indicates that the pattern continued up through the 1997 season. Other measures of competitive balance show the same pattern. Based on the baseball experience, there is no evidence at all that free agency has had negative effects on competitive balance.

While we have concentrated on major league baseball, player unions in the other pro team sports have also had impressive success in negotiating changes in their leagues' player reservation systems, although the results have not been as striking as in baseball. There is a modified form of free agency in all sports, with MLB and the NBA having the freest systems, followed by the NFL, while the most restrictive rules apply in the NHL. Free agency in some form or other has become so much a part of the labor picture in sports that the focus of team owners has shifted away from restoring the old reserve system to a new idea, namely, setting salary caps (more properly termed "payroll caps") on team payrolls. The objective is the same—to restrict the extent of competitive bidding by teams for players—but the rhetoric differs and plays out better for the owners because, while the reserve clause placed restrictions on players, the salary cap places restrictions on owners.

The justification for restrictions has changed as well. Owners still occasionally talk about the need for a salary cap to "preserve" competitive balance, but the experience of baseball under free agency makes it hard to keep arguing this with a straight face. Instead, there is more talk about the need for a cap on payrolls to keep teams profitable, especially small-market ones.

The salary cap first saw the light of day in the NBA, beginning with the 1983–84 season. It's hard to believe it today but at the time, the NBA was in economic trouble; the league claimed that eighteen of its twenty-three teams lost money in the 1981–82 season. Rumors existed that five teams—the Cleveland Cavaliers, Indiana Pacers, Utah Jazz, Kansas City Kings, and San Diego Clippers—were scheduled to be dropped by the league. (In the event, all five teams survived, but the Kings later moved to Sacramento and the Clippers left for Los Angeles.)

The NBA operates under "winner take all" rules—there is no sharing of gate or local TV revenues with visiting teams. The shaky status of the weak-drawing franchises in the league in the late 1970s led to a move within the NBA by such teams to change league rules to provide for gate and local TV sharing. But such a change in the rules requires a three-fourths majority vote of league members, with six teams at the time able to veto such a move.

On December 7, 1979, the New York Knicks hosted a meeting at the 21 Club in New York City. In attendance were representatives of the five other strong-drawing NBA franchises of the time—the New Jersey Nets, Philadelphia 76ers, Boston Celtics, Los Angeles Lakers, and Chicago Bulls. The meeting was intended to develop unified resistance to any changes in the gate or local TV revenue-sharing rules of the NBA, and ran into no problems succeeding in this. The "unholy six" (as they were dubbed by some of the frustrated small-city owners) formed a blocking coalition against such a change. Consequently, the rules for sharing revenues among teams have remained unchanged in the NBA up to the present day.

Having been rebuffed in their attempt to get some help from their rich fellow league members, the weak-drawing teams and the NBA commissioner's office turned to the NBA Players Association. The league argued that major concessions were needed from the union to avoid the loss of jobs that would result from downsizing the league as marginal weak-drawing franchises were eliminated. The labor contract arrived at was one in which the league agreed to a minimum level of total salary expenditures (at 53 percent of total league revenues). At the level of the individual NBA team, a payroll ceiling and floor were imposed. The team payroll ceiling (the "cap") was fixed at 53 percent of total league revenues divided by the number of NBA teams, and the team payroll floor was set at 47 percent divided by the number of NBA teams. The idea was that, since each team would be spending roughly the same amount on player salaries, the small-market owners would be able to field teams that were competitive with the big-market teams, and this would solve the financial problems of the small-market teams.

The NBA salary cap went into effect beginning with the 1983–84 season and has been a part of NBA rules ever since. The years under the cap have been the most successful in NBA history with league revenues, profits, and player salaries skyrocketing. The experience of the NBA did not go unnoticed by owners of teams in other pro sports. In 1993, the NFL signed a seven-year labor agreement incorporating a salary cap (since extended for several more years), and owners in MLB and the NHL have both tried (unsuccessfully) to force a salary cap on their player unions. This led to the baseball strike of 1994 and early 1995 that wiped out 52 days of the 1994 regular season, along with the 1994 playoffs and World Series, and 25 days of the 1995 season; and to a 103-day lockout of players in the NHL, wiping out half of the 1994–95 season.

On the other hand, the NBAPA has had second thoughts about the cap and has been trying for years to find a way to get rid of it. After failing to eliminate the cap in labor negotiations, the union attempted to decertify itself in order to bring antitrust charges against the league for implementing a cap. The courts rejected the union bid in 1995, holding that it was disingenuous of the union to claim antitrust violations by the league in implementing something that the union had voluntarily agreed to in earlier bargaining. Because the union had voluntarily accepted a cap to help out the NBA in its bad times, the union was now saddled with the cap in the NBA's good times and the league had no interest at all in repaying the favor the union had done for the league.

An interesting aspect of the whole cap issue is that the success of the NBA since 1983 has had almost nothing to do with the cap. The cap was supposed to alleviate problems in the league by eliminating the gap between salary spending of the big-market teams and that of the small-market teams. In 1983, before the cap, the range in expenditures was from a high of $9 million (Los Angeles Lakers) to a low of $3 million (Utah Jazz). In 1993, ten years after the cap was implemented, salary expenditures ranged from a high of $35 million (the Lakers again) to a low of $15 million (Dallas Mavericks). Over the period 1990–96, *Financial World* was reporting that the Lakers were spending roughly twice as much on player costs as the lowest team, the Minnesota Timberwolves. The salary cap has not equalized salary expenditures, even after almost fifteen years.

Because the cap has been ineffective in equalizing salary expenditures, competitive balance in the NBA hasn't improved either. In the ten years prior to the cap, the Celtics won three titles, the Lakers two, and Portland, Golden State, Washington, Seattle, and Philadelphia each won one. In the ten years after the cap, the Lakers and the Bulls won three titles each, while Boston and Detroit won two each. There was actually more concentration of championships after the cap was instituted than before, and a similar story could be told about other measures of competitive balance.

Because the cap wasn't effective in equalizing salary expenditures or competitive balance, it had no effect on the spectacular success of the NBA in the post-cap (post-1983) period. What did happen was that NBA basketball went on a popularity roll that continues up to the present time. As noted in the media chapter, TV revenues for the league rose from less than $50 million in 1983 to over $600 million in 1996, and attendance soared as well. It was the huge increase in revenue, including especially the equally shared national TV revenue, which funneled money to the small-market teams as well as the big-market teams, that solved the NBA's economic problems, not the salary cap. And a big share of the credit for this goes to the presence of just three players, the true NBA superstars of the era—Magic, Bird, and Michael.

The appeal of the cap to owners, of course, is that it's a way to control salary costs. But the NBA experience shows that the cap didn't work here, either. While the league guarantees only 53 percent of revenues to players, loopholes in the cap have fueled a rise in salaries so rapid that most years players receive 60 percent or more of league revenues.

What went wrong? Why didn't the cap work as planned? The main reason is a seemingly innocuous provision, insisted upon by the big-market teams, allowing any team to violate the cap ceiling in order to match another team's offer for one of the first team's players. The problem, of course, is that the only players you as an owner would want to keep are precisely those players that other teams want to hire, and especially those that are so in demand that their salary offers from other teams go through the roof. Thus, this "innocuous" provision gets invoked over and over again every season, as players exercise their free agency rights.

So, in their 1996 negotiations the owners tried to put a "cap" on their own "cap," by bringing forth a "luxury tax" that was to apply to payroll expenditures that exceeded the cap ceiling. After acrimonious labor negotiations, this proposal was finally dropped and there was labor peace for a full two years. In June 1998, the owners exercised their right under the agreement to reopen negotiations, and, in July 1998, they announced a lockout. As of late October 1998, the lockout was still in force, resulting in the cancellation of at least part of the 1998–99 season.

Which gets us to one of the most irritating things about player unions from the point of view of fans—the confrontational nature of labor negotiations in sports, as evidenced by the frequency of strikes and/or lockouts involving the player unions. We seem to read more news about strikes, lockouts, and labor negotiations in sports than we do about the games themselves. Is this simply a case of exaggeration on the part of fans? Well, sure, but there's still some basis for fan discontentment.

Think of things this way. Over the ten-year period 1987–96, there were a grand total of 403 work stoppages in the entire U.S. economy as reported in the 1997 *Statistical Abstract* (p. 439). Of these, five involved the sports industry—a lockout in baseball in 1990 and the players' strike in 1994–95; an NFL players' strike in 1987; and an NHL players' walkout in 1992, followed by an NHL owners' lockout in 1994–95.

There are approximately 4,000 members of the players' unions in all four sports, and approximately 16 million labor union members in the United States overall. If the rest of the union labor force had been as active in work stoppages as the players, there would have been 20,000 work stoppages between 1987 and 1996, rather than 403. You couldn't have walked down the street without bumping into a picket. Yes, labor negotiations in sports are a lot more confrontational than in other industries.

The history of work stoppages in sports can be briefly summarized as follows:

League	Year	Setting
MLB	1969	Lockout by owners of spring training, to the end of February.
	1972	Player walkout through the first half of April. Complete regular season schedule played.
	1976	Lockout by owners, end of February to mid-March.
	1981	Player strike, mid-June to first week of August. Owners had strike insurance. Split-season format used to determine league champions.
	1990	Lockout by owners from mid-February to mid-March.
	1994	Player strike beginning early August. Strike wiped out 52 days of the 1994 season, playoffs, and World Series, as well as 25 days of the 1995 season.
NFL	1982	Player strike from September until the end of November. Reduced regular season schedule, with expanded playoffs.
	1987	Player strike from end of September to end of October. Replacement players used for three games; schedule reduced by one game.
NHL	1992	Player walkout on April 1.
	1994	Lockout by owners for 103 days of regular NHL season.
NBA	1998	Lockout by owners, resulting in at least partial cancellation of regular season.

This raises the question of why strikes and lockouts have been so frequent in pro sports. Primarily, there is a lot of money in the form of monopoly revenues— mainly television income— to be fought over. In addition, player costs dominate the cost picture for pro sports leagues. If owners wish to control their costs, then first and foremost, they must control payroll costs, which puts them on a collision course with the player unions.

Beyond this, strikes or lockouts are expensive undertakings for both sides in a labor dispute, so they are not undertaken lightly and not unless there are some believable grounds on both sides for expecting a positive payoff from a shutdown. One factor leading to shutdowns is that each side perceives potential weaknesses on the other due to internal problems. Unions see the opportunity to drive a wedge between the profitable big-market teams and the marginal small-market teams. Likewise, owners see the differing incentives of superstars and the journeymen players on the union side. Each side can see the weaknesses of the other as grounds for optimism if a labor confrontation gets pushed to the wall. The big-market teams have an incentive to settle disputes quickly, while the small-market teams tend to be the hardliners on the owners' side. Superstars are concerned with maintaining their free agency rights, while journeymen players are more concerned with issues such as the league minimum salary and the level of player pensions; league proposals attempt to exploit that divergence of interests.

The availability of substitutes (replacement players) has played a role in the success of owners in strikes involving the NFL Players Association, and the short careers of NFL players has also been cited as a source of weakness for the NFLPA. The fact that MLB owners were protected in 1981 by strike insurance from Lloyd's of London provided a positive incentive for the owners to take a strong stand; that particular strike was settled almost immediately after the strike insurance ran out.

The potential for conflict between superstars and journeymen players was made clear in 1995 when Charles Gourdine, executive director of the NBA Players Association, negotiated an agreement with the owners that was opposed by a group of superstars, headed by Michael Jordan, Patrick Ewing, and Scottie Pippin. The dissidents filed a petition with the National Labor Relations Board to decertify the union.

The internal battling continued for months, with Gourdine renegotiating his original agreement, which continued to be opposed by the group headed by the superstars. In the end, players supported Gourdine and his agreement by a union vote of 226–134 and the dissident group backed down. Six months later, Gourdine was fired as executive director, to be replaced by Alex English, someone more acceptable to the superstars.

The stakes at dispute in labor confrontations in sports are not trivial. Roger Noll has provided an analysis of the 1994–95 baseball strike in which players lost about $300 million in salaries and owners about $350 million in net revenues. He estimates that the salary cap–luxury tax proposal in dispute would have shifted approximately $1.5 billion in income from players to owners over the duration of the proposed agreement. In the event, of course, the players won and the salary cap–luxury tax proposal was junked, so the players' decision to strike paid off: in effect, they paid $300 million to avoid losing $1.5 billion.

And, from hindsight, the owners made a bad decision. But before the fact there was uncertainty as to which side would prevail. How optimistic would the owners have to be to justify the $350 million loss they suffered because of the strike? It turns out that if they thought that the odds were around two to one in their favor, a two-thirds chance of winning, then it would be worth their while to take the $350 million loss of a strike. At odds much below that, the rational decision would have been to avoid the strike. Given that the owners have lost every confrontation they have had with the players' association, you have to believe that two to one odds on the owners' winning was unrealistic.

In the early days of the player unions back in the 1970s, it was easy to identify the good guys and the bad guys in pro team sports. The owners in every league were definitely the ones with the black hats, the side with all the bargaining clout, supporting and defending a system of market restrictions that was blatantly unfair to players. And, of course, .240-hitting second basemen were not earning multimillion-dollar contracts either. There are some exceptions but generally speaking, the player unions, the ones with the white hats, won the early labor wars and managed to dismantle the worst of the old player market restrictions.

The balance of power in pro sports has shifted. Today it is the player unions who have obtained the upper hand in negotiations (with the exception of the NHL), and it is the player unions who are defending the current free agency system, with the owners attempting to dismantle or modify it. With average salaries in MLB hovering around the $1.5 million mark, players are no longer viewed by fans as the sympathetic victims of greedy owners. What was once a fight between the good guys and the bad guys is now widely regarded as one between rich players and rich owners, two groups of spoiled, wealthy individuals fighting with each other over the monopoly revenue that a sport generates. The reaction of most fans is, a plague on both your houses, get back to playing ball. Labor negotiations in sports continued to be bitter and confrontational, in part because of past history but also because there are big bucks involved. Generally speaking, however, the issues under negotiation simply involve how the two sides will divide the revenue melon, which is important to the two sides, of course, but is of minimal interest to the rest of us.

So what do we conclude about the role of the player unions in creating the problems that plague sports today? Certainly pro team sports is much more acrimonious with the unions around than it was back in the days when the owners ran the show with an iron fist. This, we believe, is the main charge that can be levied against unions. Of course, it takes two to tango—the owners are every bit as much responsible for the carnage of the labor negotiating process as the unions.

Player unions have been successful in revamping the player market so that player salaries are now more closely related to what players are worth to teams, which is what competitive labor markets are supposed to do. The unions cannot be tagged with direct responsibility for the outlandish salaries that players earn, any more than the motion picture actors' union or the musicians' union can be tagged with responsibility for the outlandish money earned by matinee idols or rock stars. And the evidence is overwhelming that the move to a competitive labor market has not resulted in any further deterioration of competitive balance in baseball or the other sports.

Unions do provide backup support for players in disputes relating to disciplinary infractions and the resulting penalties imposed by teams and leagues. From a formal legal point of view, such support is needed to insure that players are protected from arbitrary actions, just as every defendant, however obnoxious, is afforded the right of an attorney to defend him. In practice, it turns out that, however guilty of gross misconduct a player is, if he has enough playing ability he will find a team to give him a contract. This suggests that the problem of players out of control is not so much a union problem as it is a problem of the owners, and ultimately of the fans, who seem willing to ignore almost any crime, misdemeanor, or felony if the player helps the team to win.

All of this leads to the general conclusion that player unions possess the power they have primarily because of the monopoly revenues that sports generates, and that their role in exacerbating the problems of pro team sports is quite limited.

PLAYERS

If the reserve clause is killed, there won't be any big leagues or
any little leagues.

—Clark Griffith, 1946

Total free agency would destroy the National Football League.

—Paul Tagliabue, *Sports Illustrated*,
September 10, 1990, p. 42

David Stern, the commissioner
of the NBA, must have taken it as a sign of the Apocalypse
when news came out in early October 1997 that the Minnesota
Timberwolves had signed their twenty-one-year-old power forward, Kevin Garnett, to a six-year contract paying $126 mil-
lion, after Garnett had turned down an earlier offer of $103
million. The dollar amount was awesome, particularly since
this was not a seasoned all-star veteran such as Michael Jordan,
Patrick Ewing, or Karl Malone, but a second-year player just
two years out of high school. That amount averages $21 mil-
lion per year. The Target Center in Minneapolis seats roughly
20,000 fans, and there are 41 regular-season home NBA games

at the Center. Assuming the Target Center is sold out all season long, the T-Wolves have to set aside more than $25 per regular season seat per game just to pay Garnett's salary. Alternatively, the Timberwolves in effect will simply turn over to Garnett the team's annual check of $21 million (plus change) that it receives each year under the NBA's new national TV contract with NBC. Or think of it this way: Glen Taylor bought the T-Wolves franchise for $88 million just two years earlier, that is, for $38 million less than he now was going to pay Garnett! Insiders raised the intriguing question of where in the world the T-Wolves expected to get the money to pay the rest of the team.

Six months or so after the Garnett contract was signed, Glen Taylor was quoted as saying that the team could not afford to offer contracts comparable to Garnett's to the two other rising stars of the team, Tom Gugliotta and Stephon Marbury, and might lose these two players because of this. That's understandable; the salary cap for the 1996–97 season was $24.3 million per team. Deduct Garnett's $21 million and that leaves just $3.4 million to spread over the other 11 players on the team, assuming—admittedly contrary to the facts—that the salary cap is a hard cap, that is, strictly enforced.

At about the same time, Commissioner Stern, as noted earlier, announced that the NBA planned to reopen the labor contract the league had signed just two years earlier, because NBA salaries were out of control, salary cap or no salary cap. Stern cited the Garnett contract as evidence for this. But he might have cited the Chicago Bulls instead. With a salary cap of $24.3 million for the 1996–97 season, the Bulls managed to rack up a payroll of a cool $58 million. So much for the restraining effects of the NBA salary cap.

Ten months earlier there had been a bombshell in major league baseball comparable to that involving Garnett. All during the negotiations with the player union up to and including the 1994–95 strike, the hardest of the hardliners among the owners was Jerry Reinsdorf, the owner of the Chicago White Sox (and of the NBA Chicago Bulls). Reinsdorf argued publicly that no deal was possible unless the players accepted a salary cap, and that a cap was essential to protect the league from irresponsible owners bidding up the prices of superstar players. The owners finally caved in to the union and accepted a deal without a salary cap. Within a week, the first of those irresponsible owners to jump into the free agent market was the same Jerry Reinsdorf, who signed the Indians' controversial outfielder Albert Belle to a five-year, $55 million contract, the richest in baseball history.

Still, the $10 million per year for which Belle signed (along with a $5 million bonus) was peanuts compared to what Reinsdorf's Chicago Bulls were paying Michael Jordan—$30 million for the 1996–97 NBA season and $33 million for the 1997–98 season. (Jordan's salary alone was $5 million more than the salary cap for the entire Bulls' team in each season and was allowed under the salary cap rules only because teams are permitted to spend whatever is required to retain their free agent players.) Admittedly, we are talking about some premiere players in Belle, Garnett, and Jordan, but it does raise the question as to whether their salaries are just off-the-charts extreme cases. Have owners lost their minds, or is there some way to explain rationally what is happening to salaries in pro team sports?

A clue comes from this simple comparison from *Sports Illustrated* (May 26, 1997): in 1976, the first year of free agency, the average MLB total team payroll was $1.2 million; in 1997, according to the same report, 255 major league players, or almost 35 percent of all MLB players, made $1.2 million or more!

The average player's salary on the opening day rosters for the 1998 MLB season was $1,444,762. The list was headed by Belle and the Marlins' Garry Sheffield at $10 million each, followed by the Braves' Gregg Maddux, the Giants' Barry Bonds, Mark McGwire of the Cardinals, Toronto's Roger Clemens, and Bernie Williams of the Yankees, all earning over $8 million. A total of 72 players on the 1998 opening day rosters had salaries of $4,750,000 or more.

In the NFL, Brett Favre has a contract with the Packers that pays him around $6.5 million per year, about the same as the one that Steve Young has with the 49ers and Barry Sanders has with the Lions. In the 1997 season, the average salary in the NFL was $791,000; this was scheduled to increase by $100,000 or more in 1998 in the wake of the new TV deal signed by the league.

Dennis Rodman made $8 million per year with the Bulls in the 1997–98 season. The average salary in the NBA was just over $2.1 million in the 1997–98 season; it is expected to climb above $3 million by the turn of the century. Even the NHL is experiencing salary inflation with average salaries topping out at over the $1 million mark in the 1997–98 season.

And it's not just the players who are being paid big bucks. Pat Riley makes $4 million per year coaching the Miami Heat. Rick Pitino hit the coaching jackpot with his $7.5 million-per-year contract with the Celtics. Even the front office types make out in the go-go environment of the 1990s—in 1996, David Stern signed a five-year extension of his contract as commissioner of the NBA, for $6 million per year.

Indeed, pro sports salaries have become the standard to set against salaries elsewhere. On September 17, 1996, the *Wall Street Journal* ran a front-page story headlined, "Bear Stearns' Five-Man Starters Get $81 Million, Beat NBA," relating how the top management team at Bear Stearns, a leading securities firm, received salaries so high that they even topped the salaries being paid to the five starters for the Bulls!

Can all these players possibly be worth the salaries they are being paid? In some cases at least we have verification that the market works more or less the way it is supposed to. In 1988, Wayne Gretzky's contract was sold by the Edmonton Oilers to the Los Angeles Kings. The deal involved about $15 million in cash, paid over time, and the Kings also gave the Oilers three first-round draft picks in coming years. The Kings assumed

Gretzky's contract, which paid $333,333 per year for six years (this was before free agency in the NHL drove hockey salaries up to within shouting distance of those in other sports). Old timers in the hockey business labeled this the "Kings' Folly." Sportwriters publicly doubted whether bringing "The King" to the Kings could really boost the team.

Gretzky joined the Kings for the 1989–90 NHL season. Cable coverage of the Kings rose from thirty-seven to sixty games. Advertising and merchandising income rose dramatically. Team revenue in 1989 nearly doubled its level in 1988. All in all, Kings' management claimed that $8 million of this increase was attributable to Gretzky, based just on revenues from the 40 regular-season home games alone. That $8 million per year in added revenue made Gretzky's purchase by the Kings a very smart business move. Of course, in Gretzky's case, it was Peter Pocklington, owner of the Oilers, and Bruce McNall, owner of the Kings, who were the main beneficiaries of Gretzky's drawing power because of his long-term contract with the Oilers. This changed drastically when the contract expired and Gretzky as a free agent moved to another big-market team, the Rangers, where he was able to capture more of his value as a drawing card in salary.

In the case of Michael Jordan, there was verification of his worth to the Bulls and to the NBA as a whole when Jordan took time off from the NBA for two years with the Birmingham Barons, a minor league baseball team—time spent determining whether he could learn to hit a curve ball (fortunately for Bulls fans he couldn't). Economists Jerry Hausman and Gregory Leonard calculated the losses in TV revenue for the team and the league during the period that Jordan was gone, placing his value to the league at over $53 million for the 1991–92 NBA season. In June 1998, *Fortune* magazine estimated Jordan's contribution to NBA gate and TV revenues over his career at around $500 million, and his impact on the economy as a whole—including all of his various sponsorships and other off-court endeavors—at around $10 billion over his career.

There is no doubt that Jordan was worth every cent of his $33 million 1997–98 Bulls contract.

We don't have the same sort of detailed documentation for run-of-the-mill players, but at least we can sketch out an argument that suggests that these players also tend to be paid pretty much what they are worth to teams.

A place to start is to look at the bargaining that goes on between a player (or actually his agent) and the general manager or owner of a team when it comes time to sign a new contract. In a press story about this, George Steinbrenner stated that his Yankee players get paid on the basis of "the number of fannies they put in the seats." In effect, the general manager's job in the negotiation process is to determine for each player how many "additional fannies" that player can be credited with, that is, how much added revenue the team will gain by signing the player. An astute general manager knows all of the stats about every player he deals with—in baseball, RBIs, batting average, fielding average, and the like for nonpitchers, and won-lost record, ERA, power ratio (strikeouts to walks), and the like for pitchers—and knows how to translate those stats into wins for the team, and to translate wins for the team into added attendance and TV viewership ratings. Likewise, an astute general manager also knows which players have the charisma that transcends the statistical measures and brings fans in just to watch those few specially gifted individuals— Michael Jordan, Wayne Gretzky, Roger Clemens, Steve Young —perform, regardless of how the team itself is making out.

A little later in this book we will look into the evidence as to whether owners in sports operate their teams to make as much money as possible. We believe you will find the evidence compelling that the "sportsman" owner who ignores profits is a rare individual indeed. Taking this as given, then, the general manager's primary job is to put on the field the team that will make the most money for the owner. The most that a general manager would be willing to pay a player is the added revenue that the player is expected to bring to the team if he is signed.

If a player is expected to add, say, $2 million in revenue to a team, then the team can make money by signing the player for anything less than $2 million and will lose money by signing him for anything more than $2 million. Thus we would argue that Glen Taylor (or Kevin McHale, his general manager) concluded that Kevin Garnett was expected to add at least $21 million per year to the revenue of the T-Wolves; similarly, Jerry Reinsdorf concluded that Albert Belle would add at least $11 million per year to the revenue of the White Sox.

From the player's point of view, presumably the least that he would be willing to accept is what the player could earn in his next highest-paid position, that is, what his next best offer is. If he gets offered less than this, he would be better off not to sign with the team but rather to take advantage of that next best offer. Back in the days of the old reserve clause, when a player either signed with the team owning his contract or was out of the sport, the next best offer for a player often meant what he could earn as a manual laborer. In the free agency era, a free agent has the option of shopping his services around among all the teams in his sport, so the next best offer to his team's offer is going to be determined by his worth to other teams. Free agency makes a big difference in the level of the next best offer, which represents the lowest salary a player will accept.

From this we can conclude that in the free agency era, a player will tend to end up playing for the team for which he adds the most revenue (since that team can bid the highest for the player and still make money on him), and he will earn something between what he is worth to that team and what he would be worth to the team that places the second highest value on his services, the team that represents his "next best offer." Just where the salary ends up within these limits depends on the bargaining ability of the player's agent and the general manager. In any case, the upper and lower limits should be fairly close together. In effect, if Kevin Garnett had taken advantage of his free agency rights back in 1997, he probably would have gotten an offer at least somewhere in the neighborhood of $21 million per year from teams in the NBA other than Minnesota.

There are some qualifications to this. Free agency in sports is not unlimited; in all sports there is a waiting period between each exercise of free agency, according to the labor contract for the sport. Having once exercised his free agency rights and signed a contract, the player is bound by the terms of that contract even if the general level of salaries increases during that term and even if the player has exceptional performances. Thus, during the interim period a player might be paid less, sometimes much less, than what he could have obtained if he had been able to enter the market at this time as a free agent. This is what gives rise to attempts by players to renegotiate contracts midway into the contracts, something which the team of course is free to reject. When a team does renegotiate midway in a contract it is often because the team has decided that it wants to enter into a longer-term contract with the player, even if it involves a higher salary.

It also is true that players will sometimes accept lower salaries just to play in a certain city. The Minnesota Twins were able to retain their superstar Kirby Puckett for less money than Puckett was offered by the White Sox, because Puckett had spent his career in the Twin Cities and apparently felt that his future after baseball was brighter in this environment than in his old hometown. The Twins also acquired St. Paul hometowners Dave Winfield, Jack Morris, and Paul Molitor, and Minnesota home-staters Kent Hrbek and Terry Steinbach at bargain prices, in the twilights of their careers.

Beyond this, no one is perfect, including general managers. Occasionally, players don't perform as their previous stats would have led one to believe. There are surprises in both directions—players signed at the league minimum who outperform the superstars and players signed to multimillion-dollar contracts who would be bad buys at the league minimum. The *Wall Street Journal* (February 7, 1997) did an analysis of NBA players during the 1996–97 season to identify the players giving the most "bang for the buck" and came up with the following list of bargain players—twelve players who were providing the most output per dollar spent in salary: Domique Wilkins, Walt Williams, David Wesley, Travis Best, Terrell Brandon, Avery Johnson, Damon Stoudamire, George McCloud, Chris Mills, Doug Christie, Kevin Garnett, and Kerry Kittles. To make this list you needed to be an outstanding NBA player and you needed to be severely underpaid. Notably absent from the list were the marquee players of the league, not because they aren't outstanding players but because, by any stretch of the imagination, they are not severely underpaid. (Kevin Garnett was still playing at the time for his original rookie contract salary of $1,870,000 per year. At $21 million per year, he would definitely not have been on the *Wall Street Journal* list.)

Excluding these exceptional cases, teams presumably pretty much get what they pay for, so it seems fair to state that if player salaries seem obscenely high—and they do—this is not because players are being paid more than competent judges of talent rate their worth to their teams. Instead, the reason for the incredibly high player salaries is that pro team sports is generating incredibly large and increasing revenues, especially from television, in the hyped-up sports business of the 1990s. With free agency in place, even the salary cap, as with the NBA and the NFL, does not prevent players from siphoning off an increasing share of the pro team sports revenue stream.

Financial World estimates summarized in Table 4-1 in the back of the book show that player costs as a percent of total league revenue increased in all leagues over the period 1990–96 (and earlier as well). One interpretation of this is that the competitive players' market created under the free agency system is gradually pushing player salaries closer and closer to the maximum that teams are willing to pay, namely, what players add to team revenue. This is occurring at the very time when team revenues and hence the value of players to teams is also increasing. The combination of the two produces an explosive rate of increase in player salaries.

—

Average salaries in all sports (except for the NFL) were over the million-dollar mark as 1998 rolled around. Table 4-2 gives the total cost of the opening lineups of MLB teams in 1998, along with average salaries per team. Beyond the fact that average baseball salaries are now approaching $1,500,000 per year, the other striking thing about the data in Table 4-2 is the disparity between the spending of the top teams—the Orioles, Yankees, Indians, and Braves—and that of the bottom teams—the Pirates and Expos. In 1998, Baltimore was spending over seven times as much per year on its players as Montreal, and over five times as much as Pittsburgh.

For Montreal in particular this was the result of a deliberate decision the team owners made several years earlier, when they apparently concluded that they could not make a profit in the Montreal market fielding a high-priced pennant-contending team. Since that time, Montreal has sold or traded all of its high-salaried talent to other teams, most notably trading Pedro Martinez to the Red Sox after the 1997 season, and has gone with a lineup of journeymen players and recent minor leaguers. When San Diego did the same thing a few years back, irate season ticket holders brought suit against the team, arguing that the owners of the Padres had engaged in deliberate misinformation about the caliber of the team they were going to put on the field—and the team ended up paying off the angry fans.

The list of 1997 payrolls of NFL teams (Table 4-3) exhibits some disparity among teams but nothing like that of MLB. The perennial front-runners—Dallas, San Francisco, Kansas City, and Buffalo—are at the top of the list as expected, along with the Raiders, a team that has a long history of generous salaries to a lineup loaded with name players, some past their prime. The relatively narrow spread of payrolls reflects both the revenue-sharing rules of the NFL and a salary cap that is much closer to a "hard" cap than the comparable cap in the NBA.

Speaking of which, Table 4-4 indicates the problems the NBA is having with its cap, with essentially all the teams in the league exceeding the cap in the 1997–98 season. Still, the fact that the NBA cap places a floor as well as a (flexible!) ceiling on team payrolls explains why teams as weak as the Clippers, the Nuggets, and the two expansion teams, the Grizzlies and the Raptors, are nonetheless mainly paying average salaries of over $1.5 million to their players.

The NHL does not have a cap, but the payroll distribution among teams as shown in Table 4-5 is not that different from the NBA. What must be a matter of long-term concern in the league are the relatively low payrolls of the Canadian members of the league, when adjustment is made for the exchange rate between the American and Canadian dollars (at the time, one Canadian dollar was worth roughly seventy cents in American money).

If general managers really were perfect judges of talent, there would be no need to play the league schedule to determine the league champion—we'd simply award the title to the team with the highest payroll. What is the correspondence between payrolls and won-lost records? Do the big-payroll teams always or almost always end up as winners? The outcome in any one year is of course subject to all the uncertainties and vagaries of injuries and slumps, as well as the timing of contract renewals, free agency, and arbitration rights. A better picture of the relationship between payrolls and performance on the field is found by looking at a longer period. Tables 4-6 through 4-9 provide some evidence, using comparisons between average won-lost percents and average player costs per team for all leagues over the period 1990–96.

There are some expected results and some surprises. Atlanta dominated the NL during the period and had the highest average payroll as well. But Montreal had a string of high-finish teams in the early 1990s, including a league-leading .648 won-lost percent in the strike year of 1994, with payrolls far below the NL average. In the AL, the odd-ball entry is the Cleveland Indians, a team that began the 1990s with a roster of second-division low-salaried youngsters signed to long-term contracts, who matured into the strong teams of the mid- to late 1990s. (As Table 4-2 indicates, the pennant-winning teams of the late 1990s are no longer bargain-priced—the Indians' salaries finally caught up with their talents.)

In the NFL, the true outlier is the Pittsburgh Steelers, who had the lowest average payrolls of the entire league between 1990 and 1996 yet posted the fifth best record in the league over that period. At the other extreme are the Jets, who parlayed the seventh-highest payroll in the NFL into the second-worst playing record.

The NBA's candidate for the team with the best general manager is the Utah Jazz, which posted the fourth-best record in the league while recording the twentieth highest payroll. In the NHL, it is the Calgary Flames that qualify as the team with "the most bang for the buck," with the LA Kings getting the booby prize, perhaps because of the myriad problems besetting owner Bruce McNall.

Is there a definite positive correlation between payrolls and won-lost percent? In each of Tables 4-6 through 4-9, a measure of that correlation is given, where a value of +1 means perfect positive correlation (the higher the average player cost, the higher the average won-lost record) and –1 means perfect negative correlation (the higher the average player cost, the lower the average won-lost record). Correlations in sports are far from these ideals. The NHL has the highest correlation coefficient at .69, followed by the NBA at .677, the AL at .509, the NFL at .29, and the NL at .135. All of the correlations are positive as expected, but except for the top two, the correlations are weak. Briefly, you can do a pretty good job of predicting a team's won-lost record in the NHL and NBA by looking at the team's payroll, but payroll is not significantly related to performance in the NFL or in either the AL or the NL. To be a little more explicit, on the basis of the 1990–96 data, payrolls explained about half of the observed won-lost ranking in the NHL, about 46 percent in the NBA, and were essentially worthless in explaining the average won-lost records in the NFL or baseball. It really does make sense to play out the season—who knows, that might be the Montreal Expos, the Pittsburgh Pirates, or the Minnesota Twins chugging into the playoffs come late September. Table 4-10 gives the rank correlations between player costs and won-lost records on a year-by-year basis, 1990 through 1996.

One other thing to note about Tables 4-6 through 4-9 is that among the big spenders in most sports are the big-market teams, such as the MLB Yankees and Dodgers, the NFL Giants, the NBA Lakers and Knicks, and the NHL Rangers and Blackhawks. And at the bottom are the small-market teams, including Minnesota, Milwaukee, Edmonton, and Ottawa. Generally speaking, this agrees with the notion that the stronger revenue potential in the big-city markets provides the incentives for teams in those markets to acquire more of the better (and more expensive) talent in a league.

As salaries have continued to rise in sports, attention has been directed toward another problem, namely the concentration of salary income among a few high-priced superstars in each sport. Every one of the major sports leagues has experienced this, with more and more of the total payroll going to the top-salaried players. Interestingly, this mirrors a similar trend in the economy as a whole, where the top 5 or 10 percent in earning power are capturing an increasing share of the total income of the economy. It has been theorized that the economy is turning into a "winner-take-all" world in which those individuals who are the very best in their professions earn incomes far in excess of what is earned by those who do not quite make it into that "very best" group, even though the difference between the very best and the next lower group might be quite slight. An example is the difference in earning power between someone who can consistently run the 100-meter dash 1/100 of a second faster than anyone else and those who have to contend for second place in the race. A part of the explanation for the general "winner-take-all" phenomenon is technological advances in communications, so that, for example, the performance of the world's greatest opera company is now available to all of us, which plays havoc with the incomes of those involved in the local company, however talented it might be.

Pro team sports seems a somewhat different kind of enterprise. Even a team of the greatest superstars would have problems drawing if there were no league rivals available offering the excitement of closely contested games. Years ago, economist Simon Rottenberg pointed out that it just doesn't pay for any sports team to become "too strong" relative to the rest of the league. Undoubtedly, what is happening in sports is that free agency has benefited better players more than journeyman players. The increased concentration of income in the highest-earning brackets should be viewed as further evidence of the movement over time of salaries closer to levels equal to what players actually earn for their teams.

The traditional fan base of pro sports has been lower- and middle-income workers, many of whom feel they are barely managing to make ends meet at a time when players such as Belle, Garnett, Jordan, or Sheffield are drawing huge paychecks. But it's important to keep things in perspective. We are talking about a very small group of superstar players, admittedly drawing fabulous salaries. On the other hand, most professional athletes earn much closer to the league minimum, say, in the $200,000 to $300,000 range, than to the Belle or Jordan level. The average playing career of a pro athlete is short, rarely lasting more than five years. When it's over, it's over, and there are only a limited number of follow-on jobs in the sport that pay enough to make them worthwhile. To make it to the pros today for most players means a complete commitment to athletics from high school on, so that the fall-back income of someone who never makes it out of the minors in baseball or doesn't get drafted into the NFL or NBA is far below that of the typical college graduate.

Pro sports is theater, among other things, and, as in the theater, many are called but few are chosen. The chosen few at the very top do very well, of course, as they do in all fields. For example, on the owners' side, Michael Eisner is the top Duck at Disney, which owns the NHL Anaheim Ducks and the AL Anaheim Angels as well as ABC and ESPN. Eisner used his stock options in 1994 to boost his income that year to a little over $200 million—and Eisner does not have to have his value tested regularly in the free agent market. If Paul Allen, owner of the NFL Seattle Seahawks and the NBA Portland Trailblazers, simply put his assets in the local savings and loan earning 6 percent interest, he would take home something on the order of $900 million per year. The American economy is one that richly rewards the innovative, the risk-takers, the best in their fields, and the lucky, and we are simply observing this fact in practice in looking at superstar salaries in sports.

The high salaries of superstars in sports have become a controversial issue among fans and sportswriters. Fans tend to think that the high salaries drive up the prices of seats at games, and that if there were some way to put a lid on salaries, ticket prices would fall. This is simply a misunderstanding of the cause-and-effect chain at work in sports. The reason that salaries are high is because the demand for sports is high, as reflected in the prices that people are willing to pay for tickets to games and in the prices TV networks are willing to pay for the rights to telecast sports games. The higher ticket prices and higher TV-rights prices increase the value of star players to teams, the amounts they add to a team's revenue, which then gets reflected in the high salaries paid to those players. Salaries are high because ticket prices are high, not the other way around.

If an enforceable lid were imposed on salaries, ticket prices wouldn't fall, because it wouldn't be in the interest of owners to cut prices. As reasonable businessmen, they are already presumably charging the ticket prices that maximize their profits, so why change them just because their salary costs are down? Given the existing league and team structure of sports, the only effect of such a lid would be to transfer income from rich players to even richer owners, with no effect at all on fans and certainly no effect in the form of lower ticket prices.

The most fundamental fact underlying high player salaries is that those salaries reflect the high levels of added revenue that good pro players can earn for a team. The free agency system permits players to capture more of their value to teams than was true under the old reserve system, but free agency does not create the value of players to teams—that arises from the demand for sports by fans. Dismantling the free agency system and returning to something approaching the old reserve clause system would reduce player salaries, but only by transferring a part of the value of players to owners. Once again, fans would see no benefit from such a change.

A second fundamental fact is that high player salaries also reflect the control of a sport by a monopoly sports league. Demand by fans is of course essential, but it is the monopoly control of a sport that permits the league to capture all or almost all of the revenues that a sport can generate. The tighter the monopoly control of a sport, the larger the revenue of the league, and thus the larger the revenue potential that a star player represents to teams in that league. Under free agency, the player is able to command a salary that over time approximates his revenue potential to the league. Thus, the frustrating thing about free agency to owners is that, having successfully established a monopoly position in a sport, they now find that an increasing share of the monopoly revenues of the sport is ending up in the hands of players rather than in their own hands. It must be especially frustrating since this transference of monopoly revenue is due to their own actions in bidding against one another in the player market.

Owners have attempted to adopt various devices to impose some controls on the player market, including even an occasional call for a return to the old reserve clause arrangement. During the Peter Ueberroth era in baseball, between 1986 and 1988, the owners adopted a nice, simple, straightforward solution to the salary problem—they jointly decided not to make any bids for free agent players. The approach worked like a charm—the average salary in baseball remained essentially constant over this period.

There was a minor problem, however. In the labor agreement signed both by owners and players, one provision outlawed collusion in the free agency market by either side, owners or players. (The owners still remembered the time that Don Drysdale and Sandy Koufax informed Walter O'Malley that neither would sign his Dodger contract unless both of them got what they wanted.) Furthermore, the labor agreement provided that if collusion damages occurred, the damaged parties could bring the case to arbitration for triple damages, just as in antitrust cases. The evidence of collusion in this case was overwhelming—only one offer was made to a free agent by any owner during a two-year period and that offer was for less than half of what the player had earned the year before. The owners ended up paying out $280 million to the free agents they had stiffed, and Peter Ueberroth's role as the savior of baseball got downsized. Ueberroth was looking for work elsewhere shortly after the collusion hearing.

More recently, owners have promoted the use of a salary cap, as noted in the previous chapter. Fifteen years of experience under the cap in the NBA still leaves it a matter of much dispute as to just what bells and whistles would have to be added to the cap to have it meet the owners' objective of restraining the growth of player salaries.

There is one change in league rules that the owners could adopt unilaterally without approval by player unions, which should promote the objective of controlling salaries. However, suggestions in this direction have provoked the most intense battles within the ownership group. The idea here is that if leagues adopted more generous gate and local TV sharing rules, this would lead to lower player salaries and hence to higher incomes for owners as a group. Why is this? Well, as we have seen, player salaries reflect the added revenue that a player can earn for a team, in the form of gate receipts and TV income. With more generous gate and local TV revenue sharing, the home team gets to keep less of the revenue that it earns, so that fielding a winning team is less valuable to the owner. That means that star players are worth less to teams when there is more generous gate sharing, which gets translated into lower salaries and hence higher league-wide profits.

With such an apparently sure-fire way of reducing salaries available to them, why is it that owners don't agree to NFL-type gate-sharing arrangements and to the sharing of local TV as well? The problem is, of course, that more generous gate sharing benefits small-market teams at the expense of big-market teams. The Knicks would be paying out much more in the way of gate sharing to teams visiting the Garden than they would collect on the road over the NBA season. Clearly, the big-market teams have weighed the benefit—lower player salaries—against the cost—lower take-home gate and local TV receipts—and have judged that the cost exceeds the benefit. Still, if salaries continue to escalate, at some point a compromise arrangement might well be reached under which gate sharing is used along with the salary cap and other devices to control player salaries.

To return to the main point of this chapter, the conclusion from all of this is that, rather than being an independent cause or source of the problems that plague pro team sports, player salaries instead simply reflect the value of players to teams. The value of players is high today because pro team sports is so popular with the public and because the monopoly power of leagues and teams allows them to maximize their share of the high levels of revenue from ticket sales, TV contracts, stadium deals, and the like. Player salaries are not the cause of high ticket prices or high pay-per-view prices. However, the high level of player salaries does impact the profitability of sports teams, which is a matter of much concern to owners. In the next chapter, we look at the profitability of teams in a free agency world and the role of profit maximization in owner decision making.

5

OWNERS

When a guy buys a franchise, he knows where he's buying it.
Nobody forces anybody to buy a franchise in Cleveland or
Milwaukee. Nobody puts a gun to your head.

—George Steinbrenner, *Sporting News*,
August 24, 1992, p. 10

This whole thing is not really an issue of big market, small
market. It's larger revenue teams, with smaller revenue teams
complaining about not making as much as their bigger partners.

—Don Fehr, *Sporting News*, August 24, 1992, p. 10

Willie Sutton, a somewhat-less-than-accomplished professional felon, who spent more than a few years in federal prisons because of this, was asked on one memorable occasion, "Why do you rob banks?" Sutton went right to the heart of the matter: "Because that's where the money is." Certainly in searching through the "usual suspects" in the pro sports power game, we must pay special attention to the individuals with the money bags, those favored few who own and operate pro sports teams.

93

There was a time in the far distant past when owners were ordinary, run-of-the-mill individuals who made their living, such as it was, from their teams. The list of early owners of baseball teams included several prominent ex-players such as Cornelius McGillicuddy (Connie Mack), who caught for the Washington and Philadelphia NL clubs and for Buffalo in the Players League, and ended up owning the old Philadelphia Athletics; Clark Griffith, a star pitcher for the Yankees, later owner of the Washington Senators; John McGraw, third baseman for the Baltimore NL team and then long-time manager and minority owner of the New York Giants; and Charles Comiskey, first baseman and manager for the St. Louis Browns team, which dominated the American Association when it was a major league in the 1880s, followed by his long stint as owner of the Chicago White Sox. In the NFL, George Halas owned and coached his Chicago Bears and played end as well during the 1920s, participating in every way in those memorable early matchups with the Green Bay Packers, where Curly Lambeau was also a player-coach-owner during the first few years of that team. But that is all a thing of the past now. The single most important thing an owner needs today is neither playing nor coaching experience, nor even any knowledge whatsoever of the game. What he needs, pure and simple, is money—lots of it—and the current crop of owners certainly has this in spades. The days of team owners with limited incomes are over; as Finley Peter Dunne put it so well, "One of the strangest things in life is that the poor, who need money the most, are the very ones that never have it."

Heading the list of present-day owners is Paul Allen, the Microsoft multibillionaire who owns the NBA Portland Trailblazers and the NFL Seattle Seahawks. But there are lots of others on the Forbes 400 list of the richest in the country. Philip Anschutz made his money in fiber optics and now owns the NHL LA Kings and the NBA LA Lakers. Rupert Murdoch made his billions running the News Corporation, which owns the Fox TV network; Murdoch is the new owner of the NL LA

Dodgers. Ted Turner of CNN fame owns the NBA Atlanta Hawks and the NL Atlanta Braves. Ross Perot, Jr., son of the software billionaire, owns the NBA Dallas Mavericks. Micky Arison, the owner of the NBA Miami Heat, also owns Carnival Cruises. Bob Tisch, a part-owner of Loews Theaters, which at one time owned CBS, has 50 percent of the NFL New York Giants. Financier Lester Crown is a minority owner of the Chicago Bulls and the New York Yankees—he might be someone to go to for investment advice, all right. Up in Seattle, billionaire John McCaw is one of the owners of the AL Seattle Mariners, and he also owns the NHL Vancouver Canucks and the NBA Vancouver Grizzlies. Wayne Huizenga of Blockbuster Video fame and currently the country's leading owner of auto dealerships at one time owned three Miami teams—the NFL Dolphins, the NL Marlins, and the NHL Panthers—before putting the reeling Marlins on the market in 1998. Detroit boasts a trio of billionaire owners: William Davidson, owner of the NBA Pistons; William Clay Ford, owner of the NFL Lions; and Michael Ilitch, owner of the NHL Red Wings and the AL Tigers. In Minneapolis, Carl Pohlad, who made his one billion plus from banking interests, is the owner of the AL Minnesota Twins and was a part-owner of the NFL Vikings, before that team was sold to Red McCombs. Two multimillionaire brothers, Melvin and Herb Simon, shopping center entrepreneurs, own the NBA Indiana Pacers. In San Diego, Alex Spanos made his $600 million in construction and now operates the NFL Chargers. Glen Taylor is the billionaire publishing industry entrepreneuer who also doubles as owner of the NBA Minnesota Timberwolves. Two brothers with recent ties to the Twin Cities (at one time they owned the since-departed NHL Minnesota North Stars) are the Gunds, Gordon and George III, who made their money from Sanka and now spend their spare time on two hobby investments, the NBA Cleveland Cavaliers and the NHL San Jose Sharks. Leon Hess is an oil mogul who also happens to own the NFL New York Jets. And the DeBartolos, despite their infighting, still control the NFL's winningest franchise, the San Francisco 49ers. All of these owners are on the 1997 Forbes 400 list, which means that each is worth at least $600 million.

The fact that pro team sports is populated with billionaires should not come as a surprise. With team prices what they are today, it takes upward of $150 to $250 million to buy a team. The owners who aren't on the Forbes list, long-timers such as George Steinbrenner of the Yankees or Jerry Reinsdorf of the Bulls and the White Sox, must feel absolutely poverty-stricken when socializing with money superstars such as Paul Allen with his $14 billion in assets or Philip Anschutz with his $5 billion plus. All of that money showing up in sports leagues does raise the specter of league titles being bought by members of the Forbes 400 who are willing and able to spend to buy a winner—does a name like Wayne Huizenga (and his Florida Marlins) come to mind? And of course owners are happy to raise this specter as a justification for their ongoing attempts, some successful, to impose a salary cap or luxury tax to control team spending on player salaries.

It also raises the question of whether garden-variety economic notions, such as profit maximization and supply and demand, apply in the case of sports leagues. As Henry Aaron of the Brookings Institution has noted, the payoffs to a rich owner from owning a sports team might come mainly from the fun of being involved with the sport itself and with the players and the coaches, rather than from the profits the team generates. There is also the publicity spotlight that shines on the owner of any team—Carl Pohlad is much better known in the Twin Cities for the Twins than for his Marquette National Bank; Leon Hess' ownership of the Jets is far more a matter of common knowledge in New York City than his role in the oil industry. And all of the fun and publicity is that much more intense when the team you own is a winner.

This view of owners as "sportsmen" ignoring bottom-line considerations has its attractions, and there have been owners who really seem to have fit this image—Tom Yawkey of the

Boston Red Sox of the 1930s and 1940s is one who comes immediately to mind. Still, it pays to be a little skeptical. Billionaires don't get there by throwing their money around recklessly—they tend to be the people who let someone else pick up the tab for lunch. As important as winning is to them, it might well be a matter of ego and personal pride that they manage to do this while pocketing a good profit at the same time.

A competing view of the owners is that, their loud protestations to the contrary, they actually are minting money from their teams' TV contracts and high-priced luxury boxes and preferred seating licenses. According to this view, owners would very much like to field winning teams if there's any money in it, but otherwise, they're quite content to load up the roster with low-priced talent and have no qualms about moving the team if fans don't flock to watch a second-division turkey.

Whatever view you have of the matter, there is no doubt that almost all of the huge amount of money that pro team sports generates, through gate receipts, TV income, stadium revenues, and sales of memorabilia, passes first through the hands of the owners. But how much stays there, and how much gets passed on in the form of player and coaching salaries, traveling expenses, administrative costs, stadium rentals, and the like? To answer this question authoritatively would require access to the books of sports teams and their owners. Unfortunately, we do not have that access. There are a few— the Boston Celtics, Cleveland Indians, and Florida Panthers— that are publicly traded businesses, so their revenues, costs, and profits are public information. But most sports teams are closely held businesses, organized as limited partnerships or subchapter S corporations, with no legal requirement to open their books to the rest of us. What we have instead is a set of estimates of income of the various sports teams, prepared on an annual basis since 1990 by *Financial World* magazine. Tables 5-1 through 5-4 in the back of the book give estimated annual operating income figures for all teams in MLB, the

NFL, the NBA, and the NHL, covering the period 1990 through 1996, along with per-team averages over the period. This is the best available information concerning sports teams and we will treat it as such, but keep in mind that these are estimates, not true inside information on the finances of teams.

The term "operating income" in the tables might be a trifle obscure—accountants can be every bit as confusing as lawyers or economists when they want to be, or when it would be helpful to their clients. Operating income in any year is revenue minus costs for the year, excluding interest costs of the team and depreciation of player contracts. This means that operating income is larger than the pretax profits of the team, the figure the team has to report to the IRS, because in calculating pretax profits, the team will deduct its interest cost and player contract depreciation from operating income. Thus, from Table 5-1 on average over the 1990–96 period, the New York Yankees had $24.2 million per year available to pay interest costs, with anything remaining after deducting that and player contract depreciation becoming the pretax profits of the Yankees.

The first thing that is abundantly clear from the data in Tables 5-1 through 5-4 is that, with just a handful of exceptions, pro team sports does not appear to be a terribly profitable business. In major league baseball, where teams were selling in the $100 to $175 million range between 1990 and 1996, an average operating income of $3.6 million per team per year over the same period wouldn't represent much of a return on investment for an average owner, even if he or she didn't have any interest costs at all—and most owners, especially the most recent ones, have substantial interest costs associated with financing the purchases of their teams. The same is true for the NFL ($5.0 million average operating income per year, teams selling for $150 to $200 million) and the NHL ($3.7 million average per year, with teams worth $50 to $100 million). Only in the NBA do owners appear to be doing much better than breaking even, with an $8.6 million average operating income (and with team prices in the early- to mid-1990s in the $75 to $125 million range). To put things in context, Albert Belle of the White Sox makes $10 million per year but Jerry Reinsdorf, the Sox owner, has an estimated average operating income of only $5 million per year.

The figures seem to make mockery of the notion that owners are making out like bandits. At most only a few teams in each league are showing impressive book profits, and they are generally the ones that all of us would have predicted—the Yankees and Orioles in MLB; the Cowboys in the NFL; the Lakers, Knicks, Pistons, Bulls, and Sun in the NBA; and the Red Wings and Blackhawks in the NHL.

Another aspect of the financial picture of sports leagues that comes through from the tables is the division between the haves and the have-nots. For simplicity, the true have-nots can be identified as the teams that show negative average operating incomes over the period between 1990 and 1996. One striking point is the relative abundance of have-not teams in baseball and hockey as compared to the other sports—11 of the 28 baseball teams fall in the have-not category, along with 6 of 29 in the NHL (and 5 more teams with positive average operating incomes of less than $1 million), as compared with only 3 of 33 in the NFL and 1 of 29 in the NBA.

The large numbers of have-nots in baseball and hockey reflect the fact that winning is more important to the bottom line in these sports than in basketball or football. NFL and NBA teams derive most of their gate revenue from season ticket sales, whereas in baseball, walk-in ticket sales are an important share of the team's gate revenues and are much more sensitive to the team's won-lost record. In the NHL, there are the regular season and the "second season," the playoffs. Playoff ticket sales are a critical part of any NHL team's finances, so missing the playoffs almost certainly means financial problems for the team.

Add to this the fact that the value of local TV rights is sensitive to the playing success of a team and that local TV plays a larger role in baseball and hockey than in the other two sports. Thus, a larger share of revenue is sensitive to the won-lost record of baseball and hockey teams, which tends to increase the value of star players to teams, so that salary costs are adversely affected as well.

The large number of have-not teams also provides a clue as to why it was major league baseball and the NHL that experienced long debilitating work stoppages in 1994 and early 1995, with the have-not owners holding out for radical changes in the rules governing their leagues' player markets. Of course, it is also true that the baseball strike in 1994 and 1995 and its after-effects account for part of the dismal operating income figures for baseball teams. If the two strike-related years are thrown out, then average income for MLB teams over the 1990–96 period rises to $5.6 million, still not much to crow about.

Predictably, most of the have-not teams are small-market teams. Oakland, Pittsburgh, Minnesota, Milwaukee, Seattle, Kansas City, and Cincinnati are have-not teams ranking among the smallest markets in MLB. It might appear that Marge Schott had front-office deficiencies to match her other public relations problems at Cincinnati, but the "Big Red" will probably be bleeding "Big Red" ink on the books even with Marge no longer around, just because of the team's limited market potential.

In the NFL, the two worst teams in terms of operating income are the expansion Carolina and Jacksonville teams, which were receiving only a fraction of the national TV income the other teams in the league get. Once their initiation period is ended and the TV spigot is turned on full force, they will no doubt move up into more favorable positions in operating income terms. On the other hand, the financial problems of the Lions appear to be systemic. But, generally speaking, the NFL shows a lot of financial balance because of the most generous revenue-sharing rules in sports, coupled with the insignificant role played by local as compared to national TV income for the league. (Gate receipts in the NFL are shared 60–40 percent between the home and visiting team; in the AL, it is roughly 80–20, and in the NL, 95–5; the NBA and NHL both have 100–0 sharing rules. As noted earlier, all leagues share national TV revenues equally, and all leagues assign all local TV revenues to the home team.)

The NBA has experienced rapid growth in revenues, including the equally shared national TV revenues, for fifteen years or so. This is reflected in the fact that only a few teams have been left by the wayside financially. The Pacers' troubles appear to be ending, especially with Larry Bird "back home again in Indiana," and most of the other weaker teams have shown some recent progress toward a break-even situation.

The NHL has problems galore. Four teams moved during the 1990–97 period because of financial problems, and they aren't doing any better at their new locations than they were at their old ones. The NHL continues to bring in more expansion teams (four more will be coming into the league in 1999), all at marginal small-market locations. The only teams in the league that are doing at all well are the true old-timers—Detroit, Chicago, Boston, the Rangers, Toronto, and Montreal (now in what will probably be a brief downturn). The present situation looks much like that of the 1920s, when the NHL also overexpanded and ultimately ended up closing down almost all of the new franchises it had added. The NHL has player union problems, franchise problems, and TV problems; it is no surprise that most teams in the league are barely hanging on.

What the figures on operating income reveal is just how successful players have been in capturing their contributions to team revenues in salaries. If TV networks simply funnel money from advertisers to teams as indicated in Chapter 2, teams seem to be simply funneling that same money through to players with not much of it sticking to the hands of owners, again with the few rare exceptions mentioned earlier. Free agency appears to be leading to the bidding away of more and more of the monopoly revenues of pro teams sports, through salary offers to the ultimate scarce factors in the industry, namely the superstar players and, to a lesser extent, the superstar coaches.

What does this suggest about the profit orientation of team owners? We would argue that the pressures that free agency has imposed on the bottom line in sports, as indicated by operating income figures, have made it all the more important for teams to act like profit maximizers, ferreting out every possible source of revenue and exploiting it to the hilt, while paring away at costs with a vengeance. It is much more expensive to be a sportsman-owner today than it was in Tom Yawkey's days, and this lesson is well known to everyone who owns a sports team. The drive for stadium subsidies and tax rebates and the hard-line stands in labor negotiations are just a few of the obvious consequences of the tightening of profit margins in sports.

Does this mean that we should be passing the hat again for Paul Allen (as Washington state voters did in 1997), or that we should erect statues to owners for their selfless and profitless task of bringing quality athletic entertainment to the masses? Well, maybe not. Let's try to count some of the ways in which an owner can still break even or do better than that, even with an operating income that is negative or barely on the plus side.

First, it is commonplace for an owner to take on a salaried job with his team, as president or chairman of the board. It's the owner's team so he can pay himself whatever salary he wishes. In the 1992 *Mackey v. NFL* case, pitting the player union against the NFL, the books of NFL teams were made available to the defense. In one extraordinary case, it was discovered that Norman Braham, then owner of the Philadelphia Eagles, paid himself $7 million in salary one year. Maybe he was worth it, but that $7 million salary shows up on the team books as a cost, and thus reduces the apparent operating income of the team, which makes it appear that the owner, Braham, was making $7 million less on his investment than he actually was.

To take another example, in the years when Calvin Griffith owned and operated the Minnesota Twins, it was widely reported that there were Griffith relations galore on the payroll of the team. There is nothing illegal or immoral about this, of course; in fact, to the contrary, it makes Griffith seem like what he in fact was, a very family-oriented person. However, it does mean that book figures on team revenues, costs, and profits for the Twins understated the income that the owner and his family derived from the team.

Second, more and more often, team owners today have complex financial interrelationships with their teams. For example, the Tribune Company owns the Chicago Cubs and also televises Cub games on its superstation, WGN. The value of the Cubs' TV rights can appear as revenue for the team; or a part can be shifted to WGN, which would have the effect of lowering the revenue and hence the operating income of the team. It's all up to the executives of the Tribune Company, who have free range to allocate the revenue where they wish. There are often incentives to shift income away from the team and to the TV station instead.

In the case of the Florida Marlins, when Wayne Huizenga owned the team, he also owned the stadium (Professional Players Stadium) in which the team played as well as the Miami TV station that aired Marlin game telecasts. Into which of Huizenga's several pockets did the stadium rental or the local TV revenue go? Questions like this have become much more than merely academic matters for the players in the NFL and NBA operating under salary cap rules, because those rules guarantee players a stated minimum percent of league revenues. League revenues will vary depending on whether the team gets the full market value of its TV revenues, or instead a part is transferred to the station, network, or superstation owned by the team owner.

Ted Turner is an especially interesting case. Turner owns the NBA Atlanta Hawks and the NL Atlanta Braves. Tables 5-1 and 5-3 indicate that both teams have been losing money (negative estimated average operating revenue), but there is no doubt that Turner's sports teams have actually made him a bundle. Turner was enough of a marketing genius to recognize in the 1970s that the one attraction cable TV needed to get public acceptance was the availability of major league sports telecasts. It was the solid schedule of telecasts of Braves and Hawks games that helped to sell his superstation WTBS to local cable operators, and that played an important role in establishing cable TV and Turner's fortune. However, the income generated for Turner by his teams through these "spinoffs" does not show up in the operating incomes of the teams themselves.

A similar situation exists in New York City where the owners of the New York Rangers and the New York Knicks also own Madison Square Garden, and the television network MSG on which Rangers and Knicks games are shown. The rentals charged the teams, and the payments made to them for the television rights, can be set at any arbitrary level by their owners, so that the operating income figures for these teams are questionable at best.

Third, ownership of a sports team provides tax sheltering opportunities that are not available to most other businesses, so that what appears to be a before-tax loss by the team can, in certain circumstances, be converted into an after-tax profit for the owner. The idea behind the tax shelter was one more contribution to the sports industry by the fertile and conniving mind of Bill Veeck, baseball's greatest hustler and team owner. Back in 1950, Veeck was in the process of selling his Cleveland Indians team to a syndicate headed by his friend Hank Greenberg, the great Tiger outfielder. (Greenberg has since gone on to much more profitable things, and has done well enough that he too is listed as one of the 1997 Forbes 400, with personal assets of over $1 billion—not bad for an ex-jock.) Veeck convinced the IRS that the purchaser of a team should be allowed to assign a portion of the purchase price of the team to the player contracts that the team owned, and then to treat this as a wasting asset, depreciating the contracts over a period of five years or less. That was an important bit of convincing, because the IRS already had in place rules allowing teams to write off as current costs signing bonuses, scouting costs, losses of minor league affiliates, and all the other costs incurred by a team in replacing its current roster of players with young players coming into the sport.

By allowing a new owner to assign a part of the purchase price of a team to player contracts and then depreciate them, the IRS in effect was allowing a team to double-count the cost of replacing players. And, since depreciation is a noncash cost, just a bookkeeping entry, this could allow the owner to convert a pretax book loss to an after-tax profit. Without getting into too much detail, an example can illustrate things.

Suppose someone buys an NFL team for $200 million. The new owner assigns 50 percent of the purchase price to player contracts (the maximum allowed under the law), that is, $100 million, and then depreciates the contracts over 5 years at $20 million per year. Suppose that revenue is $100 million per year and that costs, exclusive of player contract depreciation, are $90 million. Then, for the first five years of operation of the team, the books of the team will look like this:

Revenue	$100 million
Less costs	90 million
Less depreciation	20 million
Pretax profits	–$ 10 million

First, note that depreciation of $20 million is simply a bookkeeping entry, with no actual cash expended to cover this expense. Thus, even though the team will report a loss of $10 million to the IRS, the owner will have a positive cash flow of $10 million ($100 million in revenue minus $90 million in cost) from the operation of the team.

Suppose that the team is operated as a partnership, so that the operating income of the team becomes a part of the taxable income of the owner, which includes his or her income from outside sources. (The reason that teams are often organized as [limited] partnerships rests in large part on this fact.) As the comments earlier make clear, most owners have lots and lots of income from sources other than their teams. Suppose the owner is in the 33 percent tax bracket. Because operating income is negative, the owner can use the $10 million pretax loss to reduce his total taxable income from other sources by $10 million, thus saving him $3.3 million on his tax bill.

By the magic of accounting and the Veeck tax shelter, the team shows a loss of $10 million per year, but the owner has in fact earned $13.3 million in after-tax income from the team, equal to the $10 million cash flow from the team's operations plus the $3.3 million the owner has saved in taxes on his outside income.

The owner can continue to do this each of the first five years he owns the team, after which contract depreciation is exhausted. Moreover, because the IRS permits the team to write off the out-of-pocket costs of actually replacing players, the team should be every bit as strong on the field after five years as it was when it was purchased, despite the fact that, on the books of the team, the value of the player contracts has now been completely written off.

Now that you get the idea, let's turn to some real data. It isn't often that anybody gets to see the income statements of pro sports teams. However, the 1994–95 and 1995–96 income statements for the San Antonio Spurs, based on an independent audit by KMPG Peat Marwick in 1997, are in Tables 5-5 and 5-6. The Spurs' owners released these data to the public as part of their plea for (you guessed it) a new arena.

The Spurs were a moderately successful team, reaching the playoffs in the two years in the tables. In 1994–95, they played fifteen playoff games, eight at home, and in 1995–96, they played in ten playoff games, five at home. Including their arena management firm, SAOne, Inc., the Spurs showed net operating revenue, before depreciation and amortization, of about $4.9 million in 1994–95 and just a little over $300,000 in

1995–96. It is clear why revenues fell so dramatically. Costs, particularly player salaries and insurance, rose $5.2 million while revenues only rose $2.5 million. It would have taken a great postseason to make up for this regular-season decline but, unfortunately, such was not to be. Playoff profits in 1995–96 fell to about half the level enjoyed the previous year. All in all, over these two years, the net operating revenues of the Spurs averaged about $2.6 million.

Before we turn our attention to the player contract depreciation accounting hanky-panky as it pertains to the Spurs, it is worth noting that portions of the cost-side entries in the income statements may not be costs at all. First, "other salaries" include management and operations salaries and any salary taken out by the ownership partners. Given the example from the NFL case cited earlier, "other salaries" may be a funny kind of "cost" if they are a part of team revenues taken by *owners* in the form of salaries for themselves or for people close to them. Second, any expenses that actually are payments to the partners' other activities represent profit-taking by the partners. For example, it is common for sports team owners to gain at both ends of team borrowing and lending choices. Owners of some sports teams in the past have taken interest-free loans out from the team or loaned the team money at above market rates. Team owners might also purchase other services (broadcasting, advertising, legal, accounting, and other administration) from their own firms. Potentially all expenses except team salaries, NBA and indirect expenses, taxes, and shared revenue can actually be profit-taking. But we do not know the details behind the expense entries for the Spurs and cannot comment on the magnitude of this type of profit-taking. In what follows, we only will note again that profit-taking opportunities enhance the bottom-line return to owners.

Now, let's turn to the issue of player contract depreciation. The owners of the Spurs originally purchased the team in 1993 for $75 million and, presumably, assigned the highest percentage allowed under the tax laws, 50 percent of the purchase price of the team, to player contracts. They decided to depreciate the player contracts of the team over a 3.5-year period, making allowable straight-line player contract depreciation of about $10.7 million annually over 3.5 years. The team reported that total depreciation and amortization expenses in the 1994–95 season were $15.3 million. Ignoring player contract depreciation leaves $3.6 million as "true" depreciation of the actual capital held by the team owners.

Looking just at the 1994–95 season, if player contracts were not depreciable, the Spurs would have shown a bottom-line net profit of $1.3 million, that is, $4.9 million in net operating revenue minus the true depreciation amount of $3.6 million. Instead, with player contract depreciation added in, the net result for the Spurs becomes a book loss of $10.4 million ($1.3 million after actual depreciation, minus another $11.7 million in player contract depreciation).

But the calculation of the value of the depreciation advantage does not end here. Because the player contract depreciation shelters $11.7 million in taxable income for the owners, this means that owners can shelter an additional $10.4 million of outside income as well (the $11.7 million shelter minus the entire $1.3 million in pretax income from the Spurs). If the owners are in the 33 percent tax bracket, they save an additional $3.4 million (33 percent of $10.4 million) in taxes on income from other activities. Thus, the after-tax payoff to the owners of the Spurs from the 1994–95 season would be the sheltered $1.3 million after true depreciation, plus $3.4 million from tax savings on other income. This total of $4.7 million comes from a team that was showing a pretax book loss of around $10.4 million for the 1994–95 season! Another take on the value of owning the Spurs is that the owners would have had to have earned about $7 million in pretax income in order to have taken home the $4.7 million after taxes (again, if the owners are in the 33 percent bracket).

Things are not so clear for the 1995–96 season because the owners did not report their total depreciation for that year. So, we will stick with what the tax law allows, $10.7 million more in player contract depreciation, and assume that the Spurs had about the same depreciation of actual capital, $3.6 million. Starting from the $306,000 in net operating revenue for the season, subtracting true depreciation of $3.6 million yields a net operating loss of about $3.3 million. Deducting $10.7 million in player contract depreciation leads to a pretax book loss of $14 million. However, this permits the owners to save $4.6 million in taxes on income from other activities (33 percent of $14 million). That's a value of about $1.3 million ($4.6 million in taxes saved, minus the $3.3 million operating loss) from a team that was showing a pretax book loss of $14 million. So, over the two seasons shown in the tables, the Spurs were worth about $6 million, after taxes and true depreciation.

We do not have comparable data for the first year of the new owners' operation of the Spurs, 1993–94. But that first year should be comparable to the other two. For example, the Spurs made the playoffs in 1993–94, although they were not quite as successful as in the succeeding two years. And all of the accounting hanky-panky would have been in operation as well. So it isn't unreasonable to suppose that the owners made somewhere close to the average of the years in the tables, say, about $3 million in after-tax income for 1993–94. However, in addition to this, the Spurs' owners also shared in the expansion fees paid by the Toronto Raptors and Vancouver Grizzlies in 1994–95, adding $9.3 million in pretax income, or $6.2 million after taxes. So, in sum, it looks like the Spurs were worth about $15.2 million in after-tax income to the owners for the first three years. That's about $5 million on an annual average basis, for a rate of return in these first three years of about 7 percent per year after taxes or, equivalently, about 10.5 percent per year before taxes. And this return occurred even though their team was showing a pretax book loss of about $12.2 million annually.

Owners typically plead poverty by quoting net operating losses as the value of the team. And, for people in their wealth class, even 7 percent does not seem like an extraordinary return. Harold Seymour, the eminent baseball historian, quotes Charles Ebbets on baseball operations: "The question is purely one of business; I am not in baseball for my health." But before we agree that sports are not a high-return investment for rich people, let's remember the other values of owning a team. Profit-taking can occur under the "other salaries" heading. Most of the rest of the costs may actually be revenues, or generate even larger revenues, in other nonsports business operations of the owners. Business and government associations made during ownership tenure are valuable. And there is, after all, the fun of owning a team. Given all of these benefits, a 7 percent rate of return generating $5 million annually after taxes looks pretty good to us. Now, if only we could come up with that initial $75 million. . . .

These data on the Spurs help unravel a few of the puzzles surrounding sports team ownership. A team can show a book loss, yet pay owner-management quite well while they run the team, generate many other values not captured in the team's income statement, and end up as a very valuable commodity at sale time. After all, any subsequent owner will be starting the player roster depreciation process all over again while buying in on the same stream of value over time. The essential lesson from this analysis of the Spurs is that you can expect owners of a pretty good team to be happy for about three or four years. After that, player contract depreciation plays out, the value of ownership falls, and owners start making public statements about the losses they are suffering and the need for some sort of revenue boost in order to remain competitive in the league.

If you are an accounting freak, or if you would just like to learn more about the way the sports tax shelter works, we would suggest looking at a previous book of ours, *Pay Dirt*, also published by Princeton University Press (see Chapter 3 of that book for the gory details). Here we simply note that, under current tax law, Bill Veeck's tax shelter increases the after-tax return to an owner sufficiently to increase the value of the team by as much as 40 percent, relative to what it would have been without the shelter. The tax reforms introduced in 1986 (sponsored, interestingly enough, by another ex-player, ex–U.S. Senator Bill Bradley of New York Knicks fame) drastically reduced the benefits of tax shelters such as sports teams. However, the tax bill passed in 1997, reducing the capital gains tax rate (over time) to 20 percent, revived those benefits. Tax shelters go one up on Dracula—they are so attractive to politicians and the rich that even if you drive a stake directly into the heart of one, it will be alive and flourishing once again before you know it. Bill Veeck's tax shelter and the lowering of the capital gains tax rate together spell happier days for present and future owners to sports teams.

Finally, offsetting the bad news about operating income is the good news about the continuing increases in the prices of sports teams themselves. The capital gains that an owner gets from selling his team can more than offset the losses, if any, that the team has shown from its ongoing operations. In fact, this has been true in practically all cases involving recent sales of sports teams. Table 5-7 looks at teams that were sold between 1990 and 1998 and calculates the annual rates of return on initial investment that the owners earned from the increases in the value of the team between the time that the team was originally purchased and the time at which the team was sold. In MLB, annual rates of return range from 4.7 percent for the Tigers to 25.4 percent for the Orioles, with an average annual rate of return of around 11.3 percent. Owners in the NFL have done a little better in recent team sales, with an average rate of return from capital gains of around 12.7 percent. In the NBA, the rate of return rises to 17.7 percent, while the NHL shows an average annual rate of return of 10.7 percent.

The rates of return shown in Table 5-7 are all double-digit, except for the sales of the Tigers and the Mariners in 1992, the Cardinals in 1995, the Vikings in 1991, and the Hartford Whalers in 1994. Even given the low operating income figures discussed above, the potential capital gains from sale of the team plus the fact that interest rates in the 1990s have remained well within the single-digit range imply that almost all owners in pro team sports earned double-digit rates of return on their investments in teams in the 1990s.

Two exceptions stand out. The first is the case of Tom Monaghan, who owned the Detroit Tigers between 1983 and 1992. The Tigers have not done well at the gate for years; in addition, Monaghan sold the team for almost a fire-sale price. (The expansion fees charged the Rockies and Marlins were $95 million in 1991, just one year before the Tigers were sold for $80 million, so that we have the anomaly of an established franchise selling for $15 million less than what an expansion team was valued at.) The sale of the Tigers was triggered by cash-flow problems in Monaghan's pizza business, which might have created time pressures that affected the franchise price.

The other case is that of the former Hartford Whalers, a team that was hanging on for years by its fingernails (and by subsidies from the state of Connecticut and the city of Hartford). There was an NHL investigation into the sale of the team in 1988, and one of the principal investors in the team, Colonial Realty Co., went bankrupt a few years later. Peter Karmanos, who bought the team in 1994, suffered through several years of $10 million losses before moving the team to Carolina.

The fact that the market prices of teams keep going up, even while operating income figures remain at very low levels, raises the question as to whether what we are observing is a "bubble," much like the bubble in California real estate in the 1980s. In a bubble, the current price of an asset is determined not by what the asset is expected to earn in the future, but by what people today think buyers in the future will be willing to pay for the asset. A bubble is fueled by the "greater fool" argument: "Sure, I know this house isn't worth $300,000, but a year from now, I'll be able to sell it to some other real estate speculator for $500,000 because he'll be expecting the price the year after he buys it to be $600,000." The price is what it is today because everyone expects a "greater fool" to come around tomorrow to take the item off your hands at an even higher price.

All that economists know for sure about bubbles is that, eventually, they burst, and it's like the old game of musical chairs—whoever gets stuck with the overvalued asset at the time the bubble bursts has nowhere to get rid of it. There is a classic story about the stock market that goes something like this:

> A broker touted a small company's stock to a client and convinced him to buy 1,000 shares at $10 per share. A week later, the broker reported that the price was up to $12, and the client opted for another 1,000 shares. The price kept going up and the client kept buying for several more weeks. When the broker reported the price at $25 per share, the client said, "I'm not greedy. I'll just take my profits now. So sell my shares." There was a pause and then the broker asked, "To whom?"

If it really is a bubble that we are observing in the market for sports teams, the problem is that there isn't any way to know beforehand just when the bubble will burst. Those unlucky people who happen to be holding title to the overvalued team franchises will simply have to eat their losses and live with them. But if it is a bubble, it's been going on for quite a long time. Historical records of franchise sales in sports indicate that over the past thirty years or so, on average, NBA teams have been increasing in price at a rate of around 26 percent per year, MLB teams at around 14 percent per year, and NFL teams at around 22 percent per year.

The fact that the rates of increase in franchise prices in the 1990s, while in the double-digit range, still are lower than those in earlier years indicates that if there is a bubble in these markets, at least it is tapering off. Actually, over the period of the mid-1990s, investors were making a better rate of return simply "buying the market" with an indexed stock fund than were sports entrepreneurs with their high-visibility team investments.

Rather than being simply a bubble phenomenon, the continuing increase in team prices in sports and the capital gains being captured by owners no doubt reflect a range of factors at work in the sports industry. There are the "fun and games" and publicity aspects of ownership of a sports team. These have been increasing over time along with the media exposure that sports receives. The "spill-over" benefits of owning a sports team, those after-tax returns identified earlier that don't show up as operating income for a team, have been increasing over time as well, and get reflected in higher team prices. And there is undoubtedly something of a speculative bubble present as well, a common belief among present and prospective owners that because almost no one in the past has sold a team for less than its purchase price, future capital gains are more or less assured.

In summary, pro sports teams are now selling in the $150 to $250 million range; thus the current owners of sports teams are, by and large, very wealthy individuals. But, with teams being as expensive as they are, ownership of a team is a significant investment, even for a wealthy owner. The returns to ownership, as measured by operating income, are below market rates of return from investments of comparable risk in all sports with the possible exception of the NBA. A prime reason for the weak operating income performance of teams is free agency and the continuing escalation of player salaries. This suggests that bottom-line considerations play a critical role in team decision making, perhaps looming larger for today's owners than for owners of the past. On the one hand, this provides incentives for owners to act as aggressively as possible in attempting to exploit whatever local monopoly power the team possesses—if we don't squeeze out every cent of money from local fans and taxpayers, how can we afford to compete with the teams that do? On the other hand, the concentration on the bottom line makes it more difficult for teams to act cooperatively as members of a sports league in addressing problems of mutual interest to all teams in the league. What team can afford to sacrifice some of its income for the "common good" in a world in which lots of red ink is waiting just around the bend for any team that loses a star player to injury or ticket sales to bad weather?

There have been exceptional owners such as Phil Wrigley, who refused to schedule night games at Wrigley Park when he owned the Cubs, to keep nighttime noise, traffic, and confusion out of the northside neighborhood of the park; and Ewing Kaufman, who heavily subsidized his Kansas City Athletics when he was alive and then set up a committee of leading local citizens to operate and then sell the team after his death, to ensure that the team stayed in town. But everything about the current and historical record of pro sports suggests that if you are trying to understand what is going on in sports, your best bet is to assume that owners will be motivated by bottom-line considerations, however wealthy they are. Wayne Huizenga's decision to sell off his Florida Marlins, one by one, and then the team franchise itself after the team won the 1997 World Series but reportedly lost $30 million at the gate fits the mold nicely.

The contribution of owners to the problems of pro team sports do not arise, however, because they operate their teams to make money. After all, one of the fundamental reasons why we in America enjoy the living standards we do is that all those businessmen out there are free to operate to make as much money as they can. The argument in favor of a free enterprise, profit-oriented economy is that the way a businessman makes money is by producing the goods that consumers want, in the style and quantity that they want, at the lowest possible price. And if a businessman doesn't do this, he should be prepared to be steamrollered by other businessmen who do a better and cheaper job of producing that product.

Once again, the problem with the sports industry is the fact that leagues operate as monopolies, so that team owners in sports are not subject to the same intense market pressures to perform well as if they had to face competition from rivals. The local monopoly power of teams is limited, of course, by the availablity of substitutes. NFL football has to compete with the college game, with other pro sports such as the NBA and the NHL, and with alternative forms of entertainment. But, when combined with the monopoly power of the league it belongs to, the local monopoly power of a team is certainly significant, as evidenced, for example, by the success of teams in their campaigns for new, highly subsidized stadiums financed by cities and states. The next chapter looks into the monopoly power exercised by pro sports leagues.

6

LEAGUES

Free market economics is the process of driving enterprises out of business. Sports league economics is the process of keeping enterprises in business. There is nothing like a sports league. Nothing.

—Paul Tagliabue, *Sports Illustrated*, September 16, 1996

Tell the kids I haven't seen their fathers at the ballpark lately.

—Horace Stoneham, 1958, just before the Giants left for San Francisco, quoted in *Sporting News*, October 5, 1992, p. 5

Sports leagues are organized for the purely benevolent purposes of arranging play schedules for league teams, determining the league champion for the season, establishing the rules of play for league games and rules of eligibility for players, hiring umpires and referees, hearing protests and complaints about rules infractions, and preserving league records. But sports leagues also operate as cartels, that is, they are organizations that adopt and enforce rules on the business conduct of their members, rules that are designed to maximize the profits of the cartel, primarily by limiting competition among the members of the cartel and impeding entry into the industry. The powers exercised by leagues are juicy matters that make sports leagues prime suspects in any search for what is going wrong in pro team sports.

Cartels have a deservedly evil reputation, and it is understandable that team owners vehemently object to the application of that term to sports leagues—owners would prefer to stress the beneficial aspects of league operations and gloss over what goes on in the smoke-filled rooms at league meetings. But this is all just a matter of semantics; the important thing is how leagues actually behave in practice, not what we call them. In *The Devil's Dictionary*, that old misanthrope Ambrose Bierce came up with his typically cynical definition of a Christian: "One who believes that the New Testament is a divinely inspired book admirably suited to the spiritual needs of his neighbor. One who follows the teachings of Christ insofar as they are not inconsistent with a life of sin." Following Bierce, a sports league might be described not as a cartel but as a benevolent association that is organized to further the interests of sports fans, insofar as this is not inconsistent with extracting the maximum amount of money from them. So we won't harp on the terminology but instead look at the record.

At the very heart of the business structure of a sports league is the exclusive territorial franchise that is assigned to the owner of each member team in the league. The league franchise is a grant of a local monopoly within the league to the team owning the franchise. The specifics differ from league to league. In the NFL, for example, a team's territory is that contained within a seventy-five-mile radius of the team's home field. Under rules that apply in all leagues, no league team can schedule a game in the territory of another league team without obtaining permission from that team. Similarly, no owner can move his or her team into another location, whether occupied by a league team or not, without obtaining the consent by formal vote of three-fourths of all the owners of league teams. Supporters of the leagues argue that these rules provide the strongest incentives for owners to invest in their teams and to develop fan loyalty within their home cities, while protecting fans from capricious franchise moves. This sounds pretty benevolent, all right, but what does the record show?

League rules have been very effective in protecting the territorial rights of league members. To our knowledge, there has been exactly one documented case in pro team sports in which a league team has moved into another league team's territory without permission and has not been punished. That singular case, of course, is the one involving the peripatetic Oakland Raiders and their managing general partner, Al Davis. The story begins in 1979. Georgia Frontierre had just taken over ownership of the Los Angeles Rams from her deceased husband, Carroll Rosenbloom, and decided to implement a plan he had devised to move the team from the Los Angeles Coliseum to the Anaheim Stadium. Back in Oakland, Al Davis regarded this as a profitable opportunity and worked out a deal to move his Raiders into the Coliseum to replace the Rams, without obtaining permission from Frontierre or the other NFL owners. When the NFL refused to sanction the move of the Raiders, Davis and the Coliseum brought an antitrust suit against the league. They argued that Frontierre had abandoned the LA market, and that any attempt by the NFL to preclude entry into that market by Davis was an illegal restraint of trade. The NFL argued in reply that Anaheim Stadium was within the seventy-five-mile radius of the Coliseum, so that Frontierre was still operating within her NFL-authorized territory. The league pointed out as well that it was Davis who was abandoning his fans, not Frontierre. The case was argued out in a jury trial held in southern California, not the most favorable location for the NFL, and the NFL lost. The Raiders were permitted to move, and the NFL was assessed triple damage awards to be paid to both the Raiders and the Coliseum.

The decision hinged critically on the location of the trial, of course, and for good reason. The jury consisted of Los Angeles county tax payers who were responsible for the bills for operating the Coliseum. Georgia Frontierre had left the Coliseum in the lurch because she saw a better deal down the Santa Ana Freeway in Orange county. Now here was the NFL coming in, trying to talk an LA jury into protecting Frontierre's right to keep another team from using that same Coliseum, which otherwise would sit idle on Sunday afternoons—a tough sell under the best of conditions. And the NFL's argument that ruling for the league against Davis would protect the fans of the Raiders back in Oakland rang a little hollow, too, when it turned out that the NFL had no interest at all in allowing an expansion team to move into Oakland to replace the departed Raiders, after the case was resolved in favor of the Raiders.

Let's face it, this was a case where you could only root for all sides—the Raiders, the Rams, the NFL, and the Coliseum—to lose. There were no white hats involved. If pro sports followed the plot of a Dickens novel, there would be retribution for all sides from the fiasco of the Rams-Raiders moves, and in a sense there was. Georgia Frontierre was no Carroll Rosenbloom and over time the Rams degenerated into a second-division nonentity, with predictable low attendance results at Anaheim. Al Davis managed to field a better-than-average NFL team at the Coliseum, but the Raiders never really caught on in LA. So with all those seats to fill, the Coliseum looked very, very empty on Raider Sundays. For years, NFL fans in LA had TV blackouts every Sunday because neither the Coliseum nor Anaheim Stadium ever sold out. In 1995, the two teams left town—the Rams to St. Louis and the Raiders back to Oakland.

Unfortunately for the fans in those two cities, the very expensive publicly financed deals to obtain their new-old teams carried with them the same two owners who hadn't been able to excite the fans in LA the previous fifteen years. This was particularly unfortunate for St. Louis fans, who had already experienced twenty-five years of ineptitude under their previous owner, the football Cardinals' Bill Bidwill, who left in 1988 for Phoenix. And what about the fans in LA, the second biggest market in the country, who had been forced to live with two mediocre teams for fifteen years? The NFL was going to punish them for their lack of support for the Rams and Raiders by delaying assignment of an expansion franchise to LA for at least five years. Instead, the astute bigwigs at the NFL offices had other plans—expansion into markets such as Jacksonville (population 972,000) and Charlotte (population 1,260,000), while Los Angeles (population 15,302,000) went without an NFL team.

The court decision in the Raiders case was an aberration, as Donald Sterling, owner of the NBA San Diego/Los Angeles Clippers, discovered a couple of years later. In 1967, the Lakers left the county-owned Los Angeles Sports Arena, located just down the road from the Coliseum, for their privately financed arena, the Forum, in Inglewood. Sterling moved his Clippers from San Diego into the Sports Arena in 1984 without approval from the Lakers or the NBA. This sounds much like the Raiders-Rams case, right? The Lakers had abandoned Los Angeles for Inglewood and left a publicly financed facility without a professional team, just as the Rams had abandoned Los Angeles for Anaheim and left a publicly financed facility without a professional team. The jury didn't see it that way. The Lakers sued the Clippers and won. While the Clippers were allowed to stay in Los Angeles, they ended up paying a $6 million fee to the Lakers for invasion of Laker territory, plus legal fees.

When the All American Football Conference went out of business in 1949 under an agreement with the NFL, the Cleveland Browns, San Francisco 49ers, New York Yankees, and Baltimore Colts from the AAFC entered the NFL. The Colts paid the Washington Redskins $150,000 for invading the Redskins' territory, and there were payments as well to Tim Mara of the New York Giants for invasion of his territory. In 1966, when the AFL merged with the NFL, the AFL was required to make a payment of $18 million to the NFL over a twenty-year period. This money was paid to the San Francisco 49ers and the New York Giants for invasion of their territories by the AFL

Oakland Raiders and New York Jets. When an American League expansion franchise was assigned to Los Angeles in 1961, it occurred only with the approval of Walter O'Malley of the Dodgers, who required that the Angels play their first five seasons in O'Malley's Dodgers Stadium before the team was allowed to seek its own location. In each of these instances, as in all other aspects of league operations, the leagues did a very effective job of protecting the territorial rights of member owners.

How well do the leagues protect the fans of league teams? Well, that's a slightly different story. We are all familiar with the most outrageous cases, headed by the move of the Brooklyn Dodgers to Los Angeles in 1958. This happened at a time when Brooklyn was a veritable money machine for owner Walter O'Malley. The Dodgers accounted for 44 percent of total NL profits over the previous decade and racked up thirteen successive years of attendance over 1 million—an almost unheard-of performance for the time, save for the Yankees—before the most rabid and loyal fans in baseball. The NL vote on the move of the Dodgers and the Giants to the West Coast was unanimous—not one owner raised an objection to the joint move of the Giants and the Dodgers. So much for the vaunted protection of loyal fans by the baseball establishment.

After all these years, the move of the Dodgers still ranks as the worst sellout in the history of pro team sports, an absolute betrayal of their fans by O'Malley and the other NL owners. But there have been other moves, not quite so dramatic, all carrying much the same message to fans—"caveat emptor," loosely translated as "don't trust that rich guy who owns this team." There was the infamous move of the Milwaukee Braves to Atlanta by the "carpetbaggers," the group headed by William Barthollomay and Donald Reynolds, who had promised one and all that they had no intention of moving the team when they bought it in 1962. After alienating the fans by imposing a ban on bringing beer into the park—a long-standing Milwaukee tradition—the Milwaukee Braves, the only team in the history of major league baseball never to experience a losing season, moved to Atlanta in 1966. In 1984, there was the midnight move of the Baltimore Colts to Indianapolis by Robert Irsay, who had presided over a steady deterioration of that great football team for twelve straight years.

In 1993, Norm Green, burdened among other things by sexual harassment charges, moved his Minnesota North Stars to Dallas with the approval of the other NHL owners. This left vacant the hottest hotbed of hockey in the United States, a state that supports three leading NCAA hockey teams, that features a high school hockey tournament that far outshadows and outdraws the state basketball tournament, and that supplies a large fraction of the American players in the NHL. In a mere three years of ownership, Green had managed to carve for himself a special niche in the hearts of Minnesota hockey fans. In its story on the move, *Sports Illustrated* reported the evaluation of Green by one frustrated North Stars fan: "He's a greedy, money-hungry, egotistical country club–seeking lizard. And he looks like Satan."

A year after the team left, the NHL tried to move back into the Twin Cities market, but because of complications with the Target Center operation, was not able to accomplish this. The NHL will be back in town in 1999, over in St. Paul this time, the deal having been sealed by action of the state of Minnesota to help the city fund a $130 million renovation of Civic Center Arena, which will house the new team.

In 1988, Bill Bidwill moved the NFL St. Louis Cardinals to Phoenix after the mayor of St. Louis turned down Bidwill's request for a publicly financed 70,000-capacity football-only domed stadium. The Cardinals had been playing in Busch Stadium, owned by Anheuser Busch, which also owned the baseball Cardinals. One of Bidwill's complaints about Busch Stadium was that beer was served in the stadium at football games, making for unruly crowds. Anheuser Busch was remarkably unsympathetic to his arguments that beer should be banned from their park. Also the argument about unruly crowds rang a little hollow, given the spotty attendance at Bidwill's teams' games—what crowds was Bidwill talking about? Just why the Cardinals were going to need 70,000 seats in the proposed stadium for a team that rarely if ever sold out the 53,000 seats in Busch Stadium also remained a mystery.

Given the teams that the Cardinals put on the field, attendance at St. Louis games, averaging around 45,000, was extraordinary. The long successful history of the baseball Cardinals showed that St. Louis would support interesting teams, but Bidwill had no problem in getting NFL approval of his move to Phoenix. A few years later, of course, St. Louis bit the bullet and built that 70,000-capacity, $260 million domed stadium with public money, only to be turned down by NFL owners on a bid for an expansion franchise. St. Louis was stuck with the only available alternative and gave away the store to obtain its present team, the Rams, a team that unfortunately has brought back not-so-fond memories of the old Bidwill teams.

In 1997, an event somewhat comparable to the Brooklyn fiasco occurred, when the NFL allowed Art Modell to move his Cleveland Browns (but not the nickname!) to Baltimore. The Browns were one of the storied franchises of the NFL, with a history that ranks with that of the Bears and the Packers and fan support as strong as anywhere in the league. From the time the Browns blew into town in 1946 as a member of the newly formed All American Football Conference, through the great NFL years with Jim Brown, Cleveland has been one of the truly class teams of pro sports. But Modell had a sweetheart deal waiting for him in Baltimore, a new $200 million stadium with nominal rent and lots of cash from luxury boxes and personal seat licenses. So, with the approval of three-fourths of the NFL owners, he walked away from a proposed $160 million public refurbishing of Cleveland's Municipal Stadium, after coughing up some of his ill-gotten Baltimore gains to the rest of the league.

Commissioner Paul Tagliabue argued that the Raider decision had tied the hands of the NFL with respect to franchise moves and offered his suggestion to Congress as to how problem moves such as the Browns' should be handled: by giving antitrust exemption to the leagues when dealing with franchise moves. This would truly be letting the foxes into the chicken coop, and the amount of support for Tagliabue in Congress fortunately ranged from slim to none.

One problem for Tagliabue was that, shortly after the league approved the Browns' move, the NFL had no compunction at all about putting Ken Behring, owner of the Seattle Seahawks, back in his place. Behring had had the gall to move his team offices from Seattle down to Anaheim, in preparation for a move of his team into the LA area, before asking for NFL approval of his proposed move. Behring argued that the Seattle Kingdome was unsafe for his players and fans, because of the seismic risks in the Seattle area and the faulty construction of the dome. It is a fact that the Pacific Northwest is the second most earthquake-prone region of the country, and there have been instances of ceiling tiles dropping onto the playing surface in the Kingdome. However, one would think that if seismic risks were Behring's concerns, couldn't he have found some place other than southern California for his move?

In any case, the NFL told Behring very bluntly to move back to Seattle. The NFL made it clear that this was a stand taken on principle, not on money, which, as everyone knows, means that the decision was about money. And so it was. With no NFL teams in LA, the league stands to garner an enormous expansion fee—maybe upward of $750 million—from an investor who would like to capture that market, say, some entity such as Disney, Time Warner, or maybe Fox. The last thing the league wants is for some existing team to move in to claim the LA market and rob the other NFL teams of their share of the coming expansion fee. Behring moved his offices back to Seattle and shortly thereafter sold multibillionaire Paul Allen an option to buy the team, an option which he exercised in July 1997.

As noted earlier, one of the least endearing features of pro team sports is that when a team falls on bad times and doesn't perform well on the field, and when attendance at games drops, the owner, the players, and the league invariably blame it on the fans for lack of "loyalty to the team." In other industries, when a company does poorly, any executive who blamed his customers for not buying the firm's products would be laughed out of court before being dumped, maybe even without the traditional golden parachute. This all gets turned on its head in sports where, as a practical matter, all you need for league approval of a franchise move is poor attendance figures, regardless of the competence (or lack thereof) of the owner.

Based solely on their records, it is pretty clear that owners such as Hugh Culverhouse of the NFL Tampa Bay Buccaneers, Georgia Frontierre of the NFL Rams, Bill Bidwill of the NFL Cardinals, George Argyros of the AL Seattle Mariners, Arnold Johnson of the old AL Kansas City Athletics, and others of their ilk simply didn't understand how to build and keep a staff of people who knew how to run a successful sports team. But in pro team sports, the resulting playing and financial failures get blamed on the fans, and, short of a sale of the team to someone who does have some sports moxie, these franchises become prime candidates for moves.

Beyond the anecdotal evidence on moves are the hard numbers. Table 6-1 in the back of the book lists all of the franchise moves that have occurred in the four major pro team sports leagues between 1950 and 1997. There have been forty-seven moves during that period, an average of one per year, spread fairly evenly across sports, except that the NBA had a severe "churning" of franchises in the 1960s and 1970s. Moves of franchises during down times for a sport are understandable; the alternative might well be bankruptcy. What is a little surprising is that even during the boom periods for pro team sports, say from 1980 on, there still are franchise moves occurring with much the same regularity as in those earlier periods when a lot of teams were hanging on by their financial fingernails. In the NFL in particular, the franchise moves that are occurring these days are not due to desperate financial problems at a team's current location; none of the four teams that moved in the 1990s was in major financial trouble. Instead, the moves were generated by the lure of big-dollar stadium-related subsidies by the cities to which the teams moved. And the important thing to note is that the NFL did not move to protect the fans of the teams that moved, despite this obvious fact.

Finally, what Table 6-1 does not show is the various teams that threatened to move but did not. These are the teams that have been supplied with new stadiums or arenas, fully or partially publicly financed; with improvements to their existing stadiums or arenas; or with other public subsidies, typically in response to threats by the team, backed up the league, to move elsewhere if public funding was not forthcoming.

Here we simply note that if you haven't been paying attention these past few years, you might have missed the fact that almost every city in the country is going through the same cycle of threats to move by team owners and ultimate capitulation by politicians or voters. An example is a story involving the fair city of Minneapolis.

Back in the Twin Cities, it's known as the "Harv and Marv" story, the story of the NBA Minnesota Timberwolves; their owners, Harvey Ratner and Marvin Wolfenson; and their arena, the Target Center. Harv and Marv obtained an NBA franchise for Minneapolis in 1988 and decided to use this as a base for expanding their existing health-club business. Over objections from all sides in the Twin Cities, they built their own spanking new arena, using their own money, to house the Timberwolves, along with a downtown health club and spa. (The objections from civic leaders arose because the Twin Cities already had two existing publicly owned arenas, the Met Center [15,000 capacity] and the St. Paul Civic Arena [16,000 capacity], as well as Williams Arena [14,000 capacity] on the campus of the University of Minnesota. One more arena seemed to be overdoing things a bit.)

For the first two years, while the Target Center was being built, the team was housed in the Metrodome, where it drew an NBA record attendance the team's first year in the league. After the move to the Target Center, the team continued to draw exceptional crowds, exceeding the average of all NBA teams each of the first five years the T-Wolves were in the league. This was impressive because the T-Wolves fielded absolutely miserable teams—historically miserable teams, in fact—in part because of unbelieveably bad luck in the annual NBA draft lottery and in part because of incompetence in the team's front office.

That was the good news. The bad news was that the new arena, the Target Center, originally projected to cost $35 million, came in instead at a cost of $105 million. Another item of bad news was that competition with the other arenas in town bid up the fees for nonbasketball events at the Target Center to the point that the new arena couldn't break even on those events. By the early 1990s, Harv and Marv had run into major difficulties paying the bills for the Target Center, the arena they had insisted on building just five years earlier.

When a sports team owner has financial problems, to whom does he turn? To the local government, of course. So Harv and Marv made a pitch to the city of Minneapolis for a public buyout of the arena, along with a threat to move the team if no buyout took place. This was a team that had one of the best records of fan support in the NBA; the problem was not the team, it was the cost overrun on the arena that the owners had insisted on building.

Anywhere except in sports the threat would have been laughable. Realistically, the threat was equivalent to a robber coming into a bank with a loaded pistol, pointing the pistol at his own head, and threatening to kill himself if the teller didn't turn over the cash. What in the world would Harv and Marv have done with their arena if their team moved? Use it for kick boxing or ladies' lacrosse?

In any case, when no public buyout resulted, the team was put on the market, and an unbelievable offer came in from Top

Rank Corporation to move the team to New Orleans. The offer was for a cool $152 million, $120 million more than Harv and Marv had paid for the expansion franchise and about $50 million more than the highest valuation placed on the team by insiders. But in a rare case in which the interests of the league corresponded with those of the fans, Commissioner David Stern began working in earnest to keep the T-Wolves in the place where they had been so well supported, and so badly served by their owners.

The NBA soon found an interested suitor in Minnesota billionaire Glen Taylor. He bought the T-Wolves for a more reasonable $88.5 million, in a deal under which the city bought the Target Center from Harv and Marv for $55 million. That might sound like a bargain for a facility that cost $105 million to build. However, the city had already invested $20 million in infrastructure for the arena, so its purchase price added up to a total of $75 million. Moreover, an independent appraiser set the value of the Target Center at only $63 million, so the city had provided a $12 million subsidy to Harv and Marv, who managed to walk away from the debts incurred in the cost overrun on the arena. This is one more instance of a general rule, namely that owners never end up holding the bag—that particular task is invariably assigned to state or local governments.

In the 1990s, the monopoly power of leagues is most evident in the ways in which teams and cities hammer out stadium and arena deals. Publicly funded stadiums and arenas are the source of large subsidies to sports teams. The teams' success at obtaining those subsidies rests on the fact that threats to move a team elsewhere are not idle, as Table 6-1 makes clear. We will look in more detail at the stadium issue in the next chapter. Here we are concerned with the ways in which leagues use their monopoly power to enhance the bargaining power of teams.

To put teeth into team threats, leagues routinely leave a number of desirable locations without league teams. In baseball, Tampa, St. Petersburg, and Jacksonville filled this bill for years, popping up from season to season as potential move sites for teams such as the Indians, the White Sox, the Mariners, and the Giants, as those teams angled for publicly funded stadiums. Moreover, the monopoly power exercised by the league means that it takes league approval to obtain a replacement if the original team leaves after the proposed stadium deal is rejected, or if a team leaves for some other reason. As the Los Angeles experience with the NFL indicates, it can be a daunting task to bring a replacement team into town even in the case of a megalopolis center; and of course it is much more difficult for small-market cities. The combination of the availability of vacant team sites and the monopoly power of leagues to enforce threats makes the threats of member teams so successful.

A natural question to ask at this point is, How are sports leagues able to sustain the monopoly power that they clearly possess today? After all, in most other industries, when a monopoly develops and the monopolizing firm begins to make big profits or fails to respond adequately to its customers' demands, competitors enter into the industry, hoping to make some of those monopoly profits, too. The firms entering the industry provide lower-priced, more customer-friendly substitutes for the monopoly firm's products, eating into its market and eroding its profits. Incentives for entry are eliminated only at the point where investment in the industry yields only a market rate of return, as in other nonmonopolized industries. Why hasn't that happened in pro team sports?

The short answer is that it has happened, in the sense that there have been attempts at entry into each of the major sports at various points in time. In the early days of baseball, there were rivals galore for the National League, which was the first entrant into the sport back in 1876. In the 1880s, the American Association (AA) entered as a rival to the NL, and then came to an agreement that established the major leagues as a two-league organization. The Union League was in operation for one year as a rival league. Then in 1890, the Players League, a cooperative endeavor, took the field as a rival to the NL and AA before folding after one season. The NL became a monopoly twelve-team league in 1892 after the AA went out of business.

In 1901, the American League was organized as a rival to the NL, with the two leagues arriving at a negotiated settlement in 1903. The NL–AL settlement created a new combined monopoly structure for the sport.

In 1914, another rival baseball league, the Federal League (FL), came on the scene, competing with the NL and AL. After just two years, the FL went out of existence, following a negotiated agreement with the NL and the AL under which two FL owners were allowed to buy teams in the majors—the Cubs in the NL and the St. Louis Browns in the AL—with monetary settlements to the other FL owners. The settlement occurred only after the FL owners filed an antitrust suit against the NL and AL. One FL owner, Carroll Raisin of the Baltimore Terrapins, refused the money offer and instead opted to continue the original antitrust suit, which was heard in the court of an obscure federal district judge named Kenesaw Mountain Landis. Landis ruled that baseball was not subject to the antitrust laws, and he was upheld on appeal by the Supreme Court. Shortly after the Supreme Court reached its decision, Landis was hired by major league baseball as its first commissioner, a post he held for over twenty years. With the FL out of the picture, major league baseball reverted to its monopoly position.

Just after World War II, the Mexican League attempted to compete with the majors by signing a few major leaguers to the league's rosters, but the attempt was abandoned after just one year. The threat of the Pacific Coast League to organize as an independent major league certainly played a role in the quick and unanimous agreement of the National League to the moves of the Dodgers and the Giants in 1958. And, as noted earlier, in the late 1950s the Continental League was organized, on paper, by Branch Rickey and William Shea to bring pressure on the major leagues to add an NL team in New York to replace the Dodgers and Giants. After an agreement was reached with the majors, the Continental League went out of existence. One other paper league was organized in the early 1990s, the United League, but it failed to obtain needed financing and never reached the playing field.

The NFL has had a colorful history of rivals dating back to the first American Football League (AFL I), organized by Red Grange and his manager, C. C. "Cash and Carry" Pyle. AFL I fielded teams in 1926, after which the league went out of business. There were two more AFLs before World War II (AFL II in 1936 and 1937 and AFL III in 1940 and 1941), and then the All American Football Conference competed with the NFL from 1946 through 1949. In 1960, AFL IV came on the scene and battled with the NFL until 1966 when the two leagues merged, after Congress passed a bill exempting the merger from antitrust prosecution.

Since AFL IV, there have been two abortive attempts to enter the pro football field—the World Football League (WFL, 1974–75) and the United States Football League (USFL, 1983–85). Both leagues were underfinanced, had too many weak franchises, and did not constitute serious threats to the NFL's dominance of the sport. The USFL brought an antitrust suit against the NFL, which was won by the USFL. That was the good news for USFL owners. The bad news was that the damages assessed by the court were set at one dollar, which explains why the USFL has gone down in sports history as the "one dollar league."

In the summer of 1998, there were reports in the press that Ted Turner and NBC were on the verge of forming a new rival league in football. Earlier in the year, the new eight-year TV contracts announced by the NFL had left NBC and Turner's TNT out in the cold without pro football offerings. There were no details available concerning the proposed league, such as franchise locations, starting dates, and television exposure. The length of the NFL TV commitments combined with the financial clout of NBC and Turner make the possibility of a new rival something to be considered seriously. It should be pointed out, however, that in 1994, when CBS lost its NFL contract, CBS was reported to be considering the formation of a rival league but nothing came of that.

There have been rival leagues in basketball and hockey as well. The two most recent entries, the American Basketball Association (ABA, 1967–76) and the World Hockey Association (WHA, 1972–79), were created in the Santa Ana law offices of Gary Davidson, who also was the godfather of the WFL. Following congressional hearings designed to pressure the NBA into merging with the ABA, a merger of sorts occurred before the 1976–77 NBA season, with the New York (later New Jersey) Nets, Denver Nuggets, Indiana Pacers, and San Antonio Spurs moving to the NBA. Similarly, the Winnipeg Jets, Quebec Nordiques, Edmonton Oilers, and Hartford Whalers of the WHA moved to the NHL before the 1979 NHL season. Winnipeg, Quebec, and Hartford have since moved elsewhere, and there have been rumors of a possible Edmonton move for several years. Following the mergers, both the NBA and the NHL regained monopoly status in their sports.

There have been only two full-blown successes in the list of rival leagues—the AL in baseball and AFL IV in football. The AAFC was a qualified success, with four teams moving into the NFL, but the other rival leagues in football were all unadulterated failures. In basketball, the ABA was at best a qualified success, with four teams moving to the NBA. The same can be said for hockey, where four teams from the WHA made it into the NHL. There might be some money to be made in organizing leagues, but being an owner in a rival league is a truly hazardous occupation.

Even in the cases of the full-blown successful rival leagues, the end result of the process was the reestablishment of monopoly leagues, representing the merger of the old leagues and the rivals. One nontrivial effect of the process was that more teams were added to the sport, benefiting fans in the favored cities and in effect forcing unwanted expansion on the old league. Unfortunately, once a merger has been achieved, the new expanded league retains the same monopoly powers as the old league.

One might ask why antitrust suits weren't filed by the government in connection with the various interleague wars, or in connection with the mergers after the negotiated ends to wars. When the AL merged with the NL, the Sherman Antitrust Law was still an unknown innovation, and its application to something like baseball was regarded as ludicrous. When AFL IV came along, actions taken by the NFL to stifle the new league—including locating an expansion franchise in Dallas to combat Lamar Hunt's AFL Dallas Texans and offering the owners of the AFL Minnesota franchise a franchise in the NFL instead—did lead to an antitrust suit, not by the government but by the AFL. The AFL lost under the rather strange legal argument that, because the AFL had survived, it must not have suffered any significant damages. And the merger of the two leagues, which could have led to antitrust suits by players, was exempted from the antitrust laws by Congress.

The Justice Department has traditionally taken a hands-off position with respect to pro sports leagues. This has led to an interesting "catch-22" situation. As the brief comments above indicate, entry into pro sports by a rival league is a risky enterprise. A rival league can expect to lose money for years while it is establishing its bonafides as a major league in the sport. One wouldn't undertake an investment of this nature unless there was the prospect of rewards substantially above a market rate of return.

Because the Justice Department has a history of not filing suit against a merger of a successful rival league with an existing league, this provides incentives for entry, since a successful entry can lead to a sharing of the monopoly profits of the existing league by the rival. The problem is that this means that entry, even if successful, does not destroy the monopoly power of the league. By contrast, if the Justice Department did adopt a policy of fighting mergers, successful entry would lead to a competitive environment, with correspondingly lower profits. The only trouble is that, given the risk of entry, this would no doubt eliminate most of the incentives for entry. Welcome to catch-22 as applied to pro sports.

More recently, an even stronger barrier to entry has developed in pro sports, namely the wave of highly subsidized publicly financed stadiums and arenas of the 1980s and 1990s, in which the existing team is effectively given complete control of operation of the facility. Teams have been so successful in playing their threat cards that these new stadiums and arenas are being built all over the country. The problem they pose is that any rival league attempting to place teams in any of those cities will face an impossible hurdle, attempting to compete against a team that receives an enormous subsidy from the local government. We will look at this in more detail in the next chapter.

We have been talking about successful rival leagues. However, even when they fail, rival leagues are a problem for the existing monopoly leagues because they bid up the price of players, compete for television time and money, and spawn the inevitable, if rarely successful, antitrust suits. The best weapon a monopoly league has to deter competition from a rival league is to avoid leaving too many financially viable locations open as slots for an entering rival league. The NL made a mistake of this kind in 1901 when it dropped four cities from its league roster—Baltimore, Cleveland, Washington, and Louisville—and reverted to an eight-team league. The fledgling AL then moved franchises into three of these cities—Baltimore, Cleveland, and Washington—and found a built-in fan base there to go along with the other cities in the original AL lineup—Chicago, Philadelphia, Boston, Milwaukee, and Detroit. Within two years, the AL was outdrawing the NL. The interesting thing is that the NL had made the same mistake twenty years earlier in 1882, when it dropped markets that were picked up by the American Association.

Similarly, the NFL left too many desirable locations vacant in 1960 when AFL IV came along. The AFL went head-to-head against the NFL in New York (Titans vs. Giants) and in Los Angeles (Chargers vs. Rams), but its other member cities were newcomers to pro football—Dallas, Oakland, Boston, Houston, Buffalo, and Denver.

Pro sports leagues have certainly learned their lesson from these experiences. Table 6-2 gives a list of the leading metropolitan areas of the United States and Canada, together with the number of major league pro sports teams at each location. As the table indicates, the two countries are not completely blanketed with teams, but the leagues have done pretty good jobs of siting teams in metropolitan areas down to and below the 1 million population level. However, as the table also indicates, the teams in the megalopolises of New York and Los Angeles have much larger population bases to work with (per team) than do the smaller cities.

On the one hand, the high ratio of fans to teams in the megalopolis cities is a main reason for the lack of competitive balance in sports leagues; on the other, this provides evidence for the argument that leagues restrict the number of franchises in order to increase league-wide profits, as well as the franchise values of member teams. The profit potential of additional franchises in the megalopolis cities has been one factor driving the entry of rival leagues in the past, and might in the future as well. Still, all in all, it appears that leagues have managed to expand sufficiently to deter entry while still preserving enough vacant sites to make move threats believable, which is bad news, of course, for fans and taxpayers.

We have been searching for the source of the problems of pro sports, and all sorts of bells and whistles should be sounding at this point. The monopoly power exercised by leagues has been used to bring pressure on local governments around the country, with threats to move teams if stadiums or arenas are not built, threats that have been exercised over and over again as the record of the past twenty years makes clear. And the subsidies incorporated into the rental agreements at these new publicly financed facilities act to fix in concrete the monopoly power of leagues by establishing major impediments to the entry of others into the industry who could bring the fresh air of competition to the pro team sports business. More than this, we have seen from Chapter 2 that it is the monopoly power of leagues that has led to the leagues' capture of the lion's share of TV revenues, which in turn has fueled the escalation of player salaries in sports.

But before definitely pinning the tail on monopoly sports leagues, we don't want to forget one final group of prospective culprits—state and local politicians, the ones who feed the beasts, the ones out campaigning for those expensive stadiums and arenas.

7

STATE AND LOCAL POLITICS

I think the people now know that if we don't get a stadium, the team will be forced to leave.

—Peter Magowan, new owner of the San Francisco
Giants, after four referendum failures,
Sporting News, November 25, 1992, p. 5

We live in an era in which politicians of all stripes bend over backward to praise the virtues of state and local governments and to damn the failings of the federal government. Federal government programs such as welfare devolve to state and local governments, where politicians and government officials are theoretically closer to the people and their problems, and where innovative solutions to those problems are expected to blossom. Certainly there are strong grounds for criticizing the federal government in all of its dimensions—executive, judicial, legislative, and bureaucratic. Will Rogers once said that "No one's life or property is safe when Congress is in session." Rogers would certainly get as much support today for this sentiment as he did when he said it back in the 1920s.

However, in fairness, remember that a major function of local governments, usually the most important function both dollar-wise and impact-wise, is to operate the public school system, which is currently producing student test scores for the United States down somewhere near those of Outer Mongolia. We might have to allow some time for those innovative solutions to welfare to blossom at the state and local levels. State and local politicians are also those individuals who are involved, up to their armpits so to speak, in the booming business of providing public funds for all the stadiums and arenas being built across the country. So, however close they are to the people and their problems, they certainly deserve to be on our list of suspects of those who are abusing power in the pro sports game.

How big is the boom in stadium and arena construction? Table 7-1 in the back of the book lists some stadium and arena projects, mostly publicly financed, that have been planned or built for pro sports teams between 1991 and 1998. As the table makes clear, there are stadium and/or arena projects built or building in almost every city in the country with a major league pro sports team, and in some that are still looking for a major league team. Thirty-four new stadiums or arenas (or major renovations of existing facilities) came on line between 1992 and 1998 at a total cost of around $6.3 billion, with 70 percent or more representing public money. And there are billions of dollars worth of projects still in the pipeline.

Each one of the publicly funded facilities has had to obtain the approval of local or state governments or of the electorate itself, so there is an important political component to the building boom. Further, the publicly funded facilities all invariably involve substantial subsidies to the teams housed in them, through "sweetheart" rental arrangements that shift almost all of the costs of the facility to taxpayers while reserving all or almost all of the revenues for the team.

For an illustration in depth of what is going on, we turn to the city of Seattle. The year 1997 was a banner one in pro team sports for the citizens of Seattle and the state of Washington, something to be remembered far, far into the future. The Mariners, a team that took fourteen years from its entry into the AL back in 1976 to come up with a winning season—the worst beginning record in the history of major league baseball—won its divisional title in the AL. The team's superstar, Ken Griffey, Jr., was the unanimous choice of sportswriters for MVP of the league, after stroking out 56 homeruns, hitting .304, and once again winning a Golden Glove award in center field.

Most important, 1997 was the year that the Washington state legislature voted to fund a new stadium for the Mariners, committing the team to staying in Seattle until 2020 but along the way saddling the taxpayers of the state with a huge potential liability. Six months later, in a referendum financed by Paul Allen, the ninth richest individual in the world according to *Forbes* magazine, the citizens of Washington voted to give the NFL Seattle Seahawks and the team's new billionaire owner, Paul Allen, a new stadium, too. This was two years after the new publicly funded Key Arena opened in Seattle to house the NBA Seattle Supersonics. After the smoke cleared, the taxpayers of the state had taken on a contingent liability of something approaching $1 billion to subsidize their sports teams.

In an era in which almost every city or state seems to be building one or more stadiums or arenas for its pro sports teams, the state of Washington managed to take stadium funding "to a new level," as the jocks say. There must have been champagne corks popping in team owners' offices all over the country when the details of the Seattle stadium deals became public. Whatever the previous limits on the ability of owners to guzzle deeply from the public trough, the sky was definitely now the limit. It was as though the citizens of the state had decided to spend the next twenty years with signs on their backs reading "Kick Me." What in the world went on out there in the Pacific Northwest for all of this to come to pass?

Despite the outcome, things in Seattle and in the state of Washington all started out reasonably enough. Up until 1996, you could fire a cannon midweek at noon down Third Avenue in downtown Seattle and not hit a Mariners fan. Seattle's citizens had more important things to do in summer than watch baseball—things like boating, fishing, mountain hiking, and sitting in the sun. In fact, just about anything looked like more fun than watching the Mariners get beaten once again in the Kingdome.

In 1995, the new owners of the Mariners, who had bought the team in 1992 for $100 million and had lost a reported $10 million or so per year since, arrived at the obvious conclusion. The problem was not the general manager nor the need for better players, and certainly not the need for new owners. The problem was that the fans simply were not willing to come to the outdated Kingdome. What the team needed instead was a new stadium, financed by the taxpayers of course —or a move to some other city.

There was a public referendum on the issue and, in a close vote, the good citizens of Seattle quite reasonably defeated the proposal. Admittedly, the Kingdome had its problems—the occasional tile falling from the ceiling and a somewhat less than classic appearance—but it was only twenty years old and, given a $100 million-or-so upgrading, it was basically sound. So the election result was predictable and it was "case closed," right? Wrong. One of the things about publicly funded stadiums is that, like the phoenix, they keep arising out of the ashes of the last previous death stroke.

What happened next was the 1996 AL season, when the Mariners began to play like a real honest-to-goodness major league baseball team, and Alex Rodriguez, Junior Griffey, Jay Buhner, and Randy Johnson became almost as big local media stars as Gary Payton of the much beloved (and very successful) NBA Seattle Supersonics. It didn't hurt that Ken Behring, then owner of the Seahawks, had become public enemy number one in town, after announcing that he was going to move his team out of Seattle immediately, if not sooner, because of the earthquake hazards he had suddenly discovered in the Kingdome.

Next to Mr. Behring, the Mariners didn't look quite so greedy and rapacious.

Enter U.S. Senator Slade Gorton, a Republican who believes firmly in personal responsibility, free markets, and getting the government off our backs and out of our business. Well, within reason of course. And one place where these principles apparently do not apply is professional sports. With the Mariners making noises about moving after the 1996 season, Gorton met with the owners of the team. On December 20, 1996, Gorton then wrote a letter to Democratic Governor Gary Locke expressing his support for the Mariners' demands for a new stadium and asking the state legislature to pass legislation authorizing public funding of the stadium. In effect, Gorton was recommending that the legislature overturn the "mistake" the Seattle voters had made in the referendum the previous year.

More than any other individual, Slade Gorton can take credit for what happened next. And next to Republican Gorton in support for the stadium was Democrat Locke, who pulled out all the stops in creating a bill that could make it through a very reluctant state legislature.

What finally did make it through the legislature was a bill authorizing a $414 million open-air baseball-only stadium, including a $75 million retractable roof demanded by the team. The bill also authorized $310 million in state bonds to pay for the stadium and $26 million in bonds for a contiguous parking complex. (Of the $414 million cost, $33 million was the implicit cost of the site, a portion of city-owned land around the Kingdome donated for the new stadium by the city of Seattle.) The team agreed to provide $45 million toward the up-front cost of the stadium, seemingly adding a private touch to stadium finances. However, things are not always quite what they seem. In the stadium lease agreement, the team was given, free of charge, the "naming" rights to the stadium, that is, the rights to sell the name of the stadium to the highest industrial or commercial bidder. And what was the estimated market value of those naming rights? Make a wild guess. Those of you who guessed $45 million should congratulate yourselves—you've reached the appropriate level of cynicism about the pro team sports business and its friends and supporters in government. All during the campaign that was waged for the stadium by the local press—the *Seattle Post-Intelligencer* and the *Seattle Times*—the fact that the team was putting $45 million of its "own" money into the stadium was mentioned time and time again in asking for public support for the stadium. We will return to the naming rights below.

In the publicly funded stadiums built in the 1960s and 1970s, including the Kingdome, financing was arranged so that, under ideal conditions at least, rents paid by the teams coupled with the stadium's share of concessions, parking, and luxury box revenues would come close to covering the capital and operating costs of a stadium. So what were the terms of the Mariners' deal? First, the team agreed to pay a rent of $700,000 per year, and then to adjust the amount upward to account for inflation. Second, a 5 percent admissions tax was added to ticket prices for baseball games, the proceeds to be used to pay off the $26 million in bonds for the parking garage and to cover capital improvements to the stadium over its life. Third, the team agreed to pay 10 percent of its profits to the stadium authority, after recovering roughly $100 million in losses incurred in the period before the new stadium opened.

So what does this translate into on an annual basis? Ignoring for a moment the profit-sharing, estimated team payments per year (in constant dollars) from rent and the admissions tax amount to around $2.6 million. What about profit-sharing? In the first place, even if the team earned $10 million per year, a major turnaround from its previous history, it would be a full ten years before there would be any profits to share to cover those $100 million in past losses. Beyond that, however, the lease agreement specifies that, while the stadium authority can examine the books of the team, it cannot raise objections to any revenue or expenditure items that satisfy standard accounting practices. This is interesting. Suppose that at some time in the future, the team actually has earned enough to cover its past losses and is on the verge of showing a profit available for sharing. There is nothing in the lease that prevents the team from using the occasion to declare a bonus to its richly deserving executive-owners in an amount equal to the profits, thereby eliminating any profits for sharing. Why in the world would the team voluntarily submit itself to sharing profits with the stadium authority when there is such a simple out? The appropriate guess as to the amount of profit-sharing revenue the stadium authority will ever see is, of course, zero.

What about concessions, parking, luxury boxes? In the new Mariners stadium, things are simple, just as in the much discussed and much admired (at least among the rich) "flat tax." The lease provides for a simple 100–0 split of revenues under which the Mariners get everything—all the concession revenue, all the luxury box revenue, all the parking revenue, all the income from nonbaseball activities. To offset this, the team pays the operating costs of the stadium.

So, the team provides about $2.6 million per year toward meeting the capital costs of the stadium, which add up to around $30 million per year. The difference of $27.4 million per year ($548 million over 20 years) then represents the contingent liability that state taxpayers have incurred in order to keep the Mariners in town. This is also a good approximation of the annual subsidy that the citizens of Washington will pay to the team.

But all the problems with making interest payments and paying off the stadium bonds were way off in the future, so supporters of the team could at least congratulate themselves that they had done their part to keep the team in Seattle. And there was good news in 1997, as noted earlier, with a divisional title and an AL MVP. Another interesting bit of good news was that with an exciting and winning team in town, the Mariners began to draw, ending the season with over 3 million in attendance—in that decrepit old Kingdome that had caused all those attendance problems two years earlier.

But with good news of course comes bad. In December 1997, the team announced the proposed prices for seats when the new stadium opened (July 1999), and it was something of a shocker. Season-ticket holders in the home plate area, some of the strongest supporters of the team and their new stadium, had been paying around $22 per game in the Kingdome. They found out that they would now be paying between $125 and $195 per game for their seats in the new stadium, translating into a season ticket price of between $100,000 and $155,000 per seat—the highest in the majors—as compared to the non-trivial $17,000 fans had been paying. Those fans with somewhat less desirable season-ticket locations found that their prices would more than double, and that they would have to pay a dreaded PSL (preferred seating license) fee of from $10,000 to $20,000 when the new stadium opened, just for the privilege of buying season tickets over the next twenty years.

In hindsight, it was really incredibly naive of the supporters of the stadium to believe that the team would not take every possible advantage of the new attraction the taxpayers had provided for them—hey, those shiny bright exorbitant ticket prices are the reason the team wanted the stadium in the first place. And to turn the knife just a little more, at the same time the team announced the ticket prices, it also announced that it had decided not even to make an offer to its superstar pitcher, Randy Johnson, arguing that it "wouldn't be good business" for the team to make an offer he would even consider.

To those individuals in Seattle who complain that the only winners from the new stadium will be the owners of the Mariners, recall the old curse, "May your fondest wish be granted." With their fondest wish granted, the owners commenced construction of the stadium and began the search for some firm to which to sell the naming rights. Unfortunately, it turned out that $45 million was an overestimate of the value of the stadium's name. Instead, it brought in a bid for only $1.8 million per year (in constant dollars) from the local Safeco Insurance Company, which adds up to a present value of around $30 million, not $45 million. If the Mariners' owners were disappointed about this, the fans weren't all that pleased to learn that "their" new stadium was going to be known as Safeco Field, which somehow doesn't sound especially compelling for a $414 million stadium.

A more important problem for the team was the agreement that the Mariners had made, as part of the lease, to cover any cost overruns on the construction of the stadium beyond an allowed overrun of $25 million. By mid-June 1998, with the stadium only half built, the $25 million allowance had already been exceeded because of change orders and the tight construction schedule, and there were reports in the local press that overruns might reach into the $50 to $100 million range or beyond. This recalled major cost overruns from the past, such as the Superdome, the Target Center, or even the ultimate horror story, Montreal's Expo Stadium. The Safeco Field story was still unfolding as this book was being written in mid-1998.

The story of Safeco Field and similar stadiums raises the general question, Why did the building boom in stadiums and arenas hit in the 1990s? It also raises the question of whether there is any conceivable justification for the involvement of state or local governments in financing and building facilities for pro sports teams.

Some of the answers are immediate. There was a boom in the building of stadiums and arenas in the 1990s in part because there had been an earlier boom in stadium construction in the 1960s and 1970s, a time when a number of publicly financed multiple-use (football and baseball) stadiums—the Astrodome, Shea, Atlanta, Candlestick, Three Rivers, Riverfront, Busch, Anaheim, Veterans, and the Kingdome—opened. With a life expectancy of twenty-five to forty years, these facilities were beginning to show their age as the 1990s wore on. More important, the lease agreements that were signed when the stadiums originally opened were also expiring, permitting teams to leave without penalties and much enhancing their threat value in stadium negotiations.

Moreover, as has been emphasized in the previous chapters, teams in the 1990s, particularly small-market teams, have been under bottom-line pressures because of rising payroll costs. Given the ongoing boom in the popularity of pro team sports and the leverage from expiring stadium contracts, a predictable move by team owners was to put the squeeze on local governments to supply attractive new stadiums with lots of luxury boxes and other revenue-enhancing features, with as little cost to the team as the public could be made to swallow.

The particular event that touched off the stadium boom in earnest was the phenomenal success of Camden Yards, a publicly financed $210 million baseball-only stadium for the AL Baltimore Orioles, which opened in 1992. Camden Yards broke new ground in that it was designed specifically for baseball, with a capacity of only 48,000, a compact park with every seat close to the playing field. Camden Yards also harkened back to the old-time ballparks, the ones that were torn down in the 1950s, with its irregular outfield configuration and a background blending with local commercial and industrial buildings. The Orioles have been one of the most profitable teams in baseball since the opening of Camden Yards. Once that news got around, every team in baseball had a Camden Yards lookalike on its wish list. Camden Yards has been a smashing success from almost every point of view, including the attendance records at the park. Despite this, a study by Bruce Hamilton and Peter Kahn (1997) shows that the rental arrangement with the Orioles is such that the stadium authority operating the facility still goes in the red to the tune of $9 million per year, a bill that is picked up by Maryland taxpayers.

With only a few exceptions, the stadiums being built in the 1990s are publicly financed single-sport stadiums. The multiple-sport stadiums of the 1960s and 1970s were mainly built as football stadiums, with capacities of 60,000 or more, and baseball fields shoe-horned into the stadium configurations. MLB teams of the 1990s are demanding baseball-only stadiums seating 50,000 or fewer, such as Camden Yards, Turner Stadium (in

Atlanta), the Ballpark (in Arlington, Texas), Bank One Ballpark (BOB, in Phoenix), and the like, and in the main are getting them. With NFL lease agreements expiring along with the baseball leases, NFL teams are demanding new publicly financed football-only stadiums in the 70,000-seat range with lots of luxury boxes; they're also getting them. (NFL owners' attraction to luxury boxes in particular is that these boxes' rentals are not considered ticket revenue and hence not subject to the 60–40 home-away gate-sharing rules of the NFL.)

The process of obtaining approval for the use of public funds to finance a stadium or arena involves politicians, and it often involves the public directly, through referendums or other voting mechanisms. In their publicity campaigns, teams and leagues stress the benefits that a city or a state will gain from obtaining or retaining its pro sports team, benefits that supposedly far outweigh even the considerable costs of the facility. These publicity campaigns have been remarkably effective overall; in the end, teams win many more of these public relations battles than they lose. But putting the rhetoric to one side, what can be said factually about the benefits versus costs that a new stadium or a new team brings to a city, and what can be said about the rationale for the use of public funds to subsidize the stadium?

Regarding costs and benefits, costs are far easier to measure, even with the seemingly inevitable overruns. When you are talking about a publicly financed project, cost slippage and schedule slippage are as predictable as death and taxes. Seattle's Kingdome provides perhaps an extreme example of this: The original (1966) cost estimate for the stadium was $25 million. Ten years later, after four ballot measures and various delays, the Kingdome was completed for a cost of $67 million, 168 percent above the original estimate and six years behind the original proposed schedule.

But with all the problems of keeping tabs on costs, it is the supposed benefits of stadiums that are really difficult to measure. On the face of it, it seems completely plausible that a major facility such as a stadium must be extremely valuable to a city or state. Proponents crow about injections of spending into the local economy and the value of attaining or retaining "major league city" status for the city. But almost all of this is stuff and nonsense. Consider the following quote by Nashville Mayor Phil Bredesen, talking about the values to Nashville of building a spanking new $200 million–plus stadium for the team it lured away from Houston, the Tennessee Oilers:

> First, the economic impact, which does not totally justify the investment but justifies a piece of it. Second, the intangible benefits of having a high-profile NFL team in the community at a time when cities are competing for attention is a positive. Third, it is an amenity that a lot of people want. We build golf courses and parks and libraries and lots of things because people in the community want them, and certainly there are a substantial number of people who want this. Fourth, the location of the stadium represents the redevelopment of an industrial area close to downtown, certainly a positive in its own right and a significant factor in the public mind. Taken together, it makes a very compelling argument for going ahead wth this. (*NFL Reporter*, Summer 1996, p. 4)

Even if we accept, for the moment, that the benefits of a new stadium (and/or the new team) outweigh the costs, the argument for public involvement still makes sense only if no private investor would be able to make enough money from the stadium to make a go of it. This, in turn, depends on the level of revenues that a private investor can collect from users.

The direct revenues from stadium operation include the stadium's share of ticket sales, concession revenues, fees for personal seat licenses, luxury box rentals, parking fees, and naming rights to the stadium. A private operator will find it profitable to invest in building a stadium if these direct revenues are large enough. In certain recent instances—the Washington Redskins' $160 million stadium to replace RFK, Pro Players Stadium in Miami, the new $120 million Fleet Center in Boston, Ericsson Field in Carolina, Chicago's United Center—stadiums or arenas have been built by team owners primarily with private money, so it is not inconceivable that a new facility could pay for itself under private ownership. Of course, a stadium that just breaks even under private ownership also would provide little in the way of subsidies to the team using the stadium, which explains the high level of interest by teams in publicly rather than privately financed stadiums.

In the more likely case where direct revenues from stadium operations do not cover the costs of operating and maintaining the stadium, a privately financed stadium is not feasible. What other indirect benefits accruing to a city's population, but not available for capture by a private stadium, might make public investment in a stadium a rational economic decision? These are the so-called "spill-over" benefits that Mayor Bredesen talked about in mentioning the "economic impact" of a stadium on Nashville.

The first spill-over benefit to a city that a private investor could not capture is the economic value generated during construction of a facility. Proponents are quick to extoll the "new jobs" virtues of stadium projects. And after construction, the stadium must be supplied and operated, bringing more jobs, more income, more tax revenues. Surely this must be a boon to a city?

Nothing could be further from the truth. The arguments of proponents about the job, income, and tax benefits of stadiums are missing an essential point. What matters is not how much economic activity occurs at the stadium, but rather how much economic activity is generated over and above what already would have occurred. Only this amount represents the actual extra value generated by the stadium and its pro sports tenant.

Take the case of the new stadium for the Milwaukee Brewers, going up at a construction cost of around $250 million, employing, say, a thousand workers for eighteen months. Suppose that, rather than building the stadium, the best alternative use of the construction crew, white-collar workers, managers, and construction machinery and equipment is a reasonably sized industrial park or large retail mall somewhere in the market region of the team, costing on the order of $225 million. All of the resources that will be employed in the stadium project would otherwise earn this payment. Then, along comes the stadium and these resources are drawn off to work there instead, earning the projected stadium cost of $250 million. The net gain from having all these resources employed on the stadium is not $250 million but rather $25 million, namely $250 million less $225 million. And this is before one takes into account how much of the special construction inputs for the stadium come from outside the region. Payments made to "imported" resources are much more likely to flow outside the region and are worth that much less in terms of regional economic activity. So far as job gains are concerned, the relevant number is the difference between the number of workers employed in the stadium project and the number that would have been employed in the industrial-park or retail-mall project. In any case, the gain in employment is going to be substantially less than the one thousand workers employed to build the stadium; if the other projects also would have used one thousand workers, the net gain in employment is zero.

Proponents of stadiums stress the "gross" gains in income ($250 million in our example) and employment rather than the relevant "net" gains ($25 million in our example). As if that were not enough, the magic of the "multiplier effect" also is invoked to adjust the overstatement upward. The basic idea of a multiplier is that the income received by one person, say a construction worker, is then spent on goods produced by some other worker, thus increasing that worker's income, and so forth. While such multipliers make sense when looking at the entire economy of a country, they are hardly worth mentioning for a local or regional economy, because income "leaks" out of the region whenever it is spent on goods produced outside the region. All independent estimates place the regional multiplier for stadiums at a very low level (see the discussion in Roger Noll and Andrew Zimbalist [1997]). Moreover, even if multipliers were as large as claimed in some stadium studies, there isn't much to multiply them by in the first place because of the low "net" gain figures.

The same general argument applies to the income and employment generated from the ongoing operations of a stadium. The gross values are those associated with the stadium itself (the team, management, and maintenance and operations personnel) plus the businesses that supply the stadium or the crowds that come to the stadium. But from these gross values we have to deduct the employment and income that would have occurred if there had been no stadium to determine the relevant net values of income and employment to credit to the stadium project. Looking at the additional income and employment brought about by operation of a stadium, again all independent studies of stadium impacts show that the net values are dramatically less than the gross values and in fact approach zero in many cases.

In October 1996, Price Waterhouse prepared an estimate of the expected benefits to Los Angeles county from the Staples Center, a new arena, mainly privately financed, being built in downtown LA. According to their estimate, construction is supposed to generate $396 million in "economic growth" (new income) for LA county, along with 3,600 new jobs. Following the opening of the arena, there allegedly will be an annual impact on economic growth of $111 million, with 1,300 permanent new jobs for the county.

Needless to say, these figures are gross, not net, of what would have been produced if the facility were not built. The multiplier employed by Price Waterhouse is 2.36 (you multiply the direct increase in income by 2.36 to get the total increase in income, including all the "spill-over" spending involved). This multiplier was applied to the gross economic growth, not the net. Further, the figures on economic growth are for a facility that will simply replace the Forum out in Inglewood, which is also in LA county. Where in the world is the increase in income coming from? Not from a new team—the Lakers, Clippers, and Kings are already in town. From new attractions at the new arena? What about the loss in income from other facilities offering similar attractions in LA? And a multiplier of 2.36 is more appropriate for the United States as a whole than for one county in the United States, especially one that is noted as a world marketplace with lots of opportunities for leakages.

Despite the emphasis placed by proponents of stadiums on the "economic value" that a stadium will create, this is the weakest of all reeds on which to base a decision to engage in public financing of a stadium. In independent studies of the impacts of stadiums, there are almost no instances in which stadiums were shown to lead to a measurable increase in the economic well-being of a city. For example, Ziona Austrian and Mark Rosentraub (1997) studied the impact of Jacobs Field on economic activity in the Cleveland area. They found no evidence that construction of Jacobs Field had had a positive impact on the rate of growth of income and employment in the Cleveland area, despite the fact that Jacobs Field has been among the most successful of the new stadiums of the 1990s with season-long sellouts. This reinforces earlier studies by Robert Baade (1987) and Rosentraub and Samuel Nunn (1978), both of which found no significant correlation between stadium construction and growth of income in the ten major league cities covered by their two studies. In Noll and Zimbalist (1997), there are a number of studies of the economic impact of stadiums on major league cities, all emphasizing the marginal nature of the economic value of stadiums.

A reasonable assessment of our story so far is that there really appears to be nothing to distinguish sports stadiums as especially worthy of public subsidy relative to, say, a fair-sized industrial park or a large three-anchor retail mall. All generate about the same level of "new" direct economic activity during construction and indirect activity once built. But there are two aspects of the benefit calculations that do distinguish stadiums.

These are called the "intangible" benefits of stadiums. First, there are the so-called economic development benefits of a stadium. This is the theoretical value of being identified as a "major league" city. In touting the proposed Metrodome back in the late 1970s, Harvey McKay, a prominent Twin Cities businessman, coined the catchy phrase, "Without the Vikings and the Twins, we're just a frozen Omaha." Wisconsin state representative Martin Schneider resurrected the remark when arguing for a new stadium for the Milwaukee Brewers in 1995: "Without the Brewers, without the Bucks, without the Packers, we ain't nothing but Nebraska" (*Sporting News*, October 16, 1995, p. 5). (Irate Cornhuskers should direct their mail to McKay and Schneider, not to us.)

The implication of the "major league" city argument is that having major league teams makes some cities more desirable than others to prospective residents and businesses. But this turns cause and effect on its ear. For example, Omaha is not Minneapolis for a multitude of reasons. Minneapolis has pro sports teams for all those other reasons, including, for example, the size of the metropolitan area population. Baade's study, cited above, shows that adding a major league team to a city does not significantly change its economic status. Back in the 1970s and early 1980s, for example, Omaha was blessed with part-time tenancy of an NBA team (the Kansas City–Omaha Kings), and did not suddenly become a mecca for corporate America. Losing two NFL teams did not change LA from a "major league" city to an also-ran.

Another aspect of the argument concerning "development" benefits of a team or a stadium appears in Mayor Bredesen's comments, namely upgrading a depressed downtown area by locating a stadium (and the pro sports team) in that area. One thing that major American cities have no shortage of is depressed downtown areas, and there is no shortage either of proposed solutions to eliminate those depressed areas, almost all involving large infusions of public money. The notorious failure rate of these solutions recalls H. L. Mencken's famous remark "Every complicated problem has a simple and wrong solution."

There are one or two success stories related to the positive impact of a new stadium on a depressed part of a city—the $215 million Coors Field in Denver that opened in 1995 has apparently attracted a number of restaurants and shops into a formerly depressed area, for example. But most of the so-called success stories are stories of stadiums being located in areas that were already experiencing economic growth and revival before the stadium or arena appeared, as with Camden Yards in Baltimore or the $90 million America West Arena that opened in 1992 in Phoenix. More commonly, the stadium has next to no impact on economic activity in its neighborhood. The Metrodome in downtown Minneapolis, with multiple tenants (Vikings, Twins, Minnesota Golden Gophers), is surrounded by parking lots and warehouses, just as it was when it opened in 1982; a mile or so away, the Target Center has had no perceptible impact on its depressed downtown neighborhood, seven years after opening. In Inglewood, the Forum sits in majestic if somewhat aging isolation with its parking lot but no noticeable development thirty years after it was built. The less said about the areas around the LA Coliseum and the LA Sports Arena the better.

The problem with depressed downtown areas is that nobody with any money goes there for a variety of perfectly good reasons, including location, security, and the absence of amenities. Locating a stadium in such an area brings people into the locality for the brief period of the game on the relatively rare game days (only ten per year, preseason and season, for an NFL team). Even on the game days, the crowds are gone within an hour or two after the game finishes, and there is nothing to attract them back except another game. A sports stadium is certainly a much less effective use of public money to solve the depressed-area problem than, say, financing a commercial office building or a shopping-mall complex, which have sustained working and visiting populations over more hours in the day and more days in the year (though these also have not solved the depressed-area problem in most cities).

So much for the ambiguous development benefits of stadiums. There remains a second set of benefits to consider, the so-called "consumption" benefits of teams (and, hence, of the stadiums housing them). There are a large number of individuals who are fans of the local pro sports team but who never or only very rarely go to a game. Nonetheless, their lives are enhanced by the local presence of a sports team, which is a main topic of conversation, especially among younger men, at lunch breaks at work or when talking with neighbors. The value of these "consumption" benefits, if they could be calculated, might turn out to be small for any one person, but suppose they add up to $100 per year (about 5 family trips to McDonald's). If there are, say, half a million fans in this category, this works out to $50 million per year in benefits to fans, simply from the presence in the city or state of a pro sports team.

When the local team does well (or otherwise), it is the talk of the town even among those who never attend a game. That the dollar amounts of these types of benefits are difficult (at best!) to measure does not render them beside the point or small in magnitude. Indeed, it is just this type of identification with a team and its players that builds the foundation of the demand for sports, and it is this foundation that is tapped when public funding of stadiums becomes a matter for public debate.

The measurement problem is not an easy nut to crack. Imagine the state economic development agency taking a survey of fans to get their statements as to how much each of them would be willing to pay to keep a local team from moving. Contrast this with a survey in which the agency instead asks each fan to pay a tax equal to what the value of the team is to the fan, the money to be used to keep the team in town. In the first survey, interested fans of the team will have an incentive to overstate the value of the team in order to convince local lawmakers to act to keep the team. In the second survey, each individual has an incentive to understate the value of the team, to become a "free rider," since any one fan's contribution will be insignificant in the total collected and thus have no real effect on the decision as to whether the team will leave. Since it is only the first type of survey that is reported in the press, any numbers reported on "the value of the team to fans" should be viewed as highly suspect and highly biased upward.

The upshot of all this is as follows: There will be stadium revenues that a potential private operator can collect but other benefits that cannot be captured by a private operator. Even though stadium revenues might prove insufficient to induce a private investor to build a stadium, the state or local government, with a broader ability to make decisions that reflect the entire range of benefits of a stadium, in principle might find that the taxes and other user fees it can collect reflecting those benefits can make a stadium a desirable investment.

The spin-off benefits in the form of the economic value to the locality of construction and operation of the stadium, plus development benefits, are trivial compared to the cost of a stadium, despite the prominence given to them by stadium supporters in public debates. It is possible that the intangible benefits to nonusers of the stadium might be large enough so that the local community finds itself better off with a sub-sidized stadium than if there were no stadium at all. But it is next to impossible to obtain practical, reliable measures of the value of intangible benefits to fans, and also next to impossible to levy taxes linked specifically to those intangible benefits, so that shifting the burden of taxes to keep the team onto those who support the team simply can't be accomplished.

It is in this murky situation that political decisions are made concerning public funding of stadiums or arenas, introducing all the well-known problems of influence peddling, log rolling, and special interest money. Traditionally, mayors and governors have lined up as supporters of large-scale publicly financed construction projects in their cities and states without discrimination—they tend to be for more roads and highways, power plants, office buildings, and other such projects.

The building trades are important contributors to political campaigns, and there is a "trophy" aspect to construction projects, each of which typically carries a plaque identifying the politicians in office when it was built. Further, the benefits of big construction projects come now, when the politician is in office, while the costs come later when the bonds must be retired, and when today's politicians have long since left the scene.

In recent years, pro sports has become a much more important player in state and local politics than it was years ago. In part this reflects the increased interest of the population as a whole in pro team sports and the greater visibility of sports in the press and on television. Another factor is that the individuals who own sports teams are among the wealthiest and most influential in the city or state, as the rundown of Forbes 400 owners in Chapter 5 indicates. Owners today are leading figures in the business community, which generally supports public involvement in stadiums and arenas (so long as no new business taxes are involved, of course). Thus, campaign contributions are definitely involved in stadium issues. And, if building "trophy" projects is a political plus, being tagged with losing a "trophy" business such as a sports team is definitely a political minus. It is no surprise that mayors and governors generally lead the chorus of supporters for new stadium projects.

Politicians dealing with controversial issues such as the funding of stadiums find themselves in a difficult strategic position. Former Washington, D.C., Mayor Sharon Pratt Kelly stated quite succinctly how and why cities end up chasing sports franchises:

> The mayors of American cities are confronted with a prisoner's dilemma of sorts. If no mayor succumbs to the demands of a franchise shopping for a new home then teams will stay where they are. This, however, is unlikely to happen because if Mayor A is not willing to pay the price, Mayor B may think

it is advantageous to open up the city's wallet. Then to protect his or her interest, Mayor A often ends up paying the demanded price.

One potential safeguard against insider political control of the stadium decision process is public decision making through direct democracy, namely, initiatives and referendums, which have become an increasingly common way to make stadium decisions. While conventional wisdom holds that ballot initiatives assure that the majority will prevails, in reality the outcome of a vote like this depends on which voters turn out to vote and the amount and quality of information available to citizens on which to base a voting decision. Because both turnout and information can be biased, it is not clear that direct democracy drives the outcome closer to the "will of the people," as compared to decisions made by representative bodies such as legislatures or city councils.

Proponents of stadiums have a higher stake in the outcome of a stadium initiative and are much more likely to participate in any campaign for a ballot measure. Those in favor of the stadium subsidy almost always outspend opponents. For example, in the 1997 Seattle Seahawks ballot measure, owner Paul Allen spent $6 million while the opposition spent $160,000. Moreover, Allen had the vote scheduled as a special referendum in June by agreeing to pay for all costs of the election, something that had never occurred before in the state of Washington and perhaps never before in the entire country. Had the vote been scheduled at the time of the general election in November, this would have brought out a much larger group of voters with interest in issues other than the stadium. Stadium zealots would have constituted a smaller share of the total electorate. Even so, Allen's proposal passed by a very narrow margin, 51.1 percent of the vote.

A problem with single-issue referendums is that there is no ground for compromise. In a legislative setting, trade-offs can be identified and compromises achieved, reflecting the intensity of preferences of various groups represented in the legislature. But when decision making is transferred to the general public under a ballot measure, there is just one specific proposal to be accepted or rejected. The closer it is to an all-or-nothing proposal, the more likely it is that the voters will approve a higher level of spending. It's no surprise that the usual threat is that the owners will move the team. Thus, voters are induced to favor too much spending because the only alternative, no spending at all, is worse. In such a case, direct democracy offers no solution to the prisoner's dilemma described by Mayor Kelly.

And results in initiatives or referendums don't always end the political process. An insider's view of the situation comes from Jay Tibshraeny, the mayor of Chandler, Arizona, who discussed the issue of remodeling his town's spring training home of the Milwaukee Brewers: "I believe the citizens should have a say in this issue. If the voters pass this, we'll move forward. If the voters don't pass this, we'll still move forward." In Wisconsin, a plan to fund a stadium for the Milwaukee Brewers was turned down resoundingly by the voters before the fight was transferred to the state legislature. As noted above, voters in a Seattle referendum narrowly turned down a new stadium for the Mariners, which then led to action by the state legislature to fund the stadium, spurred on by a U.S. senator and the governor of the state.

There is one striking instance in which direct democracy brought swift and sure justice to bear on a politician in a stadium case. In 1996, the Wisconsin state legislature voted on funding a new stadium for the AL Milwaukee Brewers, to be financed by a sales tax on the residents of the five counties surrounding Milwaukee. State Senator George Petak from Racine, in one of those five counties, came out initially against the stadium when he ran for office. At the last moment, under pressure from Governor Tommy Thompson, Petak switched his vote, and the funding package passed by the slimmest of margins, 16–15. There was outrage among Racine voters, a recall election was scheduled, and, for the first time in state history, a sitting legislator was unseated. However, it was too late to reverse the vote in the legislature—the Milwaukee Brewers will be playing in a new publicly funded stadium beginning around the turn of the new century.

So much for the anecdotes and theorizing. What have we been able to observe in actual voting outcomes? There have been a large number of stadium-related votes by the general public, with widely varying purposes: increasing the sales tax, repealing previous legislation that hindered public funding, issuing bonds, increasing property taxes, specifying expenditures without identifying financing methods, raising excise taxes, enabling a sports lottery, eliciting public sentiment through "approval" votes, and increasing utility and hotel taxes. Typically, these measures get on the ballot in cities aiming to keep their current teams; and, typically, the measures do not pass, whatever the details involved. But, as noted earlier, the fact that a stadium measure does not pass does not mean that another measure might not surface later on, or that a "back door" approach might not be used to bypass the general public.

From the team's point of view, the optimal strategy in a referendum is to push spending to the highest level a majority of voters will approve. If a funding proposal is voted in by, say, 75 percent of the electorate, the proposal was aimed too low from the team's point of view. Thus, if the team and the legislators supporting the team are doing a good job in devising ballot proposals, there should be very close voting results, which, in fact, is what is typically observed in the stadium-related votes. Table 7-2 summarizes the vote results in a number of recent stadium-related initiatives. Compared to other types of referendum votes, such as votes on hospitals and nuclear power, the outcomes for stadiums are concentrated around 50 percent. More often than not, most citizens who vote in favor of stadiums would prefer less to be spent on them than is provided in the referendum.

It might be worthwhile to see how these concepts worked in practice; there is no better illustration than the long, involved history of the search by the San Francisco Giants for public funding of a stadium to replace 3-Comm (née Candlestick) Park.

The Giants' quest for a new stadium began in the early 1980s and culminated in 1996. Bay area citizens had the opportunity to speak repeatedly. Eventually, with the Giants' options reduced due to MLB expansion into Denver, Miami, Phoenix, and St. Petersburg, the team and its supporters came to the realization that the people of San Francisco wanted a privately owned and financed downtown stadium. Whether they will actually see their desires met was still a matter of contention at the time this book was written.

On November 3, 1987, San Franciscans voted on Proposition W, which proposed that a new ballpark be built on land close to the Bay Bridge. Under the city charter, the mayor was allowed to put this proposition on the ballot on his own initiative, which was backed by signatures from a few supervisors. The proposition provided that the park would be built at no cost to the city, but the grant of public land would forestall the use of that land for any other city purpose, a nontrivial cost to the city given land prices in the Bay area. The proposal specified that taxes would not increase and that all debt incurred would be repaid with nontax money. The team would pay no city property taxes on the new site.

While the ballot statement seemed innocuous enough, debate was heated. Proponents argued that passage would keep the Giants in town, help invigorate parts of the downtown area, and squelch the growing opinion that San Francisco was dying. Supporters included most of the city supervisors, the chamber of commerce, and organized labor. Bob Lurie, owner of the Giants, made his position clear: "The issue is not whether or not we should build a ballpark for Bob Lurie or for the Giants. This franchise will be around for a lot longer than I, and they will always have a place to play. I just think it would be tragic if it is not in San Francisco."

Opponents, a much more diverse mix, including the Sierra Club and the Coalition for San Francisco Neighborhoods, countered mostly with concerns about quality-of-life issues near the stadium location. But the most insightful of them pointed out that nothing in the referendum prohibited diversion of existing taxes. The proposition failed, 96,445 to 85,005.

Two years later, on November 7, 1989, two more stadium-related issues appeared on the San Francisco ballot. Proposition P sought voter approval of a joint stadium venture agreement between the city and the nationally known stadium management company Spectacor, relating to development, financing, land, amended zoning, revenue sharing, and ownership of a new stadium. Again this proposition was put on the ballot by the mayor. The proposition failed by the very narrow margin of 87,850 to 85,796. Perhaps an explicitly stated mix of public and private financing and the new location were more favorable in the voters' eyes.

The second issue on the same ballot was much less successful. Proposition V, placed on the ballot by petition of citizens, asked the voters if the Board of Supervisors should explore proposals to improve Candlestick Park at private expense instead of constructing a downtown baseball stadium. This referendum failed by a much wider margin, 98,875 to 83,599.

Taken as a whole, the early voting results in San Francisco indicated that the people preferred a downtown ballpark to Candlestick and that, at most, there should be a mix of private and public funding.

Following the 1989 vote, there were three votes taken in nearby localities. San Jose held city votes in 1990 and 1992, and voted with the rest of Santa Clara county in 1990. The Giants were willing to move the team to San Jose if the proper amount of subsidies was forthcoming, but voters rejected the Giants' proposals in all three elections.

After failing to generate public funding all over the Bay area, the Giants did receive voter approval for a stadium. On March 26, 1996, Proposition B passed, 101,343 to 85,313. The referendum was simple: whether to approve the China Basin site for the construction of a ballpark. The measure as written and voted on did not discuss financial arrangements, but promises were made that there would be no use of public funds for construction, no new taxes, no use of general fund money, and no taxpayer liability.

Given the history of this nearly ten-year pursuit, a final synopsis would be that the voters felt that the Giants belonged downtown, they rejected the many ways that public funding was requested to subsidize the Giants, but they expressed a willingness to provide a valuable public site for the stadium. In a very real sense, direct democracy eventually made the preferences of the voters clear.

Still, this might not be the end of the road. This referendum may not be perceived by anyone—voters, political leaders, or the Giants—as the final word. Even though the Giants have faced opposition to proposed moves to San Jose, other areas in northern California—notably Sacramento—still pose a threat. There may be more referendums before the issue is finally settled.

But perhaps the most important unknown is the Giants' share of costs if a new stadium is built. Nothing exists on paper as to whether or not the Giants should pay for the site and the other public expenditures on police and transportation access that go with a stadium. As a result, the promises of no public financing by proponents of the stadium may be somewhat misleading. It would be naive to ignore the history of other cities where ambiguous provisions in a referendum and manipulation of the final outcome have gone hand in hand (as in Cleveland and Cincinnati).

Stadium financing is such an important public-policy issue that it deserves at least one more illustration. Consider a somewhat different example of decision making by a city mayor and city council, and the consequences for a second California city, San Diego.

Qualcomm Park (you might know it better under its old name, Jack Murphy Stadium) houses the NFL San Diego

Chargers and the NL San Diego Padres. The owner of the San Diego Chargers is Alex Spanos, described by *Forbes* magazine (March 10, 1997) as follows:

> Even in an industry known for bloated egos, real estate developer Alexander Gus Spanos is in a class by himself. "Goddamn, Alex, you are good," Spanos exclaims as he watches a videotape of himself hamming it up with his longtime golfing buddy, Bob Hope. To a visitor, "I'm so good, it's unbelievable!"

In 1995, Spanos negotiated a new lease agreement with the city of San Diego, under which the city agreed to add 9,000 seats to the stadium, increasing its capacity from 62,000 to 71,000 and adding lots of luxury boxes, at a cost to the city of $78 million. In the new lease, Spanos agreed to continue paying a rent equal to 10 percent of ticket revenue, one of the highest rentals in the NFL. In return, the city agreed to guarantee the sale of 60,000 tickets to all Chargers games for the next 10 years. Mayor Susan Golding and a majority of the city council supported the deal, but a survey by the *San Diego Union-Tribune* indicated that if it were put to a public vote, it would fail by a four-to-one margin. However, an attempt to force the city to put the deal on the ballot as a referendum measure was turned down by the courts.

The ticket guarantee by the city is interesting. The city doesn't actually buy any unsold tickets up to 60,000 at a game; instead, it reduces the team's rental payment by the lost ticket revenue. As pointed out by the *Union-Tribune,* what this means is that with an average ticket price of, say, $40, if ticket sales are below 60,000, the team has the choice of selling one more ticket and retaining $21.60 ($40 less the visiting team's share of $16, less the NFL league office share of $2.40), or not selling the ticket and having its rent reduced by $40. The city has created a situation in which there are positive incentives for the team to raise ticket prices to a level such that there are never more than 60,000 fans in the stadium, and there are positive incentives in effect to "sell tickets" to the city rather than to fans. One estimate of the cost of the ticket guarantee is $9 million per year for the next 10 years, but that might not reflect all the incentives that exist in the guarantee. For example, the Chargers had a 1997 season record of four and twelve. What effect does the ticket guarantee have on the owner's incentive to field a decent football team?

If that wasn't bad enough, recall that Qualcomm is the home not only of the Chargers but also the Padres. With the beefing up of the size and configuration of the stadium to meet the demands of the Chargers, guess what? The Padres now find the new stadium completely unsuitable for baseball. So the $78 million renovation of the stadium carried along with it the unintended consequence of digging into the city coffers to build a new baseball-only stadium, in the $300 million range, for the Padres. San Diego voters approved the baseball park in a November 1998 referendum.

The citizens of San Diego have lived with the controversy since 1995, and it has reportedly tarnished the reputation of the mayor to the point a proposed run for the U.S. Senate was put on hold. Welcome to the very murky politics of pro team sports in the 1990s.

For most state and local politicians, it's a case of "damned if you do and damned if you don't": lose a team by not caving in and you'll hear about it at the next election; keep a team by caving in and you'll hear about it at the next election. It's reminiscent of the story of the mother who goes to visit her bachelor son at his apartment on his birthday. Her gift is two ties, a red tie and a blue one. The son goes into the bedroom and puts on the blue tie. He comes out, and his mother says, "What's the matter—you don't like the red tie?"

After this extended and rather negative look at state and local politicians, it seems only fair that we should not miss the chance to ding the feds—the U.S. Congress—as well. The role of Congress in sports goes back a long way, at least to the Supreme Court's baseball decision in 1922. While Judge Friendly's remark that this was not one of Justice Holmes' best is an opinion that most in the legal profession would probably support, it is entirely possible that Holmes was actually crazy like a fox. In an age when the judiciary shunned legislating by the judicial branch, creating a legal fiction like Federal Baseball put the decision about the commercial status of professional sports clearly in Congress's court.

Now, over 75 years later, Federal Baseball still stands, providing MLB with its much-discussed "antitrust exemption." Until 1998, Congress had never taken Justice Holmes up on his implied invitation to pass judgment on the market power of MLB. At any time from the 1950s on at the latest, Congress could have acted to end the exemption, with no backlash from the Supreme Court. In 1998, Congress finally passed a bill bringing labor negotiations in MLB under antitrust regulation. In other respects, the exemption still stands.

This isn't the only choice that Congress has made to carefully nurture the market power enjoyed by pro sports leagues. Despite the findings of the Celler committee hearings of the 1950s, Congress took no action respecting MLB. Congress actually granted a special exemption from the antitrust laws for the merger of the NFL and AFL in 1966. Congress adopted almost the same stance during the merger talks between the NBA and the ABA. And it has also allowed TV blackouts to stand in order to minimize broadcast competition, and to facilitate the careful restrictions by sports leagues on the number of games fans get to watch on television.

Congress has also exempted league-wide broadcasting contracts of pro sports leagues from the antitrust laws. This clear monopoly behavior has continued unabated despite the fact that the Supreme Court struck down precisely the same practice by the NCAA.

The record of Congress's consistency on issues involving the monopoly power of leagues is truly impressive—the leagues have no more fervent fans than congressmen. The explanation is the same for the Congress as for state and local politicians. Suppose that you are a congressman with a team in your district or state. A vote to limit the monopoly power of the league can possibly cost an important city in your state its team, and can trigger organized opposition from sports fans and other interested parties. This problem faces members of Congress from states with roughly the top thirty population centers in the country, a group that is certain to include many of the most influential members of the House and Senate. Asking these individuals to support checks on pro sports leagues' monopoly power would be asking them to violate the careful political balancing act they must maintain to secure re-election. This would go over about as well as serving rum at an Alcoholics Anonymous meeting. Congress is not the place to look for help in controlling the monopoly power of leagues.

So, this is how things stand. Fans and the general public are unhappy about the stadium mess. They resent the blackmail tactics of teams and the fact that their state and local politicians cave in to those tactics—generally the first person on board the stadium bandwagon is the mayor of the city in which the team is located, followed by the state's governor. They also resent the fact that the taxes used to subsidize the stadium and the team are not targeted at those who are most vocal in support of the stadium but instead affect the entire population. But fans also want to keep "their" team. Thus, they end up voting for stadium subsidy proposals that almost all of them agree simply funnel too much money to sports. And if one of the politicians is courageous enough to stand up against the new stadium and the team leaves, he or she is going to find it hard—impossible!—to raise money from the business community in the next campaign, where the departure of the team will be a central issue.

Should we end up blaming the politicians? Or the fans? Or should we place the blame where it really lies, with the way sports leagues operate? As monopolies, sports leagues artificially restrict the number of teams below the number that would be in business if there was competition in the sport. By constantly keeping a supply of possible host cities—cities that could support a league team—on line, current host cities are in the unenviable position of being pressured to provide exorbitant subsidies to their teams or risk losing them.

In summary, the market power possessed by pro sports leagues and teams, coupled with the workings of the local political process, has been used to extract large subsidies in the form of funding for new stadiums and sweetheart rental agreements at those stadiums. The current team is the only game in town, and the political support for its presence is practically guaranteed. If there were active rival leagues in a sport, any city that could support a team in the sport would find a league willing to locate in the city, and there would be no need for public subsidies or intrusion of politicians or the political process into the picture. Given the market power that does exist, local politics typically isn't able to overcome the advantages that leagues have in the stadium game, and Congress has no interest in limiting those advantages, either.

8

BREAKING UP THAT OLD GANG OF MINE

Organized baseball affords this subcommittee with almost a classroom example of what may happen to an industry which is governed by rules and regulations among its members rather than by the free play of competitive forces. Without knowing at this time whether such regulation is in the best interest of baseball because of its many unique characteristics, we may at least learn something of importance about how an industry operates it- self instead of being forced to comply with the antitrust laws.

—Congressman Emmanuel Celler, at the opening of
his committee's hearings, 1951

It is almost fifty years since the Celler committee met, but baseball's antitrust exemption still persists. The other pro team sports remain subject to the antitrust laws, but the last case in which the Justice Department moved against a league was also back in 1951, when a federal court enjoined the NFL from enforcing its television blackout rules. Today, as in the past, sports leagues operate as cartels in the form of monopoly leagues, largely immune from the "free play of competitive forces."

There certainly have been some major changes from the pro team sports world of 1951—the emergence of television as a dominant factor in sports finances, the rise of player unions, free agency replacing the old reserve clause, movement of league franchises, state and local government financing of stadiums and arenas, league expansion—but one fundamental verity persists, namely the monopoly power of pro sports leagues. What can we say about the implications of this monopoly power, of this continuing immunity from competitive forces?

In an era in which television revenues have become an increasingly important aspect of the pro sports business, we have seen that the monopoly position of the sports leagues has enabled them and their member teams to siphon off essentially all of the net revenues that televising games generates. Competition among the networks for pro sports television rights has bid up these rights in price to the point where the networks do little more than break even on their investments. The media might be a dominating factor in our daily lives, but, from a financial point of view, it is the league and not the media that dominates the pro team sports television business.

The emergence of strong player unions in all sports has moved the market for player services closer to the competitive norm, with players demanding and getting salaries that more closely reflect their value to teams. In turn, the value of a player to a team depends on the revenues that the player can generate for the team, and this depends on the monopoly power of the team and its league. The stronger the monopoly power, the larger the revenues that a team can earn from TV, gate receipts, stadium deals, and memorabilia sales. In the free-agent era, the larger the revenues, the larger the player salaries.

Strikes and lockouts are the inevitable outcome of owners and players battling, arguing, and scheming over who gets what share of the monopoly revenues. In recent years, it is the players who are forging ahead in this battle, with salaries taking an ever larger share of league revenues, and with leagues searching for devices, such as the salary cap or luxury tax, to stem the rising tide of salaries.

Competitive balance problems continue to persist in all sports leagues, essentially unchanged from what they were when Congressman Celler's committee met in 1951. The reserve clause, which was supposed to solve these problems, didn't work, and free agency, which was supposed to intensify the problems, has had no apparent effect. Competitive balance problems arise in the first place because of the imbalance of revenue potential among league cities. Competitive balance continues to be a problem because leagues protect the franchise rights of the richer teams, those located in the megalopolis cities, from entry by other league teams.

Sports leagues have learned to use their monopoly powers to coerce host cities into building expensive publicly financed stadiums and arenas with accompanying sweetheart rental agreements. Cities that refuse to do this are threatened with the loss of their teams, and the threats have been enforced by league action authorizing the moves of franchises elsewhere. The expansion policies of leagues are geared to adding new teams at a rate designed to protect the value of existing franchises and to minimize competition among teams within the league, while carefully husbanding credible threats of relocation against the current host cities in the league. Expansion fees are set at levels that transfer most of the prospective monopoly profits of new teams back to the league.

All in all, there is a lot going on in the sports business beyond just playing the game. As Clark Griffith, then owner of the AL Washington Senators, remarked in a different context back in 1951 at the Celler hearings, "You know, there is more to this thing of baseball than you can see on the surface."

Make no mistake about it. There is substantial and valuable market power present in professional sports. This is reflected, for example, in the prices of teams. When the Los Angeles Dodgers changed hands, as they did in 1998, for around $300 million, that price should be interpreted as the best guess of buyer and seller alike as to what the level of expected future payoffs are from the team. Thus, if the market rate of return on comparable investments is, say, 10 percent, the $300 million price tag suggests that the buyer and seller both expect the team to yield net payoffs from all sources— operating income, executive salaries, spill-over benefits to related investments of the owner, tax sheltering benefits, and capital gains from franchise price appreciation—that average around $30 million per year.

All the franchise prices or expansion fees that you see reported on TV and in the press reflect what both sides of the market, buyer and seller, think a team is worth. In particular, a team's value incorporates the payoff from the monopoly power that the team possesses and the corresponding monopoly revenues that the team can capture. Thus we have the interesting paradox that a new owner who operates the team to maximize the monopoly profits the team can make typically finds that he is just making a "market rate of return" on his investment, because the price of the team when he buys it already reflects the monopoly profit potential of the team.

To take another example, the new Cleveland Browns expansion team carried an expansion fee of around $530 million. One way to understand this is to consider what the other teams in the NFL are giving up to bring Cleveland in. The NFL TV contract pays $73 million per team per year to the 30 teams in the league. Splitting the pot 31 ways with the Browns added means that about $70 million is lost to the existing teams to make room for Cleveland's share. The loss of $70 million per year into the indefinite future is a loss worth around $600 or $700 million today to the league. This is partially offset in that adding a team back in Cleveland increases the TV audience in the Cleveland area, which will be reflected in higher TV rights prices in the future. In any case, looking at things this way, one could say that the NFL simply can't afford to put an expansion team into Cleveland at an expansion price much less than $500 to $600 million! Think of this as a built-in brake on expansion by the NFL, since cities and owners that can't afford a price tag of this magnitude are automatically excluded from the league.

Player salaries also reflect the monopoly power of leagues. Michael Jordan is either the greatest basketball player of all time or the second greatest—for some of us, Wilt still stands by himself. The reason Jordan is paid $33 million per year is that his presence in the Bulls' lineup adds that much, and more, to the Bulls' revenue from gate receipts at the United Center, from the Bulls' local TV and pay-TV contracts, and from the NBA national TV contract. If there were rival leagues in pro basketball, that wouldn't change Michael Jordan's unique status as a player. However, it would change the revenue potential that he can generate for the Bulls. With a rival league, the NBA's national TV contract wouldn't be worth as much to NBC or the other networks, because there would be more pro basketball on the tube competing with the existing NBA national telecasts. The presence of a rival league, with a team in Chicago for instance, would also eat into the ticket prices at the United Center and the value of the Bulls' local TV contract.

While Michael Jordan is unique, he can't do it all by himself, and competition for players between the leagues would lead to a dilution of the talent that Jordan and other NBA stars play with and against, which also impacts gate and TV revenues. So the monopoly power of leagues plays a major role in determining the value of player salaries as well as franchise prices.

What we have seen is that the monopoly power of leagues is at the root of essentially every problem that plagues pro team sports, from competitive balance to out-of-sight player salaries to the blackmailing of cities. The question is, what can be done about this?

A number of suggestions have come from different sources. Mark Rosentraub, an academic economist who has done a considerable amount of research into the impact of teams and stadiums on employment and income of cities, has suggested the formation of a cooperative group of cities. Members would be those small- to medium-sized cities capable of supporting a team profitably that have been bypassed in the assignment of pro sports teams. The group would file an antitrust suit against individual leagues, demanding an increase in the number of expansion franchises to satisfy their unfulfilled desires.

Ralph Nader has announced the organization of an association of sports fans who have banded together with the objective of putting pressure on the existing monopoly leagues, through negative publicity and other devices, to force the leagues to cease and desist from their current practices of anticompetitive behavior. Minnesota's attorney general, Hubert Humphrey III, has brought suit against the Minnesota Twins and MLB, claiming antitrust violations in the use of threats by teams to force cities or states to provide subsidized stadiums for them. U.S. Senator Patrick Moynihan has introduced a bill in the Senate to remove the federal tax exemption from state and local bonds issued to finance stadiums and arenas.

We are completely sympathetic with the goals of these proposals, but we don't think they go far enough. Patchwork proposals such as these, aimed at curing specific abuses, even if successful, still leave leagues in the monopoly position they currently occupy, except with respect to the specific area covered by the proposal.

The most effective way to correct monopoly abuses is not through legislative action, lawsuits, public relations campaigns, or the public utility approach, but through entry into the industry by outside firms seeking a share of the excess profits of the monopolist controlling the industry. There are good reasons why a market solution like this is always the preferred solution to the problems of monopoly power—if it can be accomplished.

But that's the rub with the pro team sports industry. As we have seen, entry into the industry in the past, even when successful, has only led to the re-establishment of an expanded monopoly league. And the possibility of entry has been made much less likely by the recent wave of publicly financed stadiums and arenas. Not only has this led to massive subsidies by cities and states to pro sports teams, it also has erected almost insurmountable barriers to entry into a sport by rival leagues. How can a rival league compete with an existing league when, in the vast majority of the sports markets in the country, the existing league's team controls access to the only state-of-the-art facility in town, a publicly financed facility that operates under a rental contract that provides tens of millions of dollars in subsidies per year to the existing team?

Under these circumstances, with entry essentially foreclosed as a solution to the monopoly problem and with monopoly abuses as widespread as they are in pro team sports, the appropriate step to take is for the Justice Department to file suit under the antitrust laws to break up the existing monopoly leagues into several independent competing leagues, with the antitrust laws to apply to the industry thus created. This policy recommendation mirrors similar proposals put forward earlier by antitrust law expert Steven Ross and sports economist Roger Noll, among others.

It might seem that the remedy we are recommending is too extreme, that there exists a less drastic application of sanctions under the antitrust laws that could control the market power of pro team sports leagues. The problem is, however, that a piecemeal patchwork approach of identifying specific antitrust violations and imposing detailed rules for eliminating them ends up, in effect, converting the sports industry into a regulated industry. What we know from lots of experience with regulated industries is that this is a recipe for disaster, for customers of the regulated industry and for the industry itself. We don't want the courts or regulatory bodies to be micromanaging the sports industry—instead, we want owners and general managers of teams to make the same kinds of decisions they make today, but in a competitive market environment, not in the present monopoly league setup. If there is one thing about which economists are in agreement, it is that decentralized decision making in a competitive market environment leads to outcomes that are in the best interests of consumers, and that is all that we are proposing here.

There are certainly legal issues involved in this proposal, including baseball's current exemption from antitrust, which, however, can be eliminated simply by congressional action. But beyond the legal issues are the questions of what the effect of introducing competition into sports would be on the pro team sports industry and whether a competitive structure is financially viable in sports.

Suppose that the current monopoly leagues in each sport, consisting of roughly thirty-two teams each, were broken up into four competing leagues, each with eight teams. These leagues would compete with one another for players and coaches, for franchise locations, for stadiums, for TV contracts, and for fans. Under the antitrust laws, there could be no agreements among the leagues to control access to markets, so that, whatever the initial list of franchise locations in a league, all leagues would be free to enter the New York, Los Angeles, and Chicago (or any other) markets.

Given the high ratio of population to teams of the megalopolis markets (see Table 6-2), one of the predictable consequences of introducing competition into sports would be the location of more teams in the presently protected big city markets. In fact, teams would be added to, say, the New York City market, to the point that there are no stronger incentives to locate a team in that market than anywhere else in the country. If this means three, four, or five (or more) NFL teams in New York City, so be it. For skeptics, note that in the 1930s there was a Brooklyn Dodgers team in the NFL and a Staten Island Stapletons team as well, together with the Giants, and the world didn't collapse. MLB supported three teams in New York—the Dodgers, Giants, and Yankees—from 1903 until 1958; it is certainly only monopolistic restrictions that have led to the siting of only two MLB teams there since 1961.

Beyond this, competition would certainly lead to an expansion in the number of cities possessing major league sports teams. Under competition, no city capable of supporting a profitable team in a sport would be left without one. If a league moved a team out of such a location, other leagues would jump at the chance to replace it with an expansion franchise. Thus, the present situation in which Washington, D.C., is left without a major league baseball team would be corrected, and cities such as Portland, Vancouver, Sacramento, Norfolk, Indianapolis, and San Antonio would definitely be candidates for major league teams as well. Instead of zero pro football teams, the Los Angeles area would be blessed with three or four at a minimum. St. Louis, Pittsburgh, San Diego, and Cincinnati would see a return of pro basketball. Green Bay might have problems surviving in a competitive football industry, but not if there were a return to the old Green Bay–Milwaukee arrangement in which the Packers split their season between the two cities.

With competition acting to eliminate the current set of restrictions on entry into protected markets, the competitive balance problems of leagues would be effectively eliminated as well. With, say, four baseball teams in New York City, a New York City team begins to look more like a Twin Cities or Seattle team in terms of drawing potential. Free entry into markets combined with profit incentives will act to eliminate the current division of sports leagues into the "haves," the big-market teams, and the "have-nots," the small-market teams, as drawing potential within the league equalizes. This would obviate the need for artificial restraints on the player market, such as salary caps, luxury taxes, or the old-fashioned reserve clause; a simple, open, freely competitive market for player services could result.

In contrast to the present, there is no way that leagues could "stockpile" potentially profitable locations to use as threats in negotations by league teams with host cities. With threats put to rest, decisions with respect to the building of publicly funded stadiums or arenas could be taken using the same criteria that apply to other public investments. Once again, competition would be at the heart of the matter. Teams in the same or different leagues would compete with one another for desirable locations. The result would be multiple bidders for the stadium services provided by any host city. Any attempt by a team to demand a large stadium subsidy would be undercut by competitive bids. Undoubtedly this would lead to fewer stadiums being built, and to rental arrangements under which team subsidies, if any, would be substantially reduced.

On the revenue side, competition among leagues for national TV contracts would drastically reduce or eliminate the monopoly profits from such contracts currently enjoyed by leagues. One way in which monopoly profits are maximized by leagues is by restricting the number of games that can be shown on television. With leagues competing with one another for TV coverage, there would be more games on TV in all sports. In turn, this reduces the value of game broadcasts to advertisers, lowering the fees paid to the networks. Thus competition would result in an expansion in the number of games televised, a lowering of the revenues earned by TV networks, and a bidding away of the profits that remain, which used to accrue to the monopoly leagues.

Local TV revenues of teams would also fall in a competitive league structure. If there were two or more teams operating in a city, competition between the two would act to increase the number of games shown on local TV and reduce advertising revenues, with the resulting profits being bid away from the teams by the competition among them for TV coverage. Even with only one team in a city, the presence of more national TV resulting from competition between leagues has the effect of reducing the market value of local TV, because there are more close substitutes for local TV now available. So TV revenues of pro sports leagues at the national and local levels both will fall under a competitive regime in sports.

Using the same arguments, you can see that competition leads to lower ticket prices, so that gate receipts of teams would fall. And, with team revenues lower, player salaries would fall as well. The special status of superstars such as Michael Jordan, Roger Clemens, Pedro Martinez, Junior Griffey, Troy Aikman, and Wayne Gretzky would still enable them to command astronomical salaries but probably not comparable with what they earn today. For less exalted talents and for journeymen players, salaries would certainly be lower than in today's markets because of the lower revenues of teams, and because the power of unions would be less as well.

In a competitive environment, free agency, one of the main objectives of current player union activity, would be an accomplished fact. It is not clear what if any benefits unions would have for superstar players in a competitive environment. Journeymen players certainly would benefit from effective unions, but with superstars out of the picture, the power of unions to impose and enforce minimum salaries and fringe-benefit packages on leagues would be very much weakened. This is particularly true given that competition for fans and revenues by leagues would eliminate most of the monopoly profits that currently support the union-negotiated benefit packages. A side benefit for fans would be that, with weaker leagues and weaker unions, there would be a less confrontational labor environment than at present.

To summarize, in a competitive league environment, we expect to see more teams in big-city locations, and a team in any location that can profitably support it. Cities would provide much lower subsidies, if any, in the form of elaborate new stadiums and sweetheart stadium contracts. There would be more games on television, lower revenues to teams from TV contracts, and lower ticket prices. Competitive balance would be relegated to the status of a marginal problem. Player salaries would fall, team profits would fall, and the market value of team franchises would fall as well. Unions would play a lesser role in sports. The stadium mess would be alleviated. In effect, power would be shifted by market forces from the insiders—owners and players—to the rest of us—fans and taxpayers.

We can't guarantee that moving to a competitive environment will necessarily eliminate from pro sports all of the behavior-impaired owners and players who currently people the industry. But with accelerated expansion, especially into the big-city markets, the spill-over benefits of owning a sports team go downhill drastically, which suggests that many of the current crop of billionaire-owners will be looking elsewhere for free publicity. Moreover, the fresh, clean breeze of competition moving through an industry forces owners of any stripe to be much more focused on satisfying their customers—or else. This would certainly be a wake-up call toward a kinder, gentler, less arrogant image for any owner. The argument is less convincing with respect to the reform of the bad actors among the superstar players, whose unique abilities allow them to retain strong bargaining power, even in an otherwise competitive setting. At least competition shouldn't make them more of a pain.

Our argument is that installing a competitive environment in sports eliminates essentially all of the most vexing problems that currently plague sports. Our proposal does not involve the creation of a regulatory authority nor the intervention of the courts into the day-to-day decision making in pro team sports. Instead, under our solution, the role of the government and the courts in pro team sports would be what it is in every other industry, as a corrective to monopolistic abuses if they arise again in the future.

There have been objections raised to our proposal, to the effect that pro team sports is an industry that cannot sustain a competitive environment. Some argue that sports fans will only support that single league in a sport that contains the team or teams with the most talent, while rival leagues with teams of lesser caliber would fail to attract fans or TV contracts and would fall by the wayside. The argument is that sports fans are so attracted by "world-class" or "championship" teams and leagues that competition for this status by investors in the sport would lead to the bankrupting of all but a single surviving league. In a sense, this is a kind of "natural monopoly" argument as applied to pro team sports—competition would be great if it could be achieved, but the nature of the sports industry just precludes it.

The argument has some surface plausibility. After all, haven't we seen that all of the pro sports have been operated as monopoly cartels over almost all of their histories? And isn't it a fact that the dominating team in a sport—the Bulls in the NBA in the 1990s, the Cowboys and the 49ers in the NFL in the 1980s, the Yankees in the AL from the 1920s through the 1950s—is the recipient of large financial rewards for being not just a very good team but a "champion," and especially a repeater or threepeater and more. There's no question that fans are attracted to the best team in a sport, and isn't this going to spell trouble for competition between a league with the best team in a sport and rivals with only the second- or third-best talent?

Actually, the historical argument is a double-edged sword. While MLB as an entity is a monopoly organization, the AL and the NL have survived and in fact flourished over the past 95 years (make that almost 125 years for the NL) despite the fact that the two leagues have been competitors (with restraints, to be sure) for fans, players, and even locations. After all this time, with ups and downs in the relative strengths of the two leagues, there are still dyed-in-the-wool NL fans ("the DH rule makes a travesty of the sport") and dyed-in-the-wool AL fans ("who wants to see a pitcher bunt three times a game?"). Why hasn't the championship motive wiped out one of the leagues? In particular, why didn't the NL simply go out of business during those long spells in which the Yankees were head and shoulders above any other team in baseball?

When the AFL merged with the NFL in the 1960s, the AFL was the inferior league, as the early Super Bowls showed. But the AFL had developed its own fan base, with loyalties as strong as those of the NFL fans. There was at least one informed insider in the AFL who argued against the merger at the time, someone who claimed that the AFL could make it on its own without the NFL. This was then-commissioner of the AFL, Al Davis. Davis was of course overruled—monopoly profits look a lot better than profits in a competitive industry—but the AFL was more than holding its own against the NFL for six years, without the championship motive working to destroy fan support for the league. There are sports historians who say that one of Pete Rozelle's worst mistakes as commissioner was not maintaining the AFL as a separate entity within the NFL when merger occurred, to capitalize on the rivalry that had already developed by the late 1960s. An even more striking case is NCAA football where fan loyalty persists for teams and for leagues that have long since abandoned the fight to achieve top-flight standing.

When a league is strong enough, both in terms of its roster of team locations and in terms of its roster of players, as was the case with the AFL, fans seem willing to take a chance on the future of the league, even if they are aware that, at present, the league isn't quite in the class of the premiere league. If this was true for the AFL, how much more so in the case of leagues established through breaking up the existing monopoly league? Moreover, leagues created in a breakup would consist of teams that already enjoy the sense of tradition and the base of fan loyalty that carries a team through the bad years. The investment in goodwill that teams and leagues have made over their histories would be carried forward in the new competitive environment, bypassing the difficult problems posed for entering rival leagues and new teams of establishing their bona fides in the sport.

Even if the championship motive is as strong as critics of introducing competition into sports argue, there are devices that can be employed to mitigate the impact of the motive on the finances of a sport. We know that's true, because the championship motive is almost as much a potential problem for a single monopolistic league as it would be for a sport in which competing leagues were playing. Why haven't the rewards of being a dominant championship team led the Yankees, for example, to raid other teams' rosters by bidding away their star players to the point of bankrupting the rest of the teams in the AL?

The answer is that all existing pro team sports leagues have adopted rules to limit the financial rewards from being a dominant championship team. They include gate-sharing and national TV revenue-sharing, so the dominant team doesn't get to keep all of the added revenue its classy roster of players brings to the league. There are the reverse-order-of-finish rules concerning a team's place in the annual rookie draft—if you're strong this year, you don't get first crack at the best players coming into the league next year. League rules provide equal sharing of revenue from licensed products such as souvenirs and paraphernalia. The NFL provides special penalties on winning teams by scheduling the best teams in the league to play against them in the next season.

Most important, all leagues have introduced playoffs—sometimes seemingly endless playoffs as in the NHL—to determine the league champion. Playoffs maintain fan interest in league games during the last weeks of a season, particularly for teams with good, but not the best, records. But playoffs also serve a more important function. They introduce greater uncertainty about which team will be the league champion as compared to the old-fashioned rule of crowning as champion the team with the best season-long winning percentage. Thus playoffs reduce the incentives for risk-averse team owners to invest large sums of money on talent in pursuit of a league championship and the payoffs this provides.

The added uncertainty associated with playoffs is a real thing. In the 1998 NCAA basketball championship, the four top-ranked teams in the tournament—Duke, North Carolina, Kansas, and Arizona—all were eliminated before the final game, in which Kentucky beat Utah. The 1997 World Series did not match the two teams that were the consensus choices as best teams in their leagues, namely Atlanta in the NL and Baltimore in the AL. Instead, Atlanta and Baltimore were defeated in the championship playoffs, with Florida and Cleveland ending up in the Series. The 1998 Super Bowl did feature the best team from the NFC, Green Bay, but Kansas City, with the best season record in the AFC, didn't make it to the Super Bowl. Instead, it lost to Denver in the playoffs, with Denver going on to win the big game.

In brief, we would agree that the championship motive is something to be concerned with in assessing the prospects for creating and maintaining a competitive structure in pro team sports. We think, though, that the case has been oversold, that the experiences of the AL and NL in baseball, the AFL in football, and, even much earlier on, the old American Association and NL in the baseball of the 1880s, indicate that competitive leagues can coexist without leading to bankruptcy of the weaker league. We would suggest that, if a competitive environment were established in a sport with two or more independent rival leagues in existence following the breakup of the monopoly league, a limited antitrust exemption should be granted. This exemption would permit the leagues to take joint action specifically and solely for the purpose of establishing a season-end championship contest among the leagues. This would permit the leagues to agree on procedures, such as playoffs, designed to limit the problems potentially posed by the championship motive. In other matters, the usual antitrust rules would apply.

So this is our solution to the pro sports problems. Given the fact that the Justice Department has ignored these problems from time immemorial, we are not wildly optimistic about any movement from the lawyers over there. Still, it does make one wonder, doesn't anyone at Justice know an antitrust violation when it comes up and bites him or her on the hind quarters? We can only hope that this book moves things along an inch or two in the right direction.

TABLES

TABLE 2-1
MEDIA INCOME, NFL, 1990–96 (millions of $)

Team	1990	1991	1992	1993	1994	1995	1996	Average
Atlanta	28.2	32.0	26.0	40.7	38.1	41.5	44.7	35.9
Baltimore						40.7	43.9	42.3
Buffalo	27.5	31.6	35.8	40.9	38.0	40.7	44.1	36.9
Carolina						18.3	20.0	19.2
Chicago	28.5	33.6	38.1	43.6	41.3	44.6	48.0	39.7
Cincinnati	27.5	31.2	35.4	40.4	37.4	39.8	43.0	36.4
Cleveland	27.5	31.6	35.8	41.1	38.2			34.8
Dallas	30.0	34.2	38.2	42.8	40.9	43.6	47.0	39.5
Denver	28.5	32.6	36.4	41.4	39.5	43.4	46.7	38.4
Detroit	27.5	31.8	35.8	40.8	37.5	40.0	43.2	36.7
Green Bay	27.0	30.9	34.8	40.5	38.0	39.1	43.2	36.2
Houston	28.0	33.8	36.1	41.1	38.5	41.1	44.4	37.6
Indianapolis	27.0	31.0	35.0	40.0	37.2	39.6	42.8	36.1
Jacksonville						18.8	20.0	19.4
Kansas City	27.0	31.2	35.2	40.4	38.4	40.8	44.1	36.7
LA Raiders	28.5	32.7	36.8	42.0	39.2			35.8
LA Rams	28.8	32.7	36.8	41.5	39.1			35.8
Miami	28.5	32.0	36.0	41.3	38.6	41.0	44.4	37.4
Minnesota	27.5	32.2	36.1	40.9	37.8	40.2	43.5	36.9
New England	26.5	31.0	35.5	40.6	38.0	43.2	46.4	37.3
New Orleans	27.5	31.3	35.3	40.2	37.8	49.6	42.9	37.8
NY Giants	29.5	34.0	37.3	42.8	39.7	42.6	45.8	38.8
NY Jets	28.5	32.4	35.9	41.0	38.0	42.0	45.2	37.6
Oakland						41.6	44.8	43.2
Philadelphia	28.0	31.9	35.8	41.4	39.3	41.7	44.9	37.6
Phoenix	27.0	30.9	35.0	40.5	38.0	40.5	43.9	36.5
Pittsburgh	27.5	32.1	35.9	40.9	37.9	40.3	43.6	36.9
St. Louis						41.5	44.7	43.1
San Diego	27.0	31.8	35.8	40.8	37.9	40.2	43.4	36.7
San Francisco	29.0	33.0	37.0	43.5	40.8	43.1	46.7	39.0
Seattle	27.3	31.8	35.8	41.8	38.9	41.7	45.0	37.5
Tampa Bay	27.0	31.2	35.2	40.2	37.5	40.4	43.6	36.4
Washington	29.2	33.2	38.3	43.0	40.1	42.4	45.7	38.8
Total	781.5	899.7	1,001.1	1,156.1	1,081.6	1,204.0	1,289.6	1,059.1
Average/team	27.9	32.1	35.8	41.3	38.6	40.1	43.0	37.0

Note: Carolina and Jacksonville entered the league as expansion teams in 1995; Cleveland moved to Baltimore, the LA Raiders moved to Oakland, and the LA Rams moved to St. Louis, all in 1995.
Source: Financial World.

TABLE 2-2
MEDIA INCOME, MAJOR LEAGUE BASEBALL, 1990–96
(millions of $)

Team	1990	1991	1992	1993	1994	1995	1996	Average
Atlanta	20.0	18.9	17.3	35.0	16.6	22.1	30.3	22.9
Baltimore	22.5	24.4	25.0	27.4	11.4	18.9	30.6	22.9
Boston	34.1	40.5	40.1	38.0	18.0	24.2	30.9	32.3
California	24.0	27.9	28.2	26.7	8.7	12.8	18.3	20.9
Chicago Cubs	24.2	27.5	28.0	36.0	17.0	21.1	29.3	26.2
Chicago Sox	24.2	25.7	26.2	26.2	7.2	16.4	24.3	21.5
Cincinnati	21.8	24.4	24.4	25.0	8.4	13.6	21.5	19.9
Cleveland	20.0	23.7	23.0	23.7	5.4	15.7	21.6	19.0
Colorado				5.0	6.2	14.9	22.8	12.2
Detroit	22.3	28.8	28.8	30.3	12.5	18.1	24.7	23.6
Florida				5.0	12.7	19.0	23.9	15.2
Houston	24.2	25.2	24.1	25.2	8.0	15.3	22.3	20.6
Kansas Cty	19.0	20.5	21.0	21.0	5.4	10.9	16.5	16.3
LA	29.7	32.5	33.0	34.0	15.3	24.4	31.8	28.7
Milwaukee	19.0	19.4	19.8	21.5	6.3	9.6	15.1	15.8
Minnesota	20.8	20.5	20.0	22.3	5.4	14.3	20.4	17.7
Montreal	20.0	23.5	24.0	24.0	7.8	12.1	19.4	18.7
NY Mets	38.3	50.0	50.0	46.1	22.2	33.6	30.9	38.7
NY Yankees	69.4	61.0	61.0	63.0	36.4	54.3	69.8	59.3
Oakland	21.2	27.0	25.0	27.4	13.2	17.0	25.2	22.3
Philadelphia	35.0	23.2	23.7	21.0	10.3	15.9	21.4	21.5
Pittsburgh	20.0	21.9	23.3	23.5	8.6	12.2	17.7	18.2
St. Louis	27.4	25.0	25.5	27.0	10.7	19.8	25.7	23.0
San Diego	25.1	23.1	25.5	25.0	9.0	11.1	16.5	19.3
San Francisco	23.3	26.2	24.5	27.5	10.7	19.8	25.5	22.5
Seattle	17.0	22.0	22.0	21.0	6.3	11.6	17.2	16.7
Texas	24.6	25.5	26.8	27.5	10.0	16.9	24.3	22.2
Toronto	28.0	30.0	28.0	31.6	12.9	20.7	28.4	25.7
Total	675.1	718.3	718.2	766.9	322.6	516.3	706.3	632.0
Average/team	26.0	27.6	27.6	27.4	11.5	18.4	25.2	23.4

Note: Colorado and Florida entered the NL as expansion teams in 1993.
Source: Financial World.

TABLE 2-3
MEDIA INCOME, NBA, 1990–96 (millions of $)

Team	1990	1991	1992	1993	1994	1995	1996	Average
Atlanta	6.7	12.5	13.1	13.4	17.4	17.0	17.7	14.0
Boston	11.4	18.0	19.6	21.4	26.0	29.3	22.6	21.2
Charlotte	4.7	9.6	12.2	15.8	19.5	19.2	19.8	14.4
Chicago	5.6	14.2	17.5	18.3	23.3	24.1	27.3	18.6
Cleveland	6.5	13.9	13.5	13.9	18.3	18.6	19.5	14.9
Dallas	11.1	14.0	13.6	13.9	17.9	17.1	17.7	15.0
Denver	8.1	11.5	11.4	12.2	15.2	16.9	18.6	13.4
Detroit	11.9	15.5	18.9	19.9	21.7	21.3	22.1	18.8
Golden State	6.5	14.1	13.7	14.0	18.6	20.3	20.9	15.4
Houston	8.3	13.8	14.9	14.4	18.6	21.5	25.0	16.6
Indiana	4.9	11.0	11.6	10.6	13.2	17.0	16.8	12.2
LA Clippers	5.2	15.6	18.2	16.5	20.5	18.7	19.1	16.3
LA Lakers	19.3	25.1	25.4	27.7	22.0	34.0	36.5	27.1
Miami	5.0	9.7	12.2	12.6	16.6	17.8	18.8	13.2
Milwaukee	5.0	12.2	12.2	12.6	16.6	17.8	18.8	13.6
Minnesota	5.2	18.5	20.0	14.0	17.0	22.0	19.9	16.7
New Jersey	7.0	13.7	14.1	13.7	19.2	27.3	24.7	17.1
New York	6.8	13.1	12.7	16.3	20.5	25.5	30.0	17.8
Orlando	6.0	12.9	13.2	14.5	19.5	25.4	25.1	16.7
Philadelphia	9.0	14.3	14.5	12.3	16.3	19.8	24.5	15.8
Phoenix	10.1	16.2	16.5	16.8	25.9	35.3	32.5	21.9
Sacramento	4.7	9.4	9.1	9.4	13.6	14.2	15.8	10.9
San Antonio	6.2	12.8	9.4	10.8	13.3	18.6	20.2	13.0
Seattle	4.1	9.7	16.5	15.8	20.2	19.1	19.5	15.0
Toronto							17.0	17.0
Utah	4.6	11.9	12.0	12.3	16.7	16.2	15.6	12.8
Vancouver							14.5	14.5
Washington	4.5	10.6	10.2	10.4	14.5	15.4	16.2	11.7
Total	188.4	353.8	376.2	383.5	482.1	549.4	596.7	
Average/team	7.2	13.6	14.5	14.8	18.5	21.1	21.3	

Note: Toronto and Vancouver were expansion franchises in 1996.
Source: Financial World.

TABLE 2-4
MEDIA INCOME, NHL, 1990–96 (millions of $)

Team	1990	1991	1992	1993	1994	1995	1996	Average
Anaheim					5.2	4.7	5.5	5.1
Boston	5.5	10.0	10.1	10.4	11.4	11.0	11.8	10.0
Buffalo	4.8	4.8	4.2	5.2	4.6	4.2	5.1	4.7
Calgary	2.7	5.0	1.8	4.6	4.5	4.3	5.0	4.0
Chicago	3.5	3.5	2.5	5.7	5.9	5.2	6.0	4.6
Colorado						4.3	3.0	3.7
Dallas				2.7	3.2	3.4	4.3	3.4
Detroit	5.5	4.3	7.9	7.9	7.1	6.8	8.3	6.8
Edmonton	5.0	2.6	1.4	4.7	3.5	4.2	5.0	3.8
Florida					4.2	3.9	5.4	4.5
Hartford	4.7	2.0	2.6	2.9	3.5	3.4	4.1	3.3
LA	6.0	6.2	1.4	5.7	7.2	6.4	7.0	5.7
Minnesota	3.0	4.5	1.4					3.0
Montreal	7.0	7.2	6.9	7.2	6.7	6.4	7.2	6.9
New Jersey	1.6	4.3	4.2	4.6	4.6	4.8	7.2	4.5
NY Islanders	12.0	7.0	6.9	7.2	7.2	14.7	10.9	9.4
NY Rangers	5.7	6.0	6.6	6.9	6.7	7.4	8.3	6.8
Ottawa				4.2	3.3	3.9	5.5	4.2
Philadelphia	8.0	7.9	1.4	7.2	7.2	6.9	7.9	6.6
Phoenix							4.6	4.6
Pittsburgh	4.0	4.2	1.4	4.9	5.2	5.6	7.0	4.6
Quebec	3.5	6.3	1.4	5.7	5.1			4.4
St. Louis	3.0	3.5	1.4	2.7	3.7	4.4	5.2	3.4
San Jose				3.2	3.7	3.6	4.2	3.7
Tampa Bay				3.7	5.2	4.4	5.5	4.7
Toronto	5.0	8.1	1.4	8.2	7.7	7.8	8.4	6.7
Vancouver	5.6	5.1	1.4	4.5	4.6	4.8	7.3	4.8
Washington	4.7	4.4	2.3	4.2	4.3	3.9	4.7	4.1
Winnipeg	3.8	4.5	1.4	3.2	3.2	3.8		3.3
Total	104.6	111.4	70.0	127.4	138.7	144.2	164.4	123.0
Average/team	5.0	5.3	3.3	5.3	5.3	5.5	6.3	5.1

Note: San Jose, Ottawa, and Tampa Bay were expansion teams in 1993; Florida and Anaheim were expansion teams in 1994. Minnesota moved to Dallas in 1993, Quebec moved to Colorado in 1995, and Winnipeg moved to Phoenix in 1996.
Source: Financial World

TABLE 3-1
RESULTS OF SALARY ARBITRATION IN BASEBALL, 1996

Player	Team	1995 Salary ($)	Player Asked ($)	Team Offered ($)	Result ($)
		I. Cases in which the player asked for arbitration but settled before formal arbitration			
AL					
Erickson, S.	Baltimore	1,863,000	*	*	2,800,000
Huson, J.	Baltimore	265,000	*	*	320,000
Mercker, K.	Baltimore	2,250,000	3,190,000	2,600,000	2,825,000
Mills, A.	Baltimore	600,000	*	*	540,000
Alicea, L.	Boston	800,000	1,925,000	1,000,000	1,500,000
Belinda, S.	Boston	575,000	1,650,000	1,000,000	1,275,000
Cordero, W.	Boston	315,000	2,250,000	1,450,000	1,850,000
Slocumb, H.	Boston	200,000	1,690,000	1,025,000	1,400,000
Valentin, J.	Boston	637,000	2,750,000	2,200,000	2,672,500
Vaughn, M.	Boston	2,775,000	6,100,000	4,200,000	5,350,000
Alvarez, W.	Chicago Sox	2,250,000	*	*	2,700,000
Fernandez, A.	Chicago Sox	3,250,000	*	*	4,500,000
Fernandez, R.	Chicago Sox	1,275,000	*	*	1,900,000
Appier, K.	Kansas City	4,387,500	5,387,500	4,715,000	5,051,250
Haney, C.	Kansas City	220,000	740,000	400,000	500,000
Howard, D.	Kansas City	350,000	795,000	465,000	500,000
Pichardo, H.	Kansas City	350,000	795,000	465,000	575,000
Eldred, C.	Milwaukee	450,000	790,000	450,000	560,000
Jaha, J.	Milwaukee	229,000	*	*	1,050,000
Nilsson, D.	Milwaukee	290,000	1,300,000	725,000	1,050,000
Leyritz, J.	NY Yankees	1,350,000	*	*	1,330,575
Nelson, J.	NY Yankees	275,000	1,050,000	725,000	860,000
Wetteland, J.	NY Yankees	3,375,000	4,750,000	3,775,000	4,000,000
Wickman, B.	NY Yankees	220,000	1,000,000	675,000	800,000
Berroa, G.	Oakland	235,000	*	*	1,150,000
Bordick, M.	Oakland	1,350,000	*	*	1,850,000
Brosius, S.	Oakland	235,000	1,100,000	790,000	955,000
Charlton, N.	Seattle	525,000	2,500,000	1,650,000	2,075,000
Pavlik, R.	Texas	225,000	*	*	1,100,000
Quantril, P.	Toronto	242,000	*	*	775,000
Timlin, M.	Toronto	500,000	670,000	600,000	635,000
NL					
Lemke, M.	Atlanta	1,250,000	1,900,000	1,250,000	1,500,000
Wohlers, M.	Atlanta	202,000	1,650,000	1,175,000	1,400,000

(Continued)

TABLE 3-1
(*Continued*)

Player	Team	1995 Salary ($)	Player Asked ($)	Team Offered ($)	Result ($)
Castillo, F.	Chicago Cubs	250,000	2,180,000	1,200,000	1,600,000
McRae, B.	Chicago Cubs	2,650,000	*	*	3,400,000
Sanchez, R.	Chicago Cubs	675,000	1,300,000	1,100,000	1,200,000
Servais, S.	Chicago Cubs	340,000	975,000	680,000	822,500
Sosa, S.	Chicago Cubs	4,300,000	5,950,000	4,400,000	4,500,000
Galarraga, A.	Colorado	3,950,000	4,700,000	4,300,000	4,500,000
Vanderwal, J.	Colorado	300,000	590,000	435,000	492,500
Young, E.	Colorado	252,000	1,575,000	895,000	1,200,000
Alex, A.	Florida	200,000	525,000	300,000	412,500
Bowen, R.	Florida	185,000	*	*	305,000
Colbrunn, G.	Florida	225,000	1,575,000	950,000	1,200,000
Berry, S.	Houston	285,000	1,190,000	800,000	995,000
Bell, D.	Houston	1,450,000	*	*	2,600,000
May, D.	Houston	358,000	*	*	750,000
Alou, M.	Montreal	3,000,000	3,400,000	2,700,000	3,000,000
Cormier, R.	Montreal	550,000	1,100,000	800,000	950,000
Rojas, M.	Montreal	1,300,000	2,150,000	1,900,000	2,075,000
Scott, T.	Montreal	225,000	800,000	575,000	700,000
Segui, D.	Montreal	755,557	2,000,000	1,100,000	1,550,000
Gilkey, B.	NY Mets	1,625,000	3,000,000	2,550,000	2,787,500
Hundley, T.	NY Mets	975,000	2,100,000	1,525,000	1,837,500
Kent, J.	NY Mets	710,000	2,275,000	1,500,000	1,960,000
Mayne, B.	NY Mets	675,000	850,000	630,000	725,000
Longmire, T.	Philadelphia	109,000	*	*	225,000
Morandini, M.	Philadelphia	1,025,000	2,200,000	1,375,000	1,750,000
Neagle, D.	Pittsburgh	740,000	*	*	2,300,000
Webster, L.	Philadelphia	275,000	545,000	300,000	397,500
Clayton, R.	St. Louis	475,000	*	*	1,600,000
Fossas, T.	St. Louis	275,000	920,000	500,000	650,000
Lankford, R.	St. Louis	2,800,000	4,200,000	3,200,000	4,000,000
Osborne, D.	St. Louis	250,000	1,150,000	450,000	675,000
Stottlemeyer, T.	St. Louis	2,050,000	4,300,000	3,200,000	3,800,000
Ashby, A.	San Diego	775,000	2,650,000	1,900,000	1,900,000

TABLE 3-1

(Continued)

Player	Team	1995 Salary ($)	Player Asked ($)	Team Offered ($)	Result ($)
II. Cases in which the salary dispute went to full arbitration					
AL					
Rhodes, A.	Baltimore	275,000	675,000	300,000	300,000
Stanton, M.	Boston	1,500,000	1,750,000	1,200,000	1,750,000
Lewis, M.	Detroit	190,000	670,000	450,000	670,000
Knoblauch, C.	Minnesota	2,987,500	4,670,000	3,750,000	4,670,000
Williams, B.	NY Yankees	400,000	3,000,000	2,555,000	3,000,000
Rodriguez, I.	Texas	2,675,000	4,950,000	4,000,000	4,000,000
NL					
Avery, S.	Atlanta	4,000,000	4,200,000	3,600,000	4,200,000
Wilkins, R.	Houston	1,475,000	1,550,000	1,250,000	1,550,000
Fassero, J.	Montreal	1,500,000	2,800,000	2,000,000	2,800,000
Banks, W.	Philadelphia	240,000	590,000	240,000	240,000

*Settlement occurred before formal player and owner bids were filed.

Source: USA Today, February 23, 1996, p. 11C.

TABLE 4-1
PLAYER COSTS AS A PERCENT OF TOTAL LEAGUE
REVENUES, ALL LEAGUES, 1990–96

League	1990	1991	1992	1993	1994	1995	1996
MLB	33.4	45.3	49.0	56.3	71.1	61.7	53.5
NFL	52.4	47.2	60.0	64.3	67.5	67.9	67.4
NBA	39.6	40.7	43.7	48.5	41.4	46.2	46.9
NHL	29.8	32.5	37.5	41.0	41.2	38.2	51.1

Note: Player costs include salaries, deferred payments, bonuses, and fringe benefits.
Source: Financial World.

TABLE 4-2
PAYROLLS AND AVERAGE SALARIES, OPENING DAY
ROSTERS, MAJOR LEAGUE BASEBALL, 1998

Team	Payroll ($)	Average Salary ($)
Baltimore	68,988,134	2,555,116
NY Yankees	63,460,567	2,440,791
Cleveland	59,582,500	2,127,982
Atlanta	59,536,000	2,126,286
Texas	55,304,595	1,975,164
St. Louis	52,575,000	1,752,500
Seattle	52,027,136	1,678,295
Boston	51,647,000	1,780,931
NY Mets	49,517,999	1,650,600
Chicago Cubs	49,433,000	1,830,852
Toronto	48,666,000	1,738,071
Los Angeles	47,970,000	1,654,138
Colorado	47,434,648	1,694,095
San Diego	45,368,000	1,744,923
Houston	40,629,000	1,451,036
San Francisco	40,570,833	1,560,417
Anaheim	38,702,000	1,290,067
Chicago Sox	36,840,000	1,473,600
Philadelphia	34,370,000	1,227,500
Florida	33,434,000	1,238,296
Kansas City	32,962,500	1,177,000
Milwaukee	32,393,012	1,117,000
Arizona	30,571,500	1,054,190
Minnesota	26,182,500	1,090,938
Tampa Bay	25,317,500	873,017
Detroit	22,725,000	783,621
Cincinnati	21,995,000	758,448
Oakland	20,063,000	668,767
Pittsburgh	13,352,000	476,857
Montreal	9,162,000	352,385
Average	40,359,347	1,444,763

Source: Associated Press, as quoted in the Seattle Post-Intelligencer, April 15, 1998.

TABLE 4-3
PAYROLLS AND AVERAGE SALARIES, NFL, 1997

Team	Payroll ($)	Average Salary ($)
Oakland	49,100,000	1,091,100
Dallas	44,900,000	997,800
San Francisco	44,200,000	933,300
Kansas City	43,900,000	975,600
Buffalo	41,200,000	915,600
NY Jets	41,200,000	915,600
NY Giants	40,200,000	893,300
Baltimore	40,000,000	888,900
New Orleans	39,700,000	882,200
Miami	38,200,000	848,900
Seattle	36,900,000	820,000
Denver	36,200,000	804,400
Indianapolis	35,400,000	786,700
St. Louis	35,000,000	777,800
Green Bay	33,700,000	748,900
Jacksonville	33,700,000	748,900
Pittsburgh	33,700,000	748,900
Phoenix	33,600,000	746,700
New England	33,200,000	737,800
Tennessee	33,100,000	735,600
Tampa Bay	32,900,000	731,100
Cincinnati	32,500,000	722,200
Minnesota	32,500,000	722,200
Chicago	32,000,000	711,100
San Diego	30,600,000	680,000
Washington	29,900,000	664,400
Philadelphia	28,400,000	631,100
Detroit	27,700,000	615,600
Atlanta	27,000,000	600,000
Carolina	26,700,000	593,300
Average	35,577,000	789,000

Source: Sports Illustrated, February 3, 1997, p. 42.

TABLE 4-4

PAYROLLS AND AVERAGE SALARIES, NBA, 1997–98

Team	Payroll ($)	Average Salary ($)
Chicago	61,729,000	4,115,267
New York	56,534,000	4,348,769
Orlando	45,782,000	2,289,100
San Antonio	42,865,000	3,061,786
Phoenix	42,117,000	2,632,313
Washington	40,890,000	2,726,000
Indiana	38,845,000	2,285,000
Seattle	36,684,000	2,157,882
LA Lakers	36,590,000	2,613,571
Miami	34,555,000	1,919,722
Golden State	34,209,000	2,443,500
New Jersey	34,054,000	2,432,429
Atlanta	32,116,000	2,294,000
Portland	28,476,000	1,898,400
Utah	28,470,000	2,190,000
Philadelphia	28,456,000	1,897,067
Houston	27,988,000	1,865,867
Cleveland	27,798,000	1,635,176
Charlotte	27,760,000	2,135,385
Boston	27,369,000	1,609,941
Minnesota	27,277,000	1,704,813
Detroit	27,140,000	1,809,333
Sacramento	27,102,000	1,426,421
Dallas	27,042,000	1,690,125
Denver	25,859,000	1,361,000
Vancouver	25,473,000	1,592,063
Toronto	25,272,000	1,579,500
Milwaukee	24,939,000	1,781,357
LA Clippers	24,057,000	1,603,800
Average	33,360,276	2,175,848

Source: USA Today Web page, February 27, 1998.

TABLE 4-5
PAYROLLS AND AVERAGE SALARIES, NHL, 1997–98

Team	Payroll ($)	Average Salary ($)
United States (U.S.$)		
NY Rangers	44,151,893	1,766,076
Colorado	43,699,713	1,820,871
Philadelphia	37,988,855	1,651,689
Dallas	32,148,522	1,236,482
St. Louis	32,085,000	1,283,400
Washington	31,385,704	1,162,433
New Jersey	29,567,535	1,095,094
San Jose	29,020,000	1,116,154
Detroit	28,397,063	1,234,655
Florida	26,725,000	1,069,000
Carolina	25,827,344	1,033,094
Pittsburgh	25,812,000	992,769
Chicago	25,799,905	992,304
Phoenix	24,515,000	980,600
Los Angeles	22,089,000	920,375
Tampa Bay	21,500,000	895,833
Boston	20,724,219	828,969
Buffalo	20,315,833	812,633
Anaheim	18,950,000	789,583
NY Islanders	18,293,672	831,531
Average	27,949,813	1,125,677
Canada (Canadian$)		
Vancouver	32,207,500	1,341,979
Montreal	28,130,723	1,041,879
Toronto	25,307,128	973,351
Ottawa	21,850,000	910,417
Edmonton	20,354,000	814,160
Calgary	19,640,000	727,407
Average	24,581,559	968,199

Source: National Hockey League Players Association Web page, October 28, 1998.

TABLE 4-6
AVERAGE WON-LOST PERCENTAGES AND
AVERAGE PLAYER COSTS, MAJOR LEAGUE
BASEBALL, 1990–96

Team	Average Won/Lost Percentage		Average Player Costs (millions of $) per Year	
	Value	Rank	Value	Rank
NL				
Atlanta	.577	1	37.5	1
Montreal	.534	2	16.9	14
Cincinnati	.528	3	35.3	3
Los Angeles	.514	4	35.5	2
Pittsburgh	.509	5	22.4	12
Houston	.500	6	24.1	11
St. Louis	.492	7	27.3	7
San Francisco	.490	8	34.3	4
Chicago Cubs	.481	9	31.1	6
Colorado	.478	10	27.0	8
San Diego	.474	11	22.1	13
NY Mets	.464	12	31.8	5
Florida	.450	13	24.3	10
Philadelphia	.426	14	26.5	9
AL				
Chicago Sox	.545	1	31.9	5
Cleveland	.523	2	25.1	12
Boston	.514	3	36.5	3
NY Yankees	.514	3	42.7	1
Toronto	.514	3	38.8	2
Texas	.510	6	29.5	9
Oakland	.509	7	33.5	4
Baltimore	.508	8	30.5	7
Kansas City	.492	9	30.6	6
Seattle	.486	10	27.9	10
Minnesota	.482	11	20.6	14
Milwaukee	.481	12	23.0	13
CA/Anaheim	.465	13	27.6	11
Detroit	.457	14	30.1	8

Note: Average player costs for Colorado and Florida are calculated by assuming league-wide average player costs for the period 1990 through 1992.
Rank correlation coefficients: NL = .135 (insignificant); AL = .509 (insignificant).
Sources: Won-lost percentages, *World Almanac;* player costs, *Financial World.*

TABLE 4-7
AVERAGE WON-LOST PERCENTAGES AND
AVERAGE PLAYER COSTS, NFL, 1990–96

Team	Average Won/Lost Percentage		Average Player Costs (millions of $) per Year	
	Value	Rank	Value	Rank
San Francisco	.750	1	42.7	1
Dallas	.688	2	39.7	5
Buffalo	.679	3	40.6	2
Kansas City	.652	4	36.0	14
Pittsburgh	.619	5	30.1	28
Miami	.598	6	37.7	10
Philadelphia	.589	7	35.9	15
LA Raiders	.588	8	38.3	6
Denver	.554	9	34.9	18
Green Bay	.545	10	34.9	18
Minnesota	.545	10	34.5	22
Chicago	.527	12	34.9	18
Houston	.527	12	37.8	9
NY Giants	.518	14	40.5	3
Detroit	.509	15	37.6	12
San Diego	.509	15	34.5	22
New Orleans	.500	17	37.7	10
Washington	.491	18	40.0	4
Indianapolis	.420	19	38.0	7
Atlanta	.411	20	36.1	13
Cleveland	.406	21	32.3	26
Seattle	.402	22	34.3	25
New England	.359	23	35.2	17
Phoenix/Arizona	.348	24	34.9	18
Cincinnati	.340	25	34.5	22
Tampa Bay	.340	25	31.6	27
NY Jets	.322	27	38.0	7
LA Rams	.288	28	35.3	16

Note: Excluded from the table are Baltimore, Jacksonville, Carolina, St. Louis, and Oakland.

Rank correlation coefficient: NFL = .29 (insignificant).

Sources: Won-lost percentages, *World Almanac;* player costs, *Financial World.*

TABLE 4-8
AVERAGE WON-LOST PERCENTAGES AND
AVERAGE PLAYER COSTS, NBA, 1990–96

Team	Average Won/Lost Percentage		Average Player Costs (millions of $) per Year	
	Value	Rank	Value	Rank
Chicago	.721	1	18.4	9
San Antonio	.667	2	18.7	8
Phoenix	.662	3	20.3	5
Utah	.660	4	16.2	20
Seattle	.641	5	18.0	12
Portland	.636	6	19.5	7
New York	.617	7	22.1	3
Houston	.597	8	17.1	16
LA Lakers	.587	9	26.0	1
Cleveland	.563	10	21.6	4
Indianapolis	.554	11	18.2	11
Atlanta	.540	12	18.4	9
Boston	.535	13	23.9	2
Detroit	.507	14	17.0	17
Golden State	.491	15	18.0	12
Orlando	.484	16	20.1	6
Charlotte	.442	17	16.2	20
Denver	.420	18	16.4	19
Miami	.404	19	15.3	26
New Jersey	.402	20	17.9	14
Milwaukee	.401	21	16.0	23
Philadelphia	.392	22	17.7	15
LA Clippers	.383	23	16.2	20
Sacramento	.361	24	16.6	18
Washington	.335	25	16.0	23
Dallas	.319	26	15.8	25
Minnesota	.265	27	14.2	27

Note: Excluded from the table are Vancouver and Toronto.
Rank correlation coefficient: NBA = .677 (significant).
Sources: Won-lost percentages, *World Almanac;* player costs, *Financial World.*

TABLE 4-9
AVERAGE WON-LOST PERCENTAGES AND
AVERAGE PLAYER COSTS, NHL, 1990–96

Team	Average Won/Lost Percentage		Average Player Costs (millions of $) per Year	
	Value	Rank	Value	Rank
Detroit	.609	1	14.6	4
Boston	.594	2	11.7	10
Pittsburgh	.587	3	15.8	3
Chicago	.576	4	12.4	7
NY Rangers	.561	5	16.6	1
Calgary	.559	6	10.2	21
St. Louis	.559	6	14.1	5
Montreal	.556	8	11.9	8
New Jersey	.539	9	11.7	10
Washington	.538	10	11.0	16
Buffalo	.519	11	12.5	6
Philadelphia	.516	12	11.7	10
Florida	.511	13	10.2	21
Toronto	.494	14	11.5	13
Vancouver	.492	15	10.8	17
Los Angeles	.484	16	16.2	2
Dallas	.472	17	10.3	19
Edmonton	.463	18	8.4	27
Minnesota	.456	19	11.4	14
Winnipeg	.448	20	11.1	15
NY Islanders	.434	21	10.3	19
Hartford	.433	22	11.9	8
Anaheim	.428	23	9.9	23
Quebec	.425	24	10.8	17
Tampa Bay	.415	25	9.6	24
San Jose	.320	26	9.5	25
Ottawa	.213	27	9.2	26

Note: Excluded from the table are Colorado and Phoenix. For Minnesota, Winnipeg, Quebec, Dallas, Ottawa, Tampa Bay, Anaheim, San Jose, and Florida, player costs for years not in the NHL are taken to be the average player costs for those years.
Rank correlation coefficient: NHL = .69 (significant).
Sources: Won-lost percentages, World Almanac; player costs, Financial World.

TABLE 4-10

AVERAGE WON-LOST PERCENTAGES AND PLAYER COSTS, YEARLY RANK CORRELATIONS, ALL SPORTS, 1990–96

League	Rank Correlation between Team Won/Lost Percentage and Team Player Costs							
	1990	*1991*	*1992*	*1993*	*1994*	*1995*	*1996*	*Average*
NL	.29	.14	−.03	.14	.41	.70	.32	.27
AL	.09	.15	.28	.61	.56	.21	.71	.37
NFL	.39	.07	.47	.46	−.24	−.12	−.02	.14
NBA	.70	.34	.36	.27	.58	.53	.56	.48
NHL	.06	.28	.40	.41	.45	.35	.44	.34

Source: Won-lost percentages, *World Almanac;* player costs, *Financial World.*

TABLE 5-1
ESTIMATED OPERATING INCOME, MAJOR LEAGUE BASEBALL,
1990–96 (millions of $)

Team	1990	1991	1992	1993	1994	1995	1996	7-Year Average	5-Year Average
NY Yankees	24.5	30.4	25.0	18.2	8.7	24.0	38.3	24.2	27.3
Baltimore	9.6	11.1	34.2	28.9	5.5	6.0	19.0	16.3	20.6
Colorado				12.7	4.6	11.5	23.0	13.0	17.9
NY Mets	15.8	20.7	5.6	4.9	-2.2	20.8	11.0	10.9	11.6
Boston	12.3	10.7	11.7	7.4	0.2	15.4	16.3	10.6	11.7
Texas	9.1	13.9	14.8	1.1	5.2	7.6	18.9	10.1	11.6
LA Dodgers	7.6	7.3	14.7	11.1	-4.1	12.8	13.5	9.0	10.9
Chicago Cubs	9.2	6.5	5.1	7.4	3.7	4.8	18.3	7.9	9.3
Florida				12.5	9.0	6.8	2.8	7.8	7.7
Toronto	13.9	26.3	-1.3	1.3	1.4	-1.6	14.5	7.8	10.9
St. Louis	10.5	12.7	3.3	20.0	-4.0	0.9	3.2	6.7	9.9
Montreal	6.4	-4.2	11.8	12.4	-3.8	7.1	6.2	5.1	6.5
Chicago Sox	8.8	18.0	16.7	10.7	-5.8	-8.0	-5.2	5.0	9.8
Cleveland	-10.5	-4.2	13.6	13.3	-4.5	1.4	15.6	3.5	5.6
San Diego	8.5	-0.4	-0.3	17.5	-1.6	-5.1	2.5	3.0	5.6
Houston	-13.5	14.5	11.4	6.7	-8.4	-4.5	11.5	2.5	6.1
Philadelphia	11.1	4.8	-0.3	0.5	-3.7	3.4	-6.5	1.3	1.9
Oakland	12.4	-1.7	-12.8	-0.4	-10.6	-4.8	11.3	-0.9	1.8
Anaheim	8.7	-7.6	-0.3	2.6	-8.7	-3.0	-2.4	-1.5	0.2
Atlanta	7.8	-0.5	-9.0	-1.4	-5.3	-2.9	-0.4	-1.7	-0.7
Pittsburgh	-0.7	-4.0	-9.9	4.1	-6.1	-1.7	1.4	-2.4	-1.8
Minnesota	-6.5	-4.5	0.2	1.0	-9.6	2.5	-1.3	-2.6	-2.2
Detroit	5.1	-2.8	-3.2	-5.4	-15.7	-5.3	3.8	-3.4	-0.5
San Francisco	9.0	-4.4	-11.1	-0.7	-10.3	-1.4	-6.0	-3.6	-2.6
Milwaukee	3.9	-11.4	-12.8	-2.2	-12.0	1.0	6.6	-3.8	-3.2
Seattle	-3.1	2.9	-2.4	-4.0	-12.1	-9.8	-1.7	-4.3	-1.7
Cincinnati	11.0	0.2	-11.8	-5.0	-16.8	-11.8	-14.0	-6.9	-3.9
Kansas City	-9.8	-7.2	-5.1	-6.3	-17.4	-6.9	4.7	-6.9	-4.7
MLB average	6.2	4.9	3.4	6.0	-4.4	2.1	7.3	3.6	5.6

Note: Colorado and Florida were expansion teams in 1993. Five-year average excludes the two strike years, 1994 and 1995.
Source: Financial World.

TABLE 5-2
ESTIMATED OPERATING INCOME, NFL, 1990–96 (millions of $)

Team	1990	1991	1992	1993	1994	1995	1996	Average
Dallas	15.2	7.9	10.7	15.6	32.2	16.4	30.2	18.3
St. Louis						12.2	16.4	14.3
Miami	12.5	14.6	0.0	1.3	13.2	13.3	20.7	10.8
Philadelphia	7.9	12.7	10.9	4.7	8.4	15.1	6.7	9.5
Chicago	11.6	11.8	9.3	5.4	9.1	14.1	2.9	9.2
Pittsburgh	9.9	10.3	13.6	10.0	3.1	6.4	4.9	8.3
Kansas City	8.7	7.8	9.9	5.3	3.4	11.5	10.9	8.2
Baltimore						5.8	9.0	7.4
Oakland						10.2	3.6	6.9
Minnesota	9.2	5.5	2.2	6.0	1.8	10.3	8.9	6.3
Denver	9.1	6.1	7.2	1.6	7.8	11.1	0.7	6.2
Tampa Bay	3.8	4.9	10.3	1.6	1.6	9.6	8.9	5.8
LA Rams	11.4	6.8	5.3	5.5	-1.8			5.4
Cleveland	10.4	8.2	1.7	0.3	6.0			5.3
New Orleans	9.5	5.1	6.6	-3.0	1.5	12.0	4.7	5.2
Houston	6.0	10.2	7.1	-3.5	2.8	6.9	5.2	5.0
Cincinnati	8.8	1.9	4.2	6.9	1.1	1.3	10.1	4.9
Arizona	10.7	6.3	3.6	1.0	-3.4	14.9	0.8	4.8
Green Bay	5.5	2.0	1.5	-5.0	5.0	13.2	7.2	4.2
NY Giants	11.6	8.9	-2.3	-1.7	8.0	10.0	-5.7	4.1
Buffalo	10.5	10.8	1.8	-7.2	3.7	9.3	-2.5	3.8
San Francisco	5.2	3.3	-5.7	-9.3	9.2	19.0	3.6	3.6
Seattle	4.6	6.8	4.7	0.2	-6.6	12.1	3.3	3.6
San Diego	4.4	5.1	2.9	-4.1	1.1	8.2	6.7	3.5
Atlanta	4.5	4.3	-4.8	-4.7	2.1	16.3	5.4	3.3
New England	4.0	-1.0	4.2	9.4	-5.4	1.6	0.1	1.8
Indianapolis	8.9	5.5	-3.1	-7.2	-3.8	7.2	3.0	1.5
LA Raiders	10.6	6.3	-2.2	-6.2	-1.3			1.4
Washington	10.5	7.6	1.7	-11.6	-6.0	0.2	7.5	1.4
NY Jets	8.9	4.0	3.3	-6.0	-1.8	3.6	-8.0	0.6
Detroit	3.9	4.6	6.4	-17.3	-4.1	-0.1	3.3	-0.5
Carolina						-18.9	1.7	-8.6
Jacksonville						-16.7	-4.8	-10.8
NFL average	8.5	6.7	4.0	-0.4	3.1	7.9	5.5	5.0

Note: The LA Raiders moved to Oakland in 1995, the LA Rams moved to St. Louis in 1995, Cleveland moved to Baltimore in 1995, and Houston moved to Tennessee in 1997. Carolina and Jacksonville were expansion teams in 1995.
Source: Financial World.

TABLE 5-3
ESTIMATED OPERATING INCOME, NBA, 1990–96 (millions of $)

Team	1990	1991	1992	1993	1994	1995	1996	Average
Detroit	23.3	15.4	34.0	28.6	31.8	28.5	25.7	26.8
LA Lakers	30.2	30.1	32.2	27.4	15.8	6.2	19.9	23.1
New York	3.4	5.7	17.9	29.1	32.9	31.8	22.9	20.5
Chicago	7.3	16.9	17.1	14.8	22.8	26.2	33.2	19.8
Phoenix	3.9	5.1	7.8	23.8	22.6	30.4	15.3	15.6
Toronto							14.4	14.4
Portland	1.4	10.4	14.2	5.9	7.6	6.8	33.5	11.4
Charlotte	6.4	9.3	10.9	9.7	11.4	15.7	14.9	11.2
Utah	0.9	3.3	13.2	8.7	16.2	17.4	14.8	10.6
Minnesota	4.7	12.7	13.2	8.5	4.5	18.0	6.7	9.8
San Antonio	0.3	7.6	3.2	8.5	15.5	17.2	15.2	9.6
Boston	8.8	14.2	–2.4	–2.4	10.8	16.7	16.4	8.9
Cleveland	6.1	5.7	3.4	2.0	9.9	21.5	11.9	8.6
Houston	3.3	2.6	2.2	2.4	9.2	25.1	13.4	8.3
Orlando	9.2	8.6	1.9	4.9	8.3	14.5	8.5	8.0
Seattle	–1.8	–3.6	2.7	10.6	8.6	9.2	12.0	5.4
Vancouver							5.4	5.4
Miami	7.5	5.2	2.9	–0.3	4.7	10.3	4.8	5.0
Golden State	1.1	5.4	3.7	1.3	3.9	10.3	7.8	4.8
Sacramento	5.2	0.1	7.2	2.7	4.6	7.9	4.3	4.6
Dallas	2.7	3.8	–0.9	2.3	6.2	9.3	4.6	4.0
New Jersey	1.8	1.2	2.0	–1.7	6.7	10.8	7.3	4.0
Milwaukee	4.3	–1.2	–1.4	3.9	7.7	13.9	–3.5	3.4
LA Clippers	1.1	3.0	3.2	2.9	2.8	7.7	–1.4	2.8
Denver	–1.8	–3.3	–0.3	0.1	8.7	9.9	4.4	2.5
Washington	–2.4	–1.3	2.6	–4.6	4.9	10.9	4.6	2.1
Philadelphia	4.1	3.3	0.6	–7.9	1.6	6.9	2.1	1.5
Indiana	–3.5	–2.7	–5.1	–5.9	0.8	8.9	9.1	0.2
Atlanta	1.2	–1.1	–2.2	–5.4	2.1	4.2	–2.8	–0.6
NBA average	4.8	5.8	6.8	6.3	10.5	14.7	11.2	8.6

Note: Toronto and Vancouver were expansion teams in 1996–97.
Source: Financial World.

TABLE 5-4
ESTIMATED OPERATING INCOME, NHL, 1990–96 (millions of $)

Team	1990	1991	1992	1993	1994	1995	1996	Average
Detroit	6.8	15.6	25.7	19.2	17.0	13.0	9.1	15.2
Chicago	6.7	7.1	6.1	13.1	12.5	22.0	26.9	13.5
Boston	9.3	11.1	10.5	7.9	13.8	11.4	17.8	11.7
Anaheim					17.1	8.7	6.9	10.9
NY Rangers	4.8	6.0	9.8	8.6	14.8	9.7	10.2	9.1
Toronto	4.0	6.4	8.6	10.2	7.1	3.5	3.4	6.2
Philadelphia	2.2	1.2	2.8	8.7	7.4	9.6	9.7	5.9
NY Islanders	10.3	6.8	3.1	1.4	–0.8	13.1	3.9	5.4
San Jose			–1.8	–0.7	12.5	7.1	8.1	5.0
Los Angeles	1.7	10.5	7.7	6.8	3.6	0.0	–2.0	4.0
Montreal	5.8	6.9	5.5	4.9	6.6	–2.3	–0.4	3.9
Calgary	3.8	4.7	2.9	2.5	–0.3	2.7	7.8	3.4
Pittsburgh	0.6	4.4	2.1	2.7	2.2	0.8	10.1	3.3
New Jersey	0.8	2.7	2.2	0.8	0.6	5.6	4.3	2.4
Quebec	0.0	0.3	3.3	2.7	1.1			1.5
Ottawa				4.5	2.8	–2.8	0.1	1.2
Colorado						2.6	–0.6	1.0
Edmonton	4.3	3.2	1.1	–2.3	–1.9	2.7	–0.1	1.0
Florida					0.5	2.9	–0.9	0.8
Vancouver	1.1	–0.7	0.4	0.8	1.4	0.9	–0.3	0.5
Minnesota	5.0	–1.3	–2.5					0.4
Dallas				–3.0	3.1	2.2	–1.0	0.3
St. Louis	–3.5	0.8	1.7	–1.7	–2.8	0.1	6.3	0.1
Washington	1.7	–1.2	–3.6	0.8	–2.8	3.4	0.5	–0.2
Buffalo	4.4	0.8	–2.1	–2.2	–6.5	–1.1	–3.3	–1.4
Tampa Bay				–1.6	0.7	–2.7	–4.2	–2.0
Winnipeg	–0.5	–1.5	–2.5	–2.6	–3.6	–3.2		–2.3
Hartford	4.1	3.1	–2.8	–5.5	–6.8	–1.0	–9.2	–2.6
Phoenix							–11.7	–11.7
NHL average	3.5	4.1	3.6	3.2	3.8	4.2	3.5	3.7

Note: Minnesota moved to Dallas in 1993, Quebec moved to Colorado in 1995, and Winnipeg moved to Phoenix in 1996. Tampa Bay and Ottawa were expansion teams in 1993; Anaheim and Florida were expansion teams in 1994.
Source: Financial World.

TABLE 5-5
SPURS NET INCOME STATEMENT, 1994–95

Category	Regular Season	Playoffs	SAOne, Inc.
Revenues			
Gate revenue	$19,125,159	$6,637,135	$2,178,570
Broadcast revenue	22,271,712	1,918,529	1,288,629
Stadium revenue	4,515,221	495,688	182,778
NBA royalties and other income	4,855,346	381,890	303,105
Total revenue	50,767,438	9,433,242	3,953,082
Costs/expenses			
Team salaries	$23,753,729	$45,000	$0
Broadcasting, advertising, and promotion	6,510,759	257,490	430,600
Other salaries	5,565,703	731,129	178,532
Interest expenses	3,655,426	0	0
NBA and indirect expenses	3,566,484	2,925,364	536,439
Sales and other taxes	2,305,618	504,985	36,186
Shared revenue	0	0	2,038,596
Other general and administrative expenses	5,255,528	607,432	334,152
Total expenses	50,613,247	5,071,400	3,554,505
Net operating revenue before depreciation	$154,191	$4,361,842	$398,577

Source: Charlotte-Ann Lucas, San Antonio Express-News.

TABLE 5-6
SPURS NET INCOME STATEMENT, 1995–96

Category	Regular Season	Playoffs	SAOne, Inc.
Revenues			
Gate revenue	$20,055,648	$3,020,335	$797,559
Broadcast revenue	24,126,334	1,275,017	1,127,701
Stadium revenue	4,497,040	296,999	111,810
NBA royalties and other income	4,577,065	283,905	172,485
Total revenue	53,256,087	4,876,256	2,209,555
Costs/expenses			
Team salaries	$26,917,914	$0	$0
Broadcasting, advertising, and promotion	7,311,916	349,459	468,378
Other salaries	5,574,112	233,452	260
Interest expenses	3,180,312	0	0
NBA and indirect expenses	3,569,964	1,366,242	182,041
Sales and other taxes	2,233,891	187,883	28,617
Shared revenue	0	0	892,901
Other general and administrative expenses	7,047,850	389,299	101,335
Total expenses	55,835,959	2,526,335	1,673,532
Net operating revenue before depreciation	–$2,579,872	$2,349,921	$536,023

Source: Charlotte-Ann Lucas, San Antonio Express-News.

TABLE 5-7
SALES OF PRO SPORTS TEAMS, 1990–98, AND
ESTIMATED RATES OF RETURN ON INVESTMENT TO OWNERS
(sales prices in millions of $)

Team	Sale (1990–98)		Previous Sale		Estimated Rate of Return (%)
	Year	Price	Year	Price	
Major League Baseball					
Montreal	1990	86	1969	12.5	9.6
San Diego	1990	75	1974	12.0	12.1
Colorado	1991	95*	None		
Florida	1991	95*	None		
Toronto	1991	134	1976	7.0	21.8
Baltimore	1992	173	1988	70	25.4
Detroit	1992	80	1983	53	4.7
Seattle	1992	100	1989	80	7.3
San Francisco	1993	95	1976	8.5	15.3
Oakland	1995	85	1980	12.7	13.5
Pittsburgh	1995	90	1985	22	15.1
St. Louis	1995	200	1953	3.8	9.9
Phoenix	1997	135*	None		
Tampa Bay	1997	135*	None		
Los Angeles	1998	311	1950	4.1	12.0
Texas	1998	250	1989	97.8	11.0
Average					11.3
NFL					
Minnesota	1991	100	1985	54.3	9.7
NY Giants	1991	150	1925	—	21.1
Charlotte	1993	140*	None		
Jacksonville	1993	140*	None		
Miami	1994	165	1965	7.5	11.3
New England	1994	153	1992	106	20.1
Philadelphia	1994	185	1985	67	11.9
Tampa Bay	1995	172	1974	16	12.0
Seattle	1997	200	1988	80	12.1
Minnesota	1998	250	1991	100	14.0
Cleveland	1998	530*	None		
Average					12.7

TABLE 5-7
(Continued)

Team	Sale (1990–97)		Previous Sale		Estimated Rate of Return (%)
	Year	Price	Year	Price	
NBA					
Denver	1991	70	1989	54	13.8
Golden State	1991	82	1962	0.9	16.8
Orlando	1991	85	1989	32.5	61.7
Sacramento	1992	80	1958	0.2	18.9
Houston	1993	85	1982	11	20.4
Toronto	1994	125*	None		
Vancouver	1994	125*	None		
Minnesota	1995	88.5	1989	32.5	18.2
Philadelphia	1996	125	1981	12	16.9
Average					17.7
NHL					
Minnesota	1990	31	1967	2	12.6
St. Louis	1991	40	1967	2	13.3
Anaheim	1992	50*	None		
Florida	1992	50*	None		
Hartford	1994	47.5	1988	31	7.4
Toronto	1994	89	1961	2	13.2
Atlanta	1997	80*	None		
Columbus	1997	80*	None		
Nashville	1997	80*	None		
St. Paul	1997	80*	None		
Edmonton	1998	85	1979	7.5**	12.8
Average					10.7

*Expansion teams.

**Fee for entering the NHL.

Note: League averages are weighted averages, with each rate of return weighted by the number of years between sales multiplied by the dollar amount of the original sales price.

Sources: New York Times and various local newspapers for recent sales; J. Quirk and R. Fort, *Pay Dirt* (Princeton University Press, 1992), Chapter 2, for previous sales.

TABLE 6-1
MOVES OF TEAMS, ALL LEAGUES, 1950–97

Major League Baseball
NL
1953	Boston Braves to Milwaukee
1958	Brooklyn Dodgers to Los Angeles
1958	New York Giants to San Francisco
1966	Milwaukee Braves to Atlanta

AL
1954	St. Louis Browns to Baltimore Orioles
1955	Philadelphia Athletics to Kansas City
1961	Washington Senators to Minnesota Twins
1966	Los Angeles Angels to California (Anaheim) Angels
1968	Kansas City Athletics to Oakland
1970	Seattle Pilots to Milwaukee Brewers
1972	Washington Senators II to Texas Rangers

NFL
1961	Los Angeles Chargers (AFL) to San Diego
1963	Dallas Texans (AFL) to Kansas City Chiefs
1983	Oakland Raiders to Los Angeles
1984	Baltimore Colts to Indianapolis
1988	St. Louis Cardinals to Phoenix
1995	Los Angeles Raiders to Oakland
1995	Los Angeles Rams to St. Louis
1997	Cleveland Browns to Baltimore Ravens
1997	Houston Oilers to Tennessee

NBA
1951	Tri Cities Hawks to Milwaukee
1955	Milwaukee Hawks to St. Louis
1957	Fort Wayne Pistons to Detroit
1957	Rochester Royals to Cincinnati
1960	Minneapolis Lakers to Los Angeles
1962	Philadelphia Warriors to San Francisco
1963	Chicago Bullets to Baltimore
1963	Syracuse Nationals to Philadelphia 76ers
1968	St. Louis Hawks to Atlanta
1971	San Diego Rockets to Houston
1971	San Francisco Warriors to Oakland (Golden State)
1972	Cincinnati Royals to Kansas City Kings
1973	Baltimore Bullets to Washington

TABLE 6-1
(Continued)

1973	Dallas Chaparrals to San Antonio Spurs
1978	Buffalo Braves to San Diego Clippers
1979	New Orleans Jazz to Utah
1984	Kansas City Kings to Sacramento
1984	San Diego Clippers to Los Angeles

NHL

1976	California Golden Seals (Oakland) to Cleveland Barons
1976	Kansas City Scouts to Colorado Rockies (Denver)
1978	Cleveland Barons merge with Minnesota North Stars
1980	Atlanta Flame to Calgary
1982	Colorado Rockies (Denver) to New Jersey Devils
1993	Minnesota North Stars to Dallas Stars
1995	Quebec Nordiques to Colorado Avalanche (Denver)
1996	Winnipeg Jets to Phoenix Coyotes
1997	Hartford Whalers to Carolina Hurricanes

Summary: Number of Franchise Moves by Decade by Sport

Decade	Major League Baseball	NFL	NBA	NHL	Total
1950s	5	0	4	0	9
1960s	4	2	5	0	11
1970s	2	0	7	3	12
1980s	0	3	2	2	7
1990–97	0	4	0	4	8
Totals	11	9	18	9	47

Source: League guides.

TABLE 6-2
MAJOR METROPOLITAN AREAS, UNITED STATES AND CANADA:
POPULATION, 1994, AND TEAM LOCATIONS,
PRO TEAM SPORTS, 1997

Metropolitan Area	Population (thousands)	NL	AL	NFL	NBA	NHL	Total	Population/ Team (thousands)
1. New York	19,796	1	1	2	2	3	9	2,200
2. Los Angeles	15,302	1	1	0	2	2	6	2,550
3. Chicago	8,526	1	1	1	1	1	5	1,705
4. Washington-Baltimore	7,051	0	1	2	1	1	5	1,410
5. San Francisco-Oakland-San Jose	6,513	1	1	2	1	1	6	1,086
6. Philadelphia	5,959	1	0	1	1	1	4	1,490
7. Boston	5,497	0	1	1	1	1	4	1,374
8. Detroit	5,256	0	1	1	1	1	4	1,314
9. Dallas	4,362	0	1	1	1	1	4	1,091
Toronto*	4,300	0	1	0	1	1	3	1,433
10. Houston	4,099	1	0	0	1	0	2	2,050
11. Miami	3,408	1	0	1	1	1	4	852
12. Atlanta	3,331	1	0	1	1	0	3	1,110
Montreal*	3,300	1	0	0	0	1	2	1,650
13. Seattle	3,226	0	1	1	1	0	3	1,075
14. Cleveland	2,898	0	1	0	1	0	2	1,449
15. Minneapolis–St. Paul	2,888	0	1	1	1	0	3	963
16. St. Louis	2,536	1	0	1	0	1	3	845
17. San Diego	2,536	1	0	1	0	0	2	1,268
18. Phoenix	2,473	1	0	1	1	1	4	618
19. Pittsburgh	2,402	1	0	1	0	1	3	801
20. Denver	2,190	1	0	1	1	1	4	548
21. Tampa	2,156	0	1	1	0	1	3	719
22. Portland	1,982	0	0	0	1	0	1	1,982
23. Cincinnati	1,894	1	0	1	0	0	2	947
Vancouver*	1,800	0	0	0	1	1	2	900
24. Kansas City	1,647	0	1	1	0	0	2	824
25. Milwaukee	1,637	1	0	0	1	0	2	819
26. Sacramento	1,588	0	0	0	1	0	1	1,588
27. Norfolk	1,529	0	0	0	0	0	0	—
28. Indianapolis	1,462	0	0	1	1	0	2	731
29. San Antonio	1,437	0	0	0	1	0	1	1,437
30. Columbus	1,423	0	0	0	0	0	0	—

TABLE 6-2
(Continued)

Metropolitan Area	Population (thousands)	NL	AL	NFL	NBA	NHL	Total	Population/ Team (thousands)
31. Orlando	1,361	0	0	0	1	0	1	1,361
32. New Orleans	1,309	0	0	1	0	0	1	1,309
33. Charlotte	1,260	0	0	1	1	0	2	630
34. Buffalo	1,189	0	0	1	0	1	2	595
35. Salt Lake City	1,178	0	0	0	1	0	1	1,178
36. Hartford	1,151	0	0	0	0	0	0	—
37. Providence	1,129	0	0	0	0	0	0	—
38. Winston-Salem	1,107	0	0	0	0	0	0	—
39. Rochester	1,090	0	0	0	0	0	0	—
40. Las Vegas	1,076	0	0	0	0	0	0	—
41. Nashville	1,070	0	0	1	0	0	1	1,070
42. Memphis	1,056	0	0	0	0	0	0	—
43. Oklahoma City	1,007	0	0	0	0	0	0	—
Ottawa*	1,000	0	0	0	0	1	1	1,000
44. Grand Rapids	985	0	0	0	0	0	0	—
45. Louisville	980	0	0	0	0	0	0	—
46. Jacksonville	972	0	0	1	0	0	1	972
47. Raleigh	965	0	0	0	0	1	1	965
Edmonton*	863	0	0	0	0	1	1	863
Calgary*	822	0	0	0	0	1	1	822

*Canadian populations are not directly comparable with U.S. populations.

Note: Rankings are in terms of population sizes of metropolitan areas, for the United States only.

Source: 1997 statistical abstract and league guides.

TABLE 7-1
STADIUMS AND ARENAS BUILT OR BEING BUILT, 1991–98

Anaheim	1993: Publicly financed arena, Arrowhead Pond, home of the NHL Anaheim Mighty Ducks, opens.
	1997: City converts publicly owned Anaheim Stadium, home field of the Anaheim Angels, from multiple-use to baseball-only status. Cost of conversion: $117 million, capacity: 44,900.
Arlington	1994: City-financed baseball stadium, The Ballpark, home field of the AL Texas Rangers, opens. Cost: $191 million (74 percent public money), capacity: 42,242.
Atlanta	1992: Publicly financed football stadium, Georgia Dome, home field of the NFL Atlanta Falcons, opens. Cost: $214 million, capacity: 71,544.
	1996: Atlanta Olympic Committee spends $207 million for construction of Olympic Stadium. Following the Olympics, the city of Atlanta spends $50 million to convert the stadium into Turner Field, home of the NL Atlanta Braves.
Baltimore	1992: Publicly financed baseball stadium, Camden Yards, home field of the AL Baltimore Orioles, opens. Cost: $210 million (96 percent public money), capacity: 48,000.
	1998: Publicly financed football stadium, home field of the Baltimore Ravens, opens. Cost: $200 million, capacity: 65,000.
Boston	1995: Privately financed arena, Fleet Center, the new Boston Garden, home ice of the NHL Boston Bruins and home court of the NBA Boston Celtics, opens. Owner: Delaware North Co., which also owns the Bruins. Cost: $160 million, capacity: 17,565.
	1997: New England Patriots mount a campaign for a new stadium to be built on public land in Boston; the stadium ($200 million) to be privately financed by Robert Kraft, Pats owner. The project is supported by Governor William Weld but opposed by Boston Mayor Tommy Menino.
Buffalo	1992: Seymour Knox, owner of the NHL Buffalo Sabres, threatens to move the team if a new arena isn't built. City council votes $2.35 million for land and planning costs.
	1996: Privately financed arena, Marine Midland Arena, home ice of the Buffalo Sabres, opens. Cost: $122 million (29 percent public money), capacity: 21,000.

—

TABLE 7-I
(*Continued*)

	1997: Ralph Wilson, the most consistent opponent of franchise moves among NFL owners and owner of the NFL Bills, threatens to move the Bills if Rich Stadium is not upgraded. New York state legislature votes $63.2 million for refurbishing the stadium, and the Bills extend their lease for six more years.
Charlotte	1996: Privately owned football stadium, Ericsson Field, home of the NFL Carolina Panthers, opens. Cost: $248 million (24 percent public financing), capacity: 72,350.
Chicago	1991: Publicly financed Comiskey Park, home of the AL Chicago White Sox, opens. Cost: $150 million, capacity: 44,321.
	1994: Privately owned arena, United Center, home of the NBA Chicago Bulls and NHL Chicago Blackhawks, opens. Owners: William Wirtz (Blackhawks) and Jerry Reinsdorf (Bulls). Cost: $175 million, capacity: 21,711.
Cincinnati	1995: NL Reds and NFL Bengals both demand new stadiums under threats to move the teams. The city council votes 5–4 to spend $540 million to build new stadiums for the Reds and Bengals, stadiums to open in 2000. Capacity of football stadium: 70,000. (76 percent public money.)
	1996: City voters approve (61–39 percent) a new half-cent sales tax to finance new stadiums.
Cleveland	1994: Publicly financed Jacobs Field, home field of the AL Indians, opens. Cost: $173 million (88 percent public money), capacity: 42,400.
	1994: Publicly financed arena, Gund Arena, home of the Cleveland Cavaliers, opens. Cost: $155 million (97 percent public money), capacity: 20,562.
	1995: City council approves $154 million increase in taxes to fund improvements to Municipal Stadium, home of the Cleveland Browns.
	1995: Browns leave anyway. The NFL avoids a threatened lawsuit under an agreement that Art Modell will pay $11.5 million to the city, the NFL will loan up to $48 million to the owner of an expansion team to assist in construction of a new stadium, and Modell will pay the league $29 million of the estimated $80 million in PSL fees he will receive from the new Baltimore stadium.
Denver	1995: Publicly financed Coors Field, home of the NL Colorado Rockies, opens. Cost: $215.5 million (72 percent public money), capacity: 50,100.

(*Continued*)

TABLE 7-1
(Continued)

	1997: Publicly financed arena, Pepsi Center, home of the NBA Nuggets and the NHL Avalanche, opens. Cost: $165 million.
Detroit	1994: Detroit voters approve (80–20 percent) funding for a new private-public stadium for the AL Tigers. Owner Mike Ilitch pays $175–200 million of the cost of the stadium, the city pays $40 million, and the state pays $55 million.
	1996: NFL Lions announce plans to move from the Pontiac Dome at the end of the 2004 season to a new domed stadium in downtown Detroit. Cost: $245 million, with $120 million paid by the team, $80 million by the city, and $45 million by the state. The team will pay $40 million for naming rights to the proposed Ford Stadium.
Hartford	1993: Governor Lowell Weicker calls a special session of the state legislature to consider a plan to spend $252 million for a new stadium for the Patriots, if they agree to move to Hartford. Plan never materializes.
	1996: The state has already lent the owners of the NHL Whalers $23.5 million, but the team is not talking about leaving Hartford.
	1997: Whalers reject a state bid to keep the team in Hartford; the state proposes building a $147.5 million arena, but the team says it can't afford the proposed $2.5 million annual rent. Team leaves for Raleigh.
Houston	1995: Bud Adams, owner of the NFL Oilers, writes to Mayor Bob Lanier to inform him that either Houston must build a new stadium to replace the Astrodome or the Oilers will leave town.
	1997: Oilers leave for Tennessee.
Jacksonville	1996: Publicly financed stadium, Gator Bowl, home field of the NFL expansion Jaguars, opens. Cost: $137 million (91 percent public money), capacity: 73,000.
Los Angeles	1995: Rams and Raiders leave town.
	1998: The city council of Los Angeles agrees to provide public land, valued at $90 million, near the Los Angeles Convention Center as the site for an otherwise privately financed arena to house the NBA Lakers and NHL Kings.
	1998: Discussions begin between the city and the NFL concerning the New Coliseum, a proposed private-public–financed replacement for the present Coliseum, to house an NFL expansion team. Cost: $500 million (estimate).

TABLE 7-I
(*Continued*)

Miami	1995: Wayne Huizenga threatens to move his NHL Florida Panthers unless he gets a new arena or a lower rent at Miami Arena. 1996: After getting no support for full public financing of a new arena, the Miami Heat announces plans for a privately financed arena with the team paying the $165 million cost of construction and taxpayers picking up $6.5 million per year in operating costs, while giving the team $2 million per year for naming rights. 1997: After being turned down in his bid for a new publicly financed baseball field for his NL Marlins, Wayne Huizenga announces plans to sell the team to a new owner who might have more luck in obtaining public funding.
Milwaukee	1995: Owner Bud Selig threatens to move the AL Brewers if a publicly financed stadium isn't built. A proposed financing plan is turned down by a large majority in a state-wide referendum. Governor Tommy Thompson pushes an alternative plan to fund the $250 million stadium, by imposing a 1/10 of 1 percent sales tax on the 5 counties around Milwaukee. This barely passes the state legislature. The new stadium will be named Miller Park. Cost: $250 million (64 percent public money), capacity: 42,500.
Minneapolis–St. Paul	1995: The city of Minneapolis buys the previously privately owned Target Center for $54.6 million as part of a deal that involves the sale of the NBA Timberwolves, keeping the team in town. 1997: Carl Pohlad, owner of the AL Twins, obtains authorization from the AL to talk with other cities above moving the team and petitions the state legislature for approval of a partially publicly funded baseball stadium. The state legislature rejects Pohlad's request. 1997: St. Paul receives an expansion franchise from the NHL, contingent on the city building a new $130 million Civic Center Arena. The city proposes a financing arrangement under which the state would provide $65 million of the funds. 1998: The state legislature approves funding of the Civic Center Arena but continues to reject funding of the proposed stadium for the Twins. Twins sign a two-year lease at the Metrodome, while owner Pohlad seeks a local buyer for the team.

(*Continued*)

TABLE 7-1
(*Continued*)

Montreal	1995: A new arena, involving public and private financing, the Molson Center, home ice of the NHL Canadiens, opens. Cost: $230 million.
	1997: Claude Brochu, president of the NL Expos, says that the team will be put up for sale unless the government of Quebec province agrees to build a $250 million baseball stadium.
Nashville	1995: City begins construction of a publicly financed arena, looking for an NBA or NHL team. There are negotiations with the NHL New Jersey Devils but they fall through.
	1996: Nashville voters approve (60–40 percent) $80 million as their share of the cost of a new football stadium for the NFL Tennessee Oilers.
	1998: A new stadium, Cumberland Stadium, is scheduled to open. Cost: $294 million (76 percent public money), capacity: 76,000.
New York	1996: George Steinbrenner, owner of the AL Yankees, talks of leaving Yankee Stadium and asks for a publicly financed stadium. Mayor Rudolph Giuliani proposes a new multisport stadium with retractable roof (seating 70,000, estimated cost $1 billion), but financing appears shaky.
	1996: Mets begin discussion of a public-private–financed stadium to replace Shea Stadium, with estimated cost of $457 million.
	1998: A falling I-beam in Yankee Stadium revives talk of $1 billion publicly financed stadium for the Yankees.
Oakland	1995: NFL Raiders move back to Oakland in a deal under which the team gets a $32 million "loan" for relocation, and the city and county agree to issue $225 million worth of bonds to finance improvements to the Oakland Stadium.
	1996: The Oakland Coliseum authority agrees to spend $121 million to upgrade its facilities. The NBA Golden State Warriors had threatened to leave if action was not taken.
Philadelphia	1996: Privately financed arena, Core States Center, opens as home arena for the NHL Flyers and NBA 76ers. Cost: $210 million (100 percent private money), capacity: 41,000.
Phoenix	1998: Publicly funded baseball stadium, Bank One Ballpark (BOB), home of the NL Arizona Diamondbacks, opens. Cost: $338 million (95 percent public money), capacity: 48,500.

TABLE 7-1
(Continued)

Portland	1995: Privately funded Rose Garden, home of the NBA Portland Trailblazers, opens. Cost: $262 million (87 percent private money), capacity: 21,400.
Quebec	1995: Marcel Aubut, owner of the NHL Nordiques, says he wants a city-financed 19,000-capacity arena or he will move the team. The city turns down the request and the team leaves for Denver.
Raleigh	1997: The city agrees to build $120 million arena for the Carolina Hurricanes, formerly the Hartford Whalers.
St. Louis	1994: Privately funded arena, Kiel Center Arena, home of the NHL St. Louis Blues, opens. Owners include Michael Shanahan, owner of the Blues. Cost: $135 million (55 percent private money), capacity: 18,500. 1995: LA Rams announce their move to St. Louis to the publicly financed dome stadium, TransWorld Dome. Cost: $299 million (96 percent public money), capacity: 65,300.
St. Petersburg	1990: Publicly funded baseball park, Thunderdome, opens with no major-league tenant. Cost: $149 million (100 percent public money), capacity: 47,600.
Salt Lake City	1991: Privately funded arena, the Delta Center, home of the NBA Utah Jazz, opens. Cost: $168 million (100 percent private money), capacity: 19,911.
San Antonio	1993: Publicly financed arena, Alamodome, home of the NBA San Antonio Spurs, opens. Cost: $186 million, capacity: 20,662.
San Diego	1995: The mayor and city council sign a new lease agreement with the NFL Chargers, which includes spending $78 million to expand and upgrade Qualcomm Stadium. The city also provides a guaranteed sale of 60,000 tickets to each Chargers game. 1998: San Diego Padres object to the new configuration of Qualcomm and raise the issue of a new publicly funded baseball-only stadium. A downtown stadium, with an estimated cost of $400 million and a completion date around 2002, was approved on a ballot referendum in November 1998.
San Francisco	1996: Voters approve (64–36 percent) the use of public land for a new privately financed NL Giants stadium, Pac Bell Park, to be ready for the 2000 season. Estimated cost of stadium: $255 million (100 percent private money, except for the land), capacity: 42,000.

(Continue

TABLE 7-1
(Continued)

	1997: Voters narrowly (50.1–49.9 percent) approve issuing $100 million in bonds to help finance a $525 million stadium-shopping mall complex. The NFL 49ers had threatened to leave if a new stadium was not built.
San Jose	1992: Voters turn down (55–45 percent) public financing of a stadium for the NL Giants.
	1993: Privately funded arena, San Jose Arena, home of the NHL San Jose Sharks, opens. Cost: $170 million (100 percent private money), capacity: 17,190.
Seattle	1995: Publicly funded arena, Key Arena, home of the NBA Seattle Supersonics, opens. Cost: $120 million (62 percent public money), capacity, 17,102.
	1995: City voters turn down a sales tax to finance a new stadium for the AL Mariners. The team threatens to leave, at which point the city council approves funding for a $325 million stadium, but runs into legal problems.
	1995: Ken Behring, owner of the NFL Seahawks, threatens to leave town but is rebuffed by the NFL.
	1996: The state legislature approves funding for $414 million Mariners' stadium, capacity 45,000 (89 percent public money, but see the discussion in Chapter 7). Later in the year, voters narrowly pass state funding for a $425 million (76 percent public money) stadium–exhibition center complex for the Seahawks and their new owner, Paul Allen. Capacity: unknown.
Tampa Bay	1996: Voters approve a publicly funded stadium for the NFL Buccaneers.
	1996: Publicly funded arena, Ice Palace, home of the NHL Tampa Bay Lightning, opens. Cost: $139 million (62 percent public money), capacity: 19,500.
	1998: Publicly funded stadium, Tampa Bay Stadium, home of the NFL Tampa Bay Bucs, opens. Cost: $265 million, capacity: 65,000.
Tempe	1992: Privately funded arena, America West Arena, home of the NBA Phoenix Sun and the NHL Phoenix Coyotes, opens. Cost: $90 million (40 percent public money), capacity: 19,023.
Toronto	1996: Privately owned arena, Air Canada Arena, home of the NBA Toronto Raptors, opens.

TABLE 7-1
(Continued)

Washington, D.C.	1992: Jack Kent Cooke, owner of the NFL Redskins, announces plans for a privately funded stadium to replace RFK Stadium. Cost: $160 million. The stadium opens in the 1997 NFL season, after being relocated.
	1994: Abe Pollin, owner of the NHL Capitols and the NBA Wizards, announces plans for a new privately financed arena for downtown Washington. Cost: $180 million.
	1997: Privately owned stadium, Jack Kent Cooke Stadium, home of the NFL Washington Redskins, opens. Cost: $180 million, capacity: 80,116.

Note: Private share of funding can include naming rights to the stadium.

Among the stadiums not covered in this table are those proposed or under construction in Houston and Pittsburgh. New stadiums for the NL Padres and NFL Broncos were approved by voters in San Diego and Denver in November 1998.

Source: Adapted from *Spokane Spokesman-Review,* June 1, 1997, pp. A7, A10.

TABLE 7-2
SPORTS FACILITY VOTES AND THEIR OUTCOMES

Location	Date	Purpose	Votes Yes	Votes No	Percent Yes
Passed					
Arlington, TX	1/19/91	Sales tax	21,924	11,936	64.7
Baltimore	1974	Enabling	91,981	45,175	67.1
Charlotte	5/3/86	Property tax	17,825	17,396	50.6
Cincinnati	3/19/96	Sales tax	na	na	61.4
Cleveland	5/8/90	Excise tax	na	na	51.7
Cleveland	11/95	Excise tax	na	na	na
Denver	8/14/90	Sales tax	na	na	54.0
Detroit	3/19/96	Bonds	na	na	na
Nashville	1996	Bonds	na	na	59.0
San Antonio	1989	Unknown	na	na	na
San Francisco	3/26/96	Approval	101,343	85,313	54.3
Seattle	6/7/97	Approval	na	na	51.1
Failed					
Chicago	1986	Enabling	3,744	3,787	49.7
Cleveland	1984	Property tax	na	na	na
Colorado Springs	8/85	Bonds	13,364	21,837	38.0
Colorado Springs	4/89	Bonds	14,965	34,597	30.2
Durham, NC	3/90	Bonds	9,051	12,984	41.1
Miami	11/2/82	Sales tax	108,963	223,774	32.7
Miami	1988	Unknown	na	na	na
Milwaukee	4/4/95	Lottery	348,818	618,377	36.1
New Jersey	1987	Bonds	473,904	972,783	32.8
North Carolina	5/5/98	Sales tax	18,261	36,796	33.2
North Carolina	5/5/98	Sales tax	21,217	30,575	41.0
Oklahoma City	na	Unknown	na	na	na
San Francisco	11/3/87	Approval	85,005	96,445	46.8
San Francisco	11/7/89	Approval	85,796	87,850	49.4
San Francisco	11/7/89	Approval	83,599	98,875	45.8
San Jose	11/6/90	Approval	85,313	89,269	48.9
San Jose	9/2/92	Utility tax	78,809	94,466	45.5
Santa Clara	11/6/90	Utility tax	126,906	129,653	49.5
Seattle	9/19/95	Sales tax	245,418	248,500	49.9

na, Not available.
Source: Adapted from Rodney Fort, "Direct Democracy and the Stadium Mess," in *Sports, Jobs, and Taxes: The Economic Impact of Sports Teams and Stadiums,* edited by Roger Noll and Andrew Zimbalist (Washington, D.C.: Brookings, 1997), p. 161.

BIBLIOGRAPHY

Austrian, Ziona, and Mark Rosentraub. 1997. "Cleveland's Gateway to the Future." In *Sports, Jobs, and Taxes: The Economic Impact of Sports Teams and Stadiums*, edited by Roger Noll and Andrew Zimbalist, 355–84. Washington, D.C.: Brookings.

Baade, Robert. 1987. *Is There an Economic Rationale for Subsidizing Sports Stadiums?* Chicago: Heartland Institute.

Davidson, Gary (with Bill Libby). 1974. *Breaking the Game Wide Open*. New York: Atheneum.

Eskenazi, Gerald. 1988. *Bill Veeck: A Baseball Legend*. New York: McGraw-Hill.

Fort, Rodney. 1997. "Direct Democracy and the Stadium Mess." In *Sports, Jobs, and Taxes: The Economic Impact of Sports Teams and Stadiums*, edited by Roger Noll and Andrew Zimbalist, 146–77. Washington, D.C.: Brookings.

Miller, Marvin. 1991. *A Whole Different Ball Game*. New York: Birch Lane Press.

Noll, Roger (editor). 1974. *Government and the Sports Business*. Washington, D.C.: Brookings.

Noll, Roger, and Andrew Zimbalist (editors). 1997. *Sports, Jobs, and Taxes: The Economic Impact of Sports Teams and Stadiums*. Washington, D.C.: Brookings.

Quirk, James, and Rodney D. Fort. 1992. *Pay Dirt: The Business of Professional Team Sports*. Princeton, N.J.: Princeton University Press.

Rosentraub, Mark, and Samuel Nunn. 1978. "Suburban City Investment in Professional Sports." *American Behavioral Scientist* 21 (January/ February):393–414.

Study of Monopoly Power, Part 6: *Organized Baseball.* House Committee on the Judiciary, 82d Congress, 1st session, July–August–October, 1951, H1365-3, Y4.J89/1:82/1/pt.6.

Veeck, Bill (with Ed Linn). 1962. *Veeck as in Wreck.* New York: Ballantine.

———. 1965. *The Hustler's Handbook.* New York: G. P. Putnam's Sons.

INDEX

CPSIA information can be obtained at www.ICGtesting.com
Printed in the USA
BVOW04s0405151013

333762BV00005B/63/P